GREAT DIVIDE

Surviving Scandal & Division in the Catholic Church

by
Thomas Rutkoski

Published by Gospa Missions

Printed in the United States of America

First Edition
October, 2002

ISBN 0-9633667-8-5

Jacket Design by Cheryl Vaca

Published by Gospa Missions

230 East Main, Street Evans City, PA 16033

724-538-3171

www.gospa.org

Contents

Dedication **7**
Acknowledgements **8**
Introduction **9**
1. The Idea of Being a Saint **13**
2. Attitude **23**
3. Desire of Sainthood **41**
4. Who Does Not Make It? **49**
5. Some of Those Who Made It **73**
Saint Maria Goretti **77**
Saint Dominic Savio **87**
Saint Joan of Arc **95**
Blessed Padre Miguel Pro **105**
Saint Teresa of Avila **119**
Saint Juan Diego **135**
6. Suffering **153**
7. Faith **157**
8. Works **165**
9. Tests **175**
10. Tithing **181**
11. Love **217**
12. Humility **227**
13. Prayer **239**
14. Evangelization **255**
15. Mass **259**
16. The Church **265**
17. Track Record **279**
18. Indulgences **293**
19. No Quitters **297**
20. And the List Goes On **305**
Epilogue **309**
An Invitation **311**
Other Works by Thomas Rutkoski **313**
The Contextual Rosary of Scripture **314**
The Chocolate Rosary **315**
St. Joseph Orphanage/School **317**

DEDICATION

At a time in history when our Church is inundated with heresy, plagued with scandal and suffering immensely, there is a class of soldier who marches to the tune of obedience.

These soldiers know they were called by God to serve, and well do they do it. These soldiers never waver in their devotion to the Bride of Christ, the Eucharist, the Blessed Virgin Mary, the Holy Father or their duty.

They are patient, kind, forbearing and forgiving. They are with us to celebrate in our greatest joy and provide us a shoulder on which to cry in our times of grief. They give us the Word that opens the door and Bread that gives the strength for the journey required to find it.

These men are endowed by their Creator with hearts that are gentle and hands that can heal. But too infrequently do they receive the support they need and so silently suffer themselves.

These men have no families, no children to care, and so adopt you and me, and for that we call them Father. Yes, these soldiers are our priests, without whom we cannot get into heaven.

Only a Catholic priest can pass his hands over plain bread and wine and turn them into the Living Jesus Christ. It is only a good Catholic priest, obedient to the Magisterium, who will sit patiently, listen to your sins, pass his hands over you in the Sign of the Cross, and absolve those sins. It is a good Catholic priest, who does what he is told, and in that obedience we find our salvation.

I dedicate this book to all those holy men who serve God and us so well. We love you. We pray for you. And we bless you for all the blessings you have brought us. Thank you for being Catholic priests in the truest sense of the word.

Thank you for doing it right.

ACKNOWLEDGEMENTS

Spiritual Director	Fr. William Kiel
Editor	Mary Rutkoski
Computer formatting	Don Gaus
Proofreading	Jenny Cygan
	Betty Diegelman
	CeCe Gallucci
	Carolyn Gaus
	Marguerite Martin
	James Paras
	Sue Roberts
Transcription	Lori Potvin

My dear friends,

As seeds of faith are planted, we know from Scripture that some fall on rocky soil, have a hard time sprouting and wither away quickly. Some fall among thorn bushes,and when they sprout, they are soon choked off. Some seeds fall on fertile soil and grow to produce much fruit.

Above is a list of people who donated their time to bring this book to fruition. For the love of God, they gave freely what was given to them freely. Now each of them becomes one of the more blessed workers of the vineyard. These workers are so loving as to help find the tiny plants trying to grow among the rocks and thorns and help them to be transplanted into good soil. They cared so much about you that they labored for free. Please pray for them in grateful thanksgiving.

I, too, will pray for you all the days of my life. Thank you.

In Jesus and Mary,

Thomas Rutkoski

INTRODUCTION

We can look on this particular time in Church history as a very dark time or a time of great opportunity, a time of hope. I prefer the latter. I prefer to think that in any time of Church scandal and great division, great saints were made. That is my prayer for you and me.

> *Father, in the name of Jesus, Your Son, send Your Holy Spirit and grant me the ability to write this book according to Your will. I pray it causes me and all who read it, to become saints.*

In this book you may find parts that you love, some that seem preachy, and some arrogant to the point that it could cause you to be not so flattering when speaking about this author. I am a Catholic author. I am used to criticism.

I am not claiming to be a saint. I am simply stating that I want to be one. I will be the first to admit that I am a long way from it. Here you will find what God has led me to compile in the way of experiences, inspirations, suggestions, and yes, some constructive criticism of what's happening in the Church today. The title, *Great Divide*, is one with many facets. As with the Continental Divide, the Great Divide, as some call it, we see two large land areas that shed water in two opposite directions. Similar to that, the division in the Church today is shedding souls in two directions, one good and one evil, one toward heaven and one toward hell. And if we know our Scripture we will also be cognizant of the *Great Divide* in the hereafter. My aim with this book is to help us all traverse this treacherous course called life and move closer to the goal of sainthood. In order to do so, we must know the pitfalls, and how to avoid them.

I ask you not to see my observations of failures in the Church today as judgmental, because that is not my point or intention. We cannot be catalysts for reparation unless we know what it is that needs to be repaired. Keep that in mind, and you will cruise over the rough spots and take refuge at the right port in this storm.

I am not so arrogant as to think this work is the one-stop shopping manual for fixing all of the problems in the Church or for sainthood. It is just a little push in the right direction. I remember having a discussion with someone about my first book, *Apostles of the Last Days*, and the person mentioned that the book was a little push towards sainthood. If that book was a little push in the direction of sainthood, then I guess this book would be more like a bulldozer. Whatever it is, I pray it works for you.

I have lived for many years with the desire to help build up the Church and become a saint. That is not accomplished by burying our heads in the sand. If we only discussed the good things we do and ignored the problems, wouldn't that be bad in itself?

From the time I was forty-four years old (1987) to this present day, I have dedicated my life to doing what Scripture calls us to do if we want to be saints. This path I have chosen has resulted in many ups and downs, and I consider myself a survivor of the Catholic Church in America. The explanation of that statement will unfold as we proceed through this material. But know that much good fruit has been produced in this grace-filled adventure, and that good fruit is the only reason I would even attempt such a dangerous project as this book. Many have a hard time turning their cheek seventy times seven each day, even religious, so I expect flak.

What God has led me to do so far has helped many. If He would choose to accomplish this through me, someone who is nothing, imagine what He might choose to do through you, if you just try.

"The further I proceed, the behinder I get." As this journey advances toward sainthood, the reality of what is placed in my path makes me feel that the beginning is still to come. It is just when I start thinking about how much I have grown in my spirituality that God opens another door to show me the next mountain to be climbed. And I realize I am just a beginner.

With this in mind, my constant prayer is that both you and I will make it. There is much here to help anyone draw closer to the Lord. The effort, if it were only mine, would have never made it between the covers of this book. I have asked for help and it has come. May God bless you in this adventure, so much so that you do obtain sainthood. And if you make it before I do, please lower a rope. It may be the only way I get to heaven. If you can't find a rope, check with the mother of Jesus. I think she is in charge of the ropes.

Oh, yes. If, when you have finished reading this book, you decide that you liked it, please tell all your friends to buy one. And if you didn't like the book, keep it to yourself!

But on the serious side, it is astounding how just a few, who acquire a negative feeling about something designed to draw us closer to God, can create so many problems. The subjects which seem to cause the strongest negative reactions are, for religious - speaking of their possible failures, and for lay people - stewardship, or tithing, as they called it in the Old Testament. The claws really come out when these are mentioned. Pray that you don't become one who reacts this way. At times, seemingly holy people do. Be careful and pray much.

The object of the book is not to cause you to become angry and seek revenge for perceived offenses. The purpose of this book is to make you uncomfortable with where you are at present in your journey of salvation and spur you on, to exit with grace. My prayer is that, at the moment of your death, you forego even purgatory, continue directly on to sainthood and live all of eternity in the glories of heaven.

You will notice there is space at the end of each chapter to write notes. This should not be a book you just read and pass on. This book should be a life-long companion. Use it for reference. Feel free to mark the book and highlight parts that are important to you. As you read this book three and four times, you will keep finding new gems to help you in your conversion. If you ever have a question, please contact me by mail, email or phone. I do not want to be just another author. I want to be your friend.

And now, *Great Divide.*

Chapter One

The Idea of Being a Saint

We are living in times no different than anybody else who ever lived since the days of Christ. Satan has tried to kill every generation and he is trying to kill us. With many he will succeed, with some he won't. The difference between the two groups is their response to God's call. Our Lord calls each one of us to be saints, and Satan calls us to division, to divide ourselves from God.

If we were baptized, God, in His mercy, took from us the stain of original sin and made us saints. Can you imagine that? We, the baptized, were once already saints. But most of us lost the title because we stumbled and sank back into the treacherous sea of sin. It is similar to what happened to Saint Peter when the Lord called him to walk on the water during a storm. When Peter's faith faltered, he sank. When he cried out to the Lord for help, he was saved.

Our only hope of surviving this world and all of its allurements is to identify Satan's work and avoid the land mines he puts in our way and call on the name of the Lord.

We can see in our past how Satan caused division by the growing number of non-Catholic churches there are. Today we see how effective he is in his attempt to divide us from our salvation by his increased efforts inside the Church. Satan has created scandal and division in the Church to the point that many are losing respect for the very leadership chosen to lead us to our Creator.

Before we even think about the division in our lives and the Church, let's focus for a moment on the end goal. Repairing the damage that Satan has caused and is still causing can only come about by our living saintly lives. Remember God's request of

Saint Francis, "Rebuild My Church?" God makes the same request of us every day. Our ultimate goal is entrance into heaven and only saints go to heaven. I can't say that often enough. Keep this constantly in your mind.

What is a saint? We have devotions to them, statues, and medals to remind us about them and history books to tell of their heroism. But what is *a saint?*

A saint was a person who did the will of God. A saint was a person who was willing to die for the teachings of Christ. A saint in-the-making is one who fashions his or her life after the life of Jesus Christ and follows through on that path and in that frame of mind until death.

Doesn't that sound exciting? At this point you may be thinking, "You have got to be kidding me. I have a life of my own to live and I am not ready to die for anybody." Okay, maybe you are just a baby saint in-the-making and never really thought about it. Or you could be someone who doesn't think he would ever be worthy of sainthood. This book is for all of the above.

Many people think that attempting to live a saintly existence would take most of the fun out of life. If this description hits dangerously close to home, this book is my effort to convince you to change your mind. You really should give sainthood your best shot. Why? As I said before, other than God and His angels, there are only saints in heaven. And there's just nowhere else for all the folks who don't make it to go. Purgatory? It is part of the seven levels of heaven. You are separated from God, but through some and possibly long-term suffering, you, one day, will be purged of the punishment due your sins and come into the presence of the Lord. You really do not want to go there. Work hard at reparation here and forego the excruciating pain of purgatory.

Right off the bat, I have some people ready to close this book because some false prophet has sold them a bad bill of goods. The false prophets are running around telling anyone who will listen that there is no hell and therefore you do not have to worry about sainthood because *everybody* is going to heaven. Hogwash! I am sorry to say even some religious are spreading this false teaching. Division! If you stick with the teaching of the one, holy, catholic and apostolic Church, you will be on safe ground. Venture away from that, go with someone's personal opinion, and who knows where you will end up?

A friend of mine from years back, Steve Bell, is an astounding Baptist singer, writer and musician. For a non-Catholic, Steve is as close to being Catholic as one can get without making the final leap to safety. He is from Winnipeg, Manitoba, Canada, and he will help me here with the words to his song, *Comfort My People.* It is a beautiful song. You should hear him sing it. It should help you to understand the idea of being on God's side. If you are not on God's side, you will not be a saint. It goes like this:

Do you know? Have you not heard?
Has it been told you from the first?
Have you not understood from the forming of the earth?
He sits enthroned above the world and spreads the heavens like a tent,
A place for us to live, a place for all to live.

Who has measured the waters in the hollow of His hand? Do you know?
Who has marked off the heavens with the breath of His word? Do you know?
Comfort my people. Comfort my people, says the Lord.

He brought out the starry host. One by one He called them by name.
But do you still complain that He doesn't know your name?
Lift your eyes and look to see who created all of these,
And never more complain that He doesn't know your ways.

Who has measured the waters in the hollow of His hand? Do you know?
Who has marked off the heavens with the breath of His word? Do you know?
Comfort my people. Comfort my people, says the Lord.

It is God-given talent, shared by people like Steve, which makes this journey more easily accomplished. Can you imagine a God so marvelous that He would make all of what we know, have and see, just for us? I take great comfort in knowing that God made all of this for me and that He wants me in heaven, no matter what wrongs I have committed. All I have to do is be sorry for my sins, change my life, and try to bring souls to the Lord. The shame of it all is that for twenty-seven years, I couldn't have cared less. What an ingrate. I didn't know God. Yet now, in His infinite mercy, He is fixing my life. Now I do care. Now I think about sainthood every day of my life. I want to be a saint, one of God's chosen.

I know many people will say there is nothing you can do to be saved outside of claiming Jesus Christ as your savior. Division! Well, people of all faiths are on different levels of believing and understanding and I happen to disagree with those who think there is nothing we can do. Martin Luther, the father of Protestantism, caused that division hundreds of years ago and Catholics live divided today because of one man choosing to alter the teachings of the Magisterium just a little bit. We probably have ninety-five percent in common regarding our faith with most of our Protestant brethren, but I disagree with them on this and several other issues. I would not want to risk the fires of hell by showing up at the gate of heaven without a resume of works, a sort of evidence of effort. Works alone cannot always be counted on to save you, but you cannot be saved without works. We can see that a little division leads to much more, can we not?

Some teach that there is no such thing as the Communion of Saints. They don't understand people like Saint Mary, Mother of Jesus, returning to help us. They believe that you die and one day you wake up and face judgment and go directly to heaven or hell. I wonder how they explain Elijah and Moses showing up at the Transfiguration of Jesus Christ. You can play with Scripture all you want, but if you change anything or lend any credence to someone who has changed a meaning, you could be in big trouble.

Mt 17:1–4 *After six days Jesus took Peter, James, and John his brother, and led them up a high mountain by themselves. And He was transfigured before them;*

> *His face shone like the sun and His clothes became white as light. And behold, Moses and Elijah appeared to them, conversing with Him. Then Peter said to Jesus in reply, "Lord, it is good that we are here. If you wish, I will make three tents here, one for You, one for Moses, and one for Elijah."*

I thought these guys were dead! Doesn't it make you wonder from whence they came? Once you get past tainted theology and understand the authority of the Catholic Church, it all goes together so well. There are too many documented instances where saints have returned to help people. And who can count the number of times that the Blessed Virgin Mary (Saint Mary) has returned to lead the flock to her Son, Jesus? So who are these people who would insult God and discriminate against women or better put, The Woman? Are only men allowed to come back and help us in our journey toward Christ?

The authority of the Catholic Church is something to study. The following Scripture will help you a bit.

> Mt 16:13–19 *When Jesus went into the region of Caesarea Philippi, He asked His disciples, "Who do people say that the Son of Man is?" They replied, "Some say John the Baptist, others Elijah, still others Jeremiah or one of the prophets." He said to them, "But who do you say that I am?" Simon Peter said in reply, "You are the Messiah, the Son of the living God." Jesus said to him in reply, "Blessed are you, Simon, son of Jonah. For flesh and blood has not revealed this to you, but My heavenly Father. And so I say to you, you are Peter, and upon this rock I will build My church, and the gates of the netherworld (hell) shall not prevail against it. I will give you the keys to the kingdom of heaven. Whatever you bind on earth shall be bound in heaven; and whatever you loose on earth shall be loosed in heaven."*

I am not going to argue the point of whether Peter was called a rock or a pebble, as some like to do. That he is the rock on which the Church was built stood as firm teaching for over fifteen hundred years until Martin disagreed with authentic teaching. Division! Keep in mind that Scripture says to hold on to the tradition that was handed down to you.

How does anyone challenge the "keys to the kingdom" Scripture or claim that you must go straight to Jesus to have your sins forgiven, when that same Scripture explicitly explains that Peter had the right to bind and loose sins on earth? The Church also has the God-given right to make and change the laws that govern the Church. Peter had the right to name a successor, and he did. This chain of command, unbroken yet today, is the authority of the one, true Church.

What is appropriate for this book to mention is that this authority has decreed the truth of the Communion of Saints and so it is. What is the Communion of Saints? The ninth article of the Apostles' Creed declares that it is the spiritual union that exists between the saints in heaven, the souls in purgatory, and the faithful living on earth. This union is one of grace and good works. In recognition of this, the faithful imitate, venerate and pray for the intercession of the saints in heaven and for the souls in purgatory.

It is so obvious that making personal choices in regard to faith rather than following those chosen by God to lead the Church have caused us much harm. If we stop fighting among ourselves and start working diligently toward sainthood, some of us might make it. But because of the amount of judging and division we are involved in, it will be a wonder if any of us makes it into heaven.

Make no mistake about this: if you do not have a desire to be a saint, you probably will not be a saint. That said, let me shift to Catholics in the Church for a second. Division is prevalent through all of Christendom and is growing inside the Church at an amazing rate. I, for one, do not believe that the walking dead who show up in churches around the world on Sundays (the sixty-minute Catholics, the ones who just occupy a pew and no more), will ever make it through the narrow gate into heaven. If you couldn't care less about singing praise to the Lord and keeping your mind focused on what is happening during the Mass, you have quite a bit of soul searching to do. If you have a hard time accepting fasting and suffering, work on it. You will notice a big difference in your faith journey if you do. If the concept of obedience is not in your realm of belief, hell may be your destination by default. Those who are not for Jesus are against Him. You need to have the idea of becoming a saint implanted in your mind, make it a lifelong goal and work every day towards that goal.

I was the chief photojournalist for KDKA Television in Pittsburgh, Pennsylvania, for most of my twenty years there and won many awards for what I did. I did not start out as an award winner or as chief photojournalist. I had to work hard at it and many times I put my life at risk for my profession. The countless flights I made in helicopters, the most dangerous form of air travel, did not rank quite up there with my trip to war-torn Beirut, Lebanon, in 1982, but both were very risky.

If someone is willing to put his life at risk for a paycheck and occasionally even work overtime to make that check bigger in order to sock some away for the golden years, then what about this retirement package called heaven? Are we to take something that only lasts for seventy or eighty years and put more effort into that, than we will for something that will last for all of eternity, which can't even be measured? How stupid are we? I am pretty foolish for not paying attention to the Lord for the entire first half of my life. But it ain't over 'til the fat lady sings!' (I'm not making fun of us fat people; it's just an expression.)

If you do not believe that hell exists, then chances are you will find out how true it is when you get there, and then it will be too late. No one ever gets out of hell. Think about that for a while. That scenario in itself should make you ponder a little more on the idea of trying to become a saint.

We will go over this and a lot more in the coming chapters, so hold on to your hat. I believe you are in for the shock of a lifetime, but maybe what we need are shock treatments. There has been far too much passive faith and far too many false prophets and theologians telling us that there is no hell, and otherwise altering Christ's teachings. Acts of disobedience, "customizing" the Mass through pride and doing one's own will are so prevalent in the Church today. These sorry souls may not only be paving their own road to hell, but risk taking multitudes with them. If you are not learning your faith from the Magisterium, you had better rethink whom you choose to follow. The Magisterium is the Holy Father and all the bishops of the world who are united with him. That scenario is becoming smaller all of the time as priests and bishops decide to create their own church within the Church.

I pray that the Lord, through this book, will open our eyes to the truth, and grant us the grace to be able to drink the deadly poison of the false prophets and theoretical theologians of our time. "Please, Lord, grant us the grace to drink it and live. Grant us the grace to be Your saints."

You will notice the word 'division' used strategically throughout this chapter. I am not going to do that everywhere, but I want you to think about division and its consequences. We need to realize just how much division there is in the Church today, so we can work to repair what is obviously a major problem that has been thus far, poorly addressed. We will direct our attention in the greater part to sainthood rather than division, because in our trying to become saints we will diminish the division. But rest assured we will talk more about problems in the Church current.

If you are one who is unwilling to admit that there many problems in the Catholic Church today, there is an excellent example which was announced on the United States Council of Catholic Bishops (USCCB) web site just days before going to press on this book.

The USCCB web site posted a document which declares unequivocally that the biblical covenant between Jews and God is valid and therefore Jews do not need to be saved through faith in Jesus. A growing respect for the Jewish tradition, teachings that date back to the Second Vatican Council, and drawing conclusions from statements by Pope John Paul II throughout his papacy, were reasons cited in the announcement.

I put in an emergency call to the Bishop of the Diocese of Pittsburgh, Donald W. Wuerl and he assured me the recent announcement was not the teaching of the Catholic Church nor the conclusion of the USCCB. He further assured me that the issue of this release, official looking as it was, would be addressed at the very next conference meeting.

The committee of bishops that released this tainted information is already involved in damage control. It only goes to show us what we are up against. There have been several such attempts by internal bishops' committees to release unofficial information in a seemingly official manner to further bad agendas. Let's continue on.

NOTES

Chapter Two

Attitude

Most people think living a sacramental, holy, or Christ-like life would be less exciting than their present lives and they are sadly mistaken. So people choose to live a truly mundane life - that which contains little or no God. As they experience all of life's challenges, both the ungodly and sainthood-bound run into snags. The ungodly, under pressure, fall apart very rapidly. They may hide the moral destruction that is going on in their lives and they may seem, on the surface, to be happy individuals, but their interior lives are extremely empty. The converse is true for those who are headed for sainthood. These fortunate individuals have latched on to a close personal relationship with Jesus Christ, their Savior. They run into exactly the same snags and pitfalls in life as the ungodly, but they have Jesus to lean on and to counsel them in these difficult situations. Therein lies the crux of our faith.

As you continue to read this book, there are a few things you need to know about your author. One, as I said before, I was once on the ungodly side. I was, and actually still am, a party kind of guy. I love a good time. Finally, in mid-life, through the grace of God, I was given the opportunity to realize where I was heading with my ungodliness. I was given the opportunity to accept a great gift from God – a total attitude adjustment. It is ironic that we can go through this life pretending to be happy and all the time be heading towards the catastrophe of hell. If I have my head screwed on with any kind of Godly perspective, that would not be a place I would choose to go. From what I've read, it is not a party. It is eternal suffering and I want no part of it. Two, I don't like to party alone, so I am working hard on trying to get as many people as possible into heaven. That, in itself, is more fun than you can imagine.

Surely those who have walked this treacherous, worldly path before me and achieved sainthood would agree - you have to plot your course towards the goal that you want to achieve. In plotting this course, you increase your chances of achieving that goal.

If you want to be a saint, you must have a game plan. You must choose on whose team you want to play in this "mortal combat." I, a bit late in the game, now choose life - eternal life. I raised the banner of Jesus Christ and said, "Lord, I am ready to fight for right. I want to be a saint."

I want to be a saint. It feels great to say that. Try it. I want to be a saint. I want to be a saint. I WANT TO BE A SAINT. Don't you want to just shout it from the rooftops? Well, I do. If you have a good, holy attitude, an obedient disposition, a kind, loving personality and you want to share what God has given to you with others, then you have a saintly attitude and you will want to shout it out. And I want you to shout it out, also; that is the reason for this book. If you do not have a Godly attitude then, more than likely, you are not much fun to be around. You have to redesign your life to bring about the desire of sainthood. I want you to find the treasure I have found in searching for sainthood, the treasure that makes me want to sing and dance, the treasure that makes me want to help you in your journey of salvation.

Drum roll, please! This is the part where I inspire you toward your attitude adjustment. And now, cue the music and pick up the tune.

Oh, when the saints, go marching in.
Oh, when the saints, go marching in.

Come on, get up and start marching around the table. And sing out loud! And now, take it from the top.

Oh, when the saints, go marching in.
Oh, when the saints go marching in.
Lord, I want to be in that number,
When the saints go marching in.

Maybe it would be best to be alone when you do this. Someone might think you have lost a few marbles if you are caught marching around the table and singing out loud. What the heck! Let them think what they want.

Oh, when the saints, go marching in.
Oh, when the saints go marching in.
Lord, I want to be in that number,
When the saints go marching in.

Lift those legs high! Move those arms! It's going to be great. Look, there's Saint Michael. Sing louder and do the grand wrap-up. Drag those last words out.

When the saints goooo marrrr-ching iiiiiinnnnnn !

Wow, I want to be in that number. How about you?

This is book three in a possible series of sixteen. To understand that comment and that number, you have to know that I lied to get out of high school. I was failing the twelfth grade and my English teacher came to me and explained that I was about to fail her class. She also explained that she chose to give me an opportunity to pass. Her proposition was this: if I would do sixteen book reports, she would give me a B in English, which would raise my grade average to a D, and I would squeak by.

I took her up on the offer and immediately went to my brother-in-law, who was a fifth grade school teacher. I found no difficulty in asking him to have his class do book reports. I explained my dilemma and the next thing I knew, I was picking through thirty or forty book reports to come up with the best sixteen. Presto, I was a high school graduate! You have to know that I was not failing because I lacked intelligence. I had dyslexia.

There was no problem for me, whatsoever, in cheating to get a high school diploma. My hatred for school was great, and with no God in my life, it was quite easy to do. That was back in 1962. In 1987, the Lord granted me a tremendous conversion and took my dyslexia away. Now, in retrospect, I can see my many mistakes. Today I'm on a mission to write sixteen books to make up for that big lie and many others. The passion I have, to do penance for that mistake, and the others, seems to have caught God's attention, because He is most certainly helping me to author these books.

I am also on the aforementioned mission, that is, this saint business. So just consider this book, the previous two and the thirteen to come, a course. Call the package *How to Become a Saint 101.* It is not that I am an expert, but I do have a lot of experience, both bad and good, that would earn me credits toward a degree in this subject. My prayer is that you can glean enough from this to take your best shot at sainthood.

I guess if you really wanted expert advice, you could read some of the lives of the actual saints. I have found much of the writing done by our saints is way over my head and possibly yours. So this just might be God's attempt at dumbing-down the sainthood process for all of us non-intellectuals. And it seems that God is using one of His biggest dummies to do it.

If I am going to try to help you to become a saint, the first thing I have to do is prove to you that there is a God. Many people, lay and religious alike, claim they believe in God, but their actions show that they are actually employed by Satan. After all, if we want to be saints and on God's winning team, we have to truly believe in Him. You could be saying, "I already believe in God." Please read on and grade yourself and your beliefs and we will see.

The following is for entertainment only. I am not your judge.

1: How often do you go to Mass? (Sunday is mandatory, unless you miss for a very good reason, or you automatically get an E.)

A. 14 times a week.
B. 7 times a week.
C. 3 times a week.
D. 1 time a week.
E. Not on a regular basis.

Maybe you are starving to death. Eat more of the Bread of Life!

2: How often, in the course of the day, do you pray?

A. Without ceasing.
B. All of my waking hours.
C. Many times in the day.
D. When I wake and when I go to sleep
E. Seldom.

No cheating. Be honest.

3: Whom do I love? (Hint: There is no middle ground.)

A. Everyone.
E. Everybody except a person or two.

You've got to love even Bill Clinton. I know it is tough.

4: How much do I fast?

A. On Eucharist and water for thirty-seven years with out fail. (Theresa Neumann)
B. Bread and water seven days a week.
C. Bread and water on Wednesdays and Fridays.
D. From meat on Fridays and maybe candy during Lent.
E No fasting at all.

Don't give me that wimpy "two small meals and one normal meal" argument. A person could get fat doing that. Surely that is not much fasting. The Church says it is fasting and so it is, but that is not the kind of which great saints are made.

5: How often do I do a holy hour?

A. Every day.
B. Six days a week.
C. Three days a week
D. One day a week.
E. Zero days a week.

Holy mackerel, does a holy hour help me be a saint?

6: How often do I say the Rosary?

A. 105 decades a day
B. 30 decades a day
C. 15 decades a day
D. 5 decades a day
E. Zero decades a day

Sniff, sniff. Do I smell something burning?

7: In tithing of time, talent and treasure – what do I give?

A. 30% or more
B. 20%
C. 15%
D. 10%
E. Less than 10%

Get the fire extinguisher.

8: How well do I follow the teachings of the Church?

A. I follow all of the rules of the Church.
B. I follow all of the rules of which I am aware.
C. I do break some of the rules, but I go to confession as soon as possible.
D. I do break some of the rules, but I go to confession once a year.
E. I am a Cafeteria Catholic, i.e. I believe what I want to believe and ignore the teachings where I think the Church is wrong (abortion, contraception, women as priests and the like.)

Amazing how many Catholics fail that one.

9: How often do I go to confession?

A. Every day - Pope John Paul II does.
B. Once a week
C. Once a month
D. Once a year
E. Less than once a year

We had better not die between long intervals of confessions.

10: How many people have you brought to or back to the Catholic faith?

A. Multitudes
B. Many
C. A few
D. One
E. None

I would imagine that investing in fireproof suits is going to be the best bet for many people.

The list could go on and on, but these few can give you a general idea of what kind of Catholic you are. Answer values are: A=5 points, B=4, C=3, D=2, E=1. Add up your points and divide by 10. If your grade point average is 1.9 or lower, you have failed and may not be a saint unless you get some things fixed. To help you figure out the rest of my grade chart, it stands to reason that if you got 5.0, you get an A. If you got 3.0 to 3.9, you got a grade of C, or average. As I asked up at Number 6, do you smell something burning? I hope it is not you. If you are a parent with children in school, are your grades on par with what you expect from your children? If not, why not?

Oh, did I assume a negative answer from you? Our Father in heaven wants to be proud of our grades, also. He would like to see every one of His children getting good grades. And as with all good parents, He will reprimand us for bad grades. If we do not take the time to check ourselves out as far as our Godly grades go, we may just end up proclaiming with our lives that God does not exist. Maybe by the end of this book we can get your grades up, but you may have to go to summer school. On with the course.

I am sure many people have tried to prove the existence of God in very theological ways. With true Christianity in a period of great decline, not in numbers, but in performance, the attempts do not seem to be effective enough to pull us out of this nosedive, do they? So let's begin there. Let's first prove that God exists. This understanding is a requirement to have a saintly attitude. How could you have a saintly attitude if you can't even prove that God exists? If today someone walks up to you and says, "Prove to me God exists," what will you say?

Let me back up for a second. Let's suppose you are an average Joe and one day you wake up wondering if there really is a God. If you wonder about that, then you may also wonder if heaven and hell really exist. With that in mind, you have to make a decision. Do you care? If you don't really care whether you become a saint or if you become trapped in hell forever, then you are basically a dim-witted person, as I was, for the twenty-seven years that I didn't care. You would really have to be stupid not to care at all. But it is astounding how many choose a life with Satan over sainthood by simple default. If you don't choose God, you get Satan. We could say you have an attitude, but it's the wrong one.

The understanding needed to make a decision on the existence of God is not rocket science. This entails only a very basic understanding of reality and reality is this - there is a God. Even the most primitive of civilizations throughout all of history understood the premise of a supreme being or beings. All may not have zeroed in on the one true God, but most civilizations knew that there was someone greater than us humans. It is the very nature of our being to know we were created, that there is someone greater than we are. This is imbedded in our soul at conception. It is only through a human being not doing battle with original sin or simply allowing the entrance of evil, that the mind becomes clouded to the point where the common sense with which we're endowed is reduced and arrogance is enhanced. You can find these lesser traits manifesting themselves in many public officials, judges and even some of our past presidents and vice-presidents, e.g., Clinton and Gore.

Imagine Supreme Court judges ruling that it is lawful to pull a child halfway out of his mother's womb, suck his brains out until he is dead, then pull him the rest of the way out and deliver the dead baby and believe you are not a murderer. News flash! It is called conspiracy. A mother, a doctor, a judge, the president, vice-president, various other politicians and voters conspired to sentence to death the most innocent of all human life. It is ungodly and there is only one place reserved for the unforgiven, ungodly person, and that is hell. There is no return from that great divide! Sorry, Judge, that's how it is. Sorry, Mr. Clinton, but you cannot be a practicing whore and expect heaven to be your home. Many people could lose their salvation just because they support a political party or a certain candidate. Take the Democrats, for instance. I was a Democrat most of my life, but because of their 'culture of death' platform, I had to change parties or risk my salvation. You can throw God out of the schools, pass laws to kill the unborn and promote homosexuality as a politician, but you cannot alter the fact that God is the Judge. And there is only one sentence for unforgiven mortal sin. Hell! This is not a judgment on my part, but revealed truth in Scripture.

There's nothing wrong with grappling with truth, but many people take it to an extreme that eventually costs them their salvation. If you want to know the truth, consider this: a basic law of physical science states that for every action there is an opposite and equal reaction. This simply says nothing can move unless something makes it move. It is remarkable how much we take this law of science for granted, or else ignore it completely.

Let's take a look at this law and its association with an automobile. Observe the action and reaction necessary to take a car from a dead stop to a forward motion. Your hand goes in your pocket for the keys. You take the correct key, insert it into the keyhole and unlock the door. You heft your heavy body inside. Just this little bit of movement on your part takes a lot of action and reaction. You had to eat celery, beans, hot dogs, and steak, and then there are all those liquids. Your body has to digest all of this and turn it into energy, the energy that makes it possible for you to move about, to operate your limbs. If you do not eat, you will die, and you don't even have your car started yet.

Let's assume that you are smart enough to eat, stay alive, get in your car and insert the key. I know that is a stretch for many people; in fact I know some from whom we should take the keys. But let's suppose you still have yours. So now you turn the key. All you hear is *errrr, errrr, errrr*, and the next thing you know, the car is running. You turn the key - an action. The reaction? A switch makes contact. Electricity is passed from a storage battery to the starting motor. The electrically driven motor spins and it turns a flywheel. The flywheel is attached to the crankshaft. Attached to the crankshaft are piston rods and pistons. Imagine that it's a V-8 gasoline engine. Because you turn that key, all these parts begin to move. The fuel pump is actuated, gasoline is pumped from a tank into a carburetor or injectors and the fuel is dispersed through intake valves into the eight combustion chambers. Also put into motion is a generator or alternator providing electricity necessary to power all of your accessories. More than this, it sends an electrical charge to eight spark plugs, one at a time, mounted at the top of the combustion chambers. When one of the eight pistons is just around top dead center, an electrical spark is introduced into the chamber that has become filled with gas vapor and a tremendous explosion ensues. In turn, each of the pistons has an explosion occur above it, causing the piston to be forced downward. This downward motion turns the crankshaft. The crankshaft is connected to a transmission, which distributes this rotating motion to the wheels, and the car moves forward.

If your car is equipped with a tachometer you can observe the revolutions per minute the engine is making. If the engine is turning at 3000 revolutions per minute, we have to multiply this times eight to find the number of explosions occurring to make the car move down the road. The answer is 24,000. It takes 24,000 explosions every minute to keep your car moving at highway speeds. And you probably didn't even know all that and more was taking place under your hood. For every action there is an opposite and equal reaction. No turning the key, no moving car. No gasoline exploding, no moving car. You must have the action to have the reaction.

I think we've proven the existence of God already. No, not because we got this car moving, but because I know all of this and I lied to get out of high school. Who gave me the ability to know all of this? God! The fact that I can tear apart a car engine and put it back together blindfolded is not my own doing, but God's. He gave me this brain, so all glory is His! But on with the subject at hand.

You may now be saying that this doesn't prove that God exists. And what does all of this action and reaction stuff have to do with sainthood? What does all of this have to do with God? Well, if I have just reminded you about the simple theory of cause and effect, action and reaction, think for a moment. If the laws of physical science say nothing moves without something or someone making it move, what made the first thing move? Nothing in the entire universe could have moved or come into being if something didn't make it move or come into being. What could have made the first thing move? It could only be God! Way cool, isn't it?

Some say we, as humans, simply evolved. Foolish men teach the theory of evolution. The very school from which I lied to graduate teaches evolution as a fact. My question is: we evolved from what? What made the first thing from which we evolved? You don't even have to try to answer that because with the discovery of DNA, we find the theory of evolution has no possibility of being true. The scientists now say that the probability of us evolving from some amino acid five billion years ago has the same probability as one million blind people all solving Rubik's Cube, all at the same moment.

Try to hit a bull's eye, one inch square, five solar systems away, with your hunting rifle. That is how realistic the theory of evolution is, yet they teach evolution and not creationism in our schools. From a scientific point of view, evolution has no probability of being true – zero. Yet creation has much scientific support and much historic fact to back it up. Still the lie of evolution is taught so that God does not have to be. There needs to be an attitude adjustment in our schools and in our children. People who teach evolution will probably not make it into heaven. How can you be a saint and teach against God? Let me explain. I am only talking about teachers who teach evolution to be the truth over creation, whether forced to teach it or not. You cannot teach a lie, live with that lie unconfessed and go to heaven. You can teach evolution as a theory that cannot possibly be, and you can teach that Darwin was in error, but you cannot teach evolution as fact.

Do you believe in the Big Bang? What made the Big Bang? No matter what your theory is, it all goes back to the simple law of action and reaction and it proves the existence of God. He is the only unexplained existence that defies science. God says He made everything and, for sure, none of us did. He says He made heaven and hell. Wouldn't it be a shame if we found out too late that He was right and we ended up in the wrong place? He says that hell is forever. That alone should scare the bejeebies out of you.

If there was a Big Bang, God caused it. You can have all the scientists and all the people in the world dispute this, but the only thing they end up trying to prove wrong is their own law of physical science. So until they change their laws, it all had to be started into motion by God. And if He did that, then where does that leave all those who do not believe in God?

A few years ago, I stumbled upon this premise in my mind. Surely it had to be sent by God, but if you want to write it off to personal inspiration, it's okay with me. I was still overwhelmed by it.

I actually believed that, at last, someone – me – had proven the existence of God in a very practical way. And then, only a short time later, God allowed me to be introduced to some writings of Saint Thomas Aquinas. Saint Thomas was a great philosopher and may well be the first person to be inspired with the theory of God being the first mover. I guess I will never know if I was the second or the millionth to think of it, but it most certainly was an original thought on my part. I did not read it first.

Now we know we can prove the existence of God. And this very fact demands a reaction from us. We can react to it in a positive way and chart our course in God's direction, toward sainthood, or we can react to it in a passive way and, by default, chart our course toward hell. We can even react to it in a negative way and actively chart our course toward hell. It all depends on our attitude.

I, for one, was charting my course toward hell for most of my life. I am not going to go through all that in this book, but if you're interested in information on how I got this far, you could find that in my first book, *Apostles of the Last Days.* That book explains how I fell away from God, the many mistakes I made while away, and how God came for me when no one else would.

The question with which we are going to deal is this: when you realize that God exists and you want to spend all of eternity with Him, what is it you must do?

If none of this is making sense to you, at this point you may need that attitude adjustment we were talking about earlier. I have some very wealthy friends who go through life without much of God in their lives and seem not to need Him. That is a prime example of where an attitude adjustment should come into play. That needs to take place first. It would be sad to think we just die and everything ends right then and there. Extremely sad, indeed, to think that this miserable world is all there is. So the attitude adjustment will help us lean toward hope and then faith. The attitude adjustment toward hope would entail our taking a hard look at this world and our role in it.

I stated above that this world is miserable and you may not agree with me, but allow me my due. I have traveled the globe extensively. I have been overseas more than fifty times. I've spent time in war zones, impoverished parts of the world and in places of abundant affluence. I have been poor and I have been rich. I was not as poor as some, but poor enough. I was not as rich as some, but rich enough. I believe that all of this gives me a broad perspective as far as the world goes. In the realm of the Catholic Church, I have gone to Mass at well over a thousand different churches, and the number is growing constantly because of the traveling involved in my being a Catholic evangelist.

I have also witnessed, firsthand, from a worldwide viewpoint, the attitudes of people. And I have witnessed the attitude in the Catholic Church and many other churches. In trying not to be too arrogant, as referenced previously, I believe I have accomplished a kind of life study in attitudes. I have observed and concluded that most people demonstrate an anti-God attitude. It does not matter whether we claim to be Christian or not. In fact, many so-called Christians demonstrate a phenomenal amount of anti-God attitude. If you had a chance to see the results of my little test from all who will read this book, it would shock you. But as with everything that tends towards sin in our lives, we find our little faith and our sins far too easy to justify.

Let's take a scenario that plays itself out quite often. A man and a woman, both claiming to have difficult marriages, get involved with each other. The woman seems to demonstrate an abundance of Catholic faith and the man is lacking in faith. Enter Satan. The woman leaves her husband for her newfound friend. He, likewise, leaves his wife. God did not put them together, but they feel He did. The man, they also believe, is drawn back to his previously abandoned Catholic faith through the influence of this new relationship. Now the two divorcés, even though they share physical relations (if only in their minds), feel free to participate at their will in the ceremonies and sacraments of the Catholic Church.

Now they each have a new title - adulterer. Both plunge headlong into mortal sin. The attitudes of those involved are altered by evil. Few live up to the promise of "until death do we part." The two who Satan brought together now are willing to revise their beliefs and standards of Catholic morality to do, not God's will, but their own. They're willing to set all of the teachings of God aside. The age-old adage, "If it feels so good, how could it be so wrong?" comes into play. The ultimate distortion of truth is when this couple seeks the advice of a priest, and they are told that they can live together without offending God. Believe me, this has happened.

The battle lines are drawn. Families take sides and the proverbial wedge is driven into what seemed to be wholesome and happy American Christian families. Satan changes attitudes quickly and dramatically. Now a once holy human being is willing to say, "I am right and the Church is wrong." Parents who love their children are now willing to let them plunge toward the depths of hell in the name of "love". The reality of the situation is this: both parties, being from a Catholic background, know full well that for them to be involved with another person, even if a civil divorce decree has been pronounced, is against God's law. All Catholics know full well, when in this kind of situation, that you cannot date, have affections for, or sexual thoughts about, another person without being in serious sin. You are not always yours to give.

What if they both go to confession? They are now free of the horrible sin, but Satan doesn't give in so easily. Their only option is to separate or continue on as though brother and sister. The latter is almost impossible to do once the physical relationship has already been established.

Seven Scriptures, like the following one, explain that associations without two annulments and one new marriage are punishable by death. The punishment for adultery is the eternal fire. At times some people will even lie to obtain an annulment. An annulment obtained under false claims and contentions is no annulment at all and dangerous territory at best.

> Mt 5:31-32 *"It was also said, 'Whoever divorces his wife must give her a bill of divorce.' But I say to you, whoever divorces his wife (unless the marriage is unlawful) causes her to commit adultery, and whoever marries a divorced woman commits adultery."*

What if they promise that they will not have relations until their annulments come through? What if the annulments don't come through? But while waiting, they have to fight off entertaining lust in their minds. The idea of loving another person while still married is a mortal sin.

> Mt 5:28-29 *"But I say to you, everyone who looks at a woman with lust has already committed adultery with her in his heart. If your right eye causes you to sin, tear it out and throw it away. It is better for you to lose one of your members than to have your whole body thrown into Gahanna."*

But there are those who say that to be with the one you love until the annulments come through is permissible. To think that way is delusion. These misguided souls need not only an attitude adjustment, but they also need a morality adjustment.

The parents who side with their child in an adulterous situation not only condone the child's sin, but, I believe, take on that sin themselves. And the same scenario extends itself to the siblings of the family. Scripture says, *"Choose today whose side you're on."* A brother or sister who supports a sibling's sin falls into sin himself.

The Lord also says,

> Mt 10:34-40 *"Do not think that I have come to bring peace upon the earth. I have come to bring not peace but the sword. For I have come to set a man against his father, a daughter against her mother, and a daughter-in-law against her mother-in-law; and one's enemies will be those of his household. Whoever loves father or mother more than me is not worthy of me, and whoever loves son or daughter more than me is not worthy of me; and whoever does not take up his cross and follow after me is not worthy of me. Whoever finds his life will lose it, and whoever loses his life for my sake will find it. Whoever receives you receives me, and whoever receives me receives the one who sent me. Whoever receives a prophet because he is a prophet will receive a prophet's reward, and whoever receives a righteous man because he is righteous will receive a righteous man's reward. And whoever gives only a cup of cold water to one of these little ones to drink because he is a disciple—amen, I say to you, he will surely not lose his reward."*

It is sad that kind, loving people who once appeared to fully embrace the true teachings of the Catholic Church so easily abandon the Lord. These kinds of examples are prophesied in the parable of the seed.

> Mt 13:1-9 *On that day, Jesus went out of the house and sat down by the sea. Such large crowds gathered around him that he got into a boat and sat down, and the whole crowd stood along the shore. And he spoke to them at length in parables, saying, "A sower went out to sow. And as he sowed, some seed fell on the path, and birds came and ate it up. Some fell on rocky ground,*

> *where it had little soil. It sprang up at once because the soil was not deep, and when the sun rose it was scorched, and it withered for lack of roots. Some seed fell among thorns, and the thorns grew up and choked it. But some seed fell on rich soil, and produced fruit, a hundred or sixty or thirty fold. Whoever has ears ought to hear."*

All of this might be put in the most precise perspective in Jeremiah:

> Jeremiah 7:3-11 *Thus says the Lord of hosts, the God of Israel: Reform your ways and your deeds, so that I may remain with you in this place. Put not your trust in the deceitful words: "This is the temple of the Lord ! The temple of the Lord ! The temple of the Lord !" Only if you thoroughly reform your ways and your deeds; if each of you deals justly with his neighbor; if you no longer oppress the resident alien, the orphan, and the widow; if you no longer shed innocent blood in this place, or follow strange gods to your own harm, will I remain with you in this place, in the land which I gave your fathers long ago and forever. But here you are, putting your trust in deceitful words to your own loss! Are you to steal and murder, commit adultery and perjury, burn incense to Baal, go after strange gods that you know not, and yet come to stand before me in this house which bears my name, and say: "We are safe; we can commit all these abominations again"? Has this house, which bears my name, become in your eyes a den of thieves? I, too, see what is being done, says the Lord .*

Satan uses attitude manipulation to his advantage all the time. It is not just in divorce and annulment scenarios, but also in every walk of life. Satan is at the work place, in the home, on the playground, in the schools, and yes, even in Catholic schools, and the Church.

To be on the safe side we should always err on the side of caution. It is better to play it safe with God than to err one time using your own mind as a measuring stick. God knew full well how the evil one would use our minds to manipulate us. It is the very reason He gave us the Church. The Church is here to guide us through all of the pitfalls. It is when we venture out on our own, away from the Church that we get into trouble. Sticking with the Church is dangerous enough with all of the wolves in sheep's clothing, so be very careful. It takes great discernment, even within the Church, but to be on your own is the most dangerous of all.

Give yourself a break. Adjust your attitude so that it relies heavily on the precepts of Jesus Christ, and you will be on the beginning path to sainthood. It is not difficult to know the difference between right and wrong. Opt for the attitude adjustment and choose right.

If you now choose to undergo a major attitude adjustment, to start analyzing your relationship with God, and decide to increase your time spent with Him (no matter how holy you think you are), you pass Lesson Two. Move on with what you have learned about survival, scandal and division thus far. Now you have the chance to sharpen your skills and your desire to be a saint in Chapter Three.

NOTES

CHAPTER THREE

DESIRE OF SAINTHOOD

"I want," is probably the most overused statement in all our lives. It all starts from that first slap on our butts as babies. The slap causes sounds to come out of the wee ones, "Wa. Wa. Wa." Translated that means, "I want. I want. I want." I want you to stop hitting me. I want food. I want to be held. And soon enough, I want to be changed.

We graduate rapidly from wanting just the basic necessities of life as babies, to those items of self-satisfaction and entertainment. One of the first things that we demand is more toys. This particular desire was ingrained in our brains by our parents, brothers and sisters, aunts and uncles and, of course, grandparents. Everyone seems to want to quiet us down or to demonstrate affection by giving us something. We soon find out that these people are easy marks and so we use the words, "I want . . . (whatever)." Quite frequently and generally, we get what we want.

Depending on the family into which one is born, the teachings of what is really necessary in life can vary greatly. If you take a serious look at the population of this world, you will find what is most needed is least given. And what is most needed is an early foundation for the teachings of Christ - say, a rattle with a picture of Jesus on it. That would be a great place to start. Your child's first word could have been or could be "Jesus".

I know of families who desired the best for their children, so they started at the age of one year, sometimes earlier, even in the womb, to teach their children about Jesus Christ. It works. It is truly something beautiful to behold - the young child with knowledge of his Creator. I don't know anything more heart warming than a two-year-old saying the Rosary.

Then there are those families who don't give much thought, if any, to the instruction of their children at an early age in the teachings of Jesus Christ. Some feel the children will not comprehend the premise of Christ and creation at one or two years old and so they delay the process. Many feel their children will learn on their own when they're ready, or worse yet, the children will choose their own faith when they are adults. This is a spiritually fatal mistake.

The difference between these two scenarios, should one do a case study, would be astounding. Children who grow up in a family with a good moral foundation carry those teachings through all their lives and it makes their lives more complete. On the other hand, the children who do not have this foundation tend to be much more materialistic and find themselves in more trouble.

I was a child brought up in a moderately Catholic family. What I mean by that is that my parents were Sunday Catholics. We, as a family, were not overly involved in our faith. Subsequently I turned out to be a rather materialistic individual. The "I wants" in my life turned out to be, "I want a new car, I want new clothing, I want more money," and not, "I want to go to Church. I want to pray." This had a devastating effect on my life and I ended up breaking all of God's laws.

The seed of desire for sainthood was not planted in my youth; therefore, it was not a desire in my adulthood. I got a great start in my baptism, but that great start, unnourished, soon gave way to the world.

I don't know why God decided to bring to fruition my conversion at age forty-four. I did find out that same year that He had been working in my life for a long time. It could have been my reluctance to accept what He was sending my way. I am studying the conversion process a bit and a pattern is starting to unfold. I am witnessing many firstborn males returning to the faith. Scripture says that all firstborn males belong to God and it seems that He is gathering them unto Himself. If my theory is correct, I am extremely grateful.

Retrospect is an astounding subject. In retrospect, I look at my life without Christ and I become a bit frustrated with myself, knowing what I could have accomplished through Christ if I had chosen the right path sooner. But how do I know that my delay was not Christ-created?

It is difficult for me to blame my parents for not giving me a better Christ-centered foundation, but where else could the fault lie? I am not bringing this up to degrade my parents, but to alert current and future parents to the damage they will cause to all humanity by not raising their children in a Christ-centered atmosphere.

Most parents do not have a clue as to the destruction they cause when they force their weak faith, or lack of faith, on their children. If someone had cared enough for these parents when they were children, they may have understood the existence of God. With that understanding, perhaps they would have had a desire for sainthood, which they might then have passed along to their children. Without this early ingraining, there is little chance that the desire for sainthood will exist. If you do not have this desire, then what is life all about - possessions and death?

Take a look at most parents today. Do you see them drilling their children on their faith? Do you see them placing a firm understanding in their children's minds that there is a heaven and hell? It is a shame, but parents spend more time figuring out how to get their next new car than they do trying to get the children into heaven. Most parents are far more concerned about their children's academic and athletic conditioning, and that demonstrates clearly who their god is. It is just a matter of priorities. Too many people take heaven and hell in a very passive or an "I couldn't care less" way. Thus by the path of evasion, they choose hell for themselves and their children.

I personally believe that there are no adults in heaven who did not have a great desire to go there. I don't believe you get to heaven with a casual consideration. Not long ago, I wrote an editorial for our *Gospa Missions Newsletter* on the subject of lukewarmness. Why don't I just reprint that particular commentary here?

Lukewarm

> Rev 3:11–22 *I am coming quickly. Hold fast to what you have, so that no one may take your crown. "The victor I will make into a pillar in the temple of my God, and he will never leave it again. On him I will inscribe the name of my God and the name of the city of my God, the new Jerusalem, which comes down out of heaven from my God, as well as my new name. Whoever has ears ought to hear what the Spirit says to the churches. To the angel of the church in Laodicea, write this: 'The Amen, the faithful and true witness, the source of God's creation, says this, "I know your works; I know that you are neither cold nor hot. I wish you were either cold or hot. So, because you are lukewarm, neither hot nor cold, I will spit you out of my mouth. For you say, 'I am rich and affluent and have no need of anything,' and yet do not realize that you are wretched, pitiable, poor, blind, and naked. I advise you to buy from me gold refined by fire so that you may be rich, and white garments to put on so that your shameful nakedness may not be exposed, and buy ointment to smear on your eyes so that you may see. Those whom I love, I reprove and chastise. Be earnest, therefore, and repent. Behold, I stand at the door and knock. If anyone hears my voice and opens the door, (then) I will enter his house and dine with him, and he with me. I will give the victor the right to sit with me on my throne, as I myself first won the victory and sit with my Father on his throne. Whoever has ears ought to hear what the Spirit says to the churches."*

The Scripture above has been altered and distorted by modern Bible writers and so Pope John Paul II has called for a new Bible to be written that will more authentically represent the *Latin Vulgate*. He has a desire for all of us to find sainthood and so tries to lead the flock correctly, but he gets so much flak from his bishops and priests. The crux of this Scripture is supposed to be that if you are lukewarm, the Lord will *begin to vomit you* from His mouth. There is a big difference in the teaching by today's politically correct writers and what Christ really taught.

I guess all we have to do is figure out what *hot* is. It stands to reason from Scripture that if we are lukewarm, we probably won't be going to heaven. What then is hot? In the thesaurus, we find words like *sweltering, scorching, blazing, boiling* and *passionate.*

Are you passionate for the Lord? Are you blazing and on fire for the Lord? If you are not asking yourself these kinds of questions, then maybe the idea of being hot, cold or lukewarm never crossed your mind. Maybe you feel that occupying a seat in church on Sunday is a ticket to heaven and chances are good that you are wrong. To be wrong about your salvation is the biggest mistake you can make and it is uncorrectable after your death.

Is it really going to kill any of us to stop one day and analyze where we stand with God? At what point do we decide that we love ourselves enough to make an effort toward our salvation?

If we take a chance on the lotto and lose, what difference does it make? But to gamble on salvation . . . you don't even want to go there.

I am the first to admit that when I buy a product that comes equipped with an owner's manual, I almost always fail to read it. I attempt to put the product together on my own and find it, without fail, very difficult to accomplish. As a last resort, I delve into the manual and soon the product is working fine. The same goes for God. His product of salvation comes with a manual, but who takes the time to read it? And therein lies the reason for being lukewarm. We do not have a full understanding of what salvation consists of, therefore, have little desire for salvation.

I am not going to take the time in this editorial to explain all of the parameters that it takes to rise above *lukewarm* and fall into the realm of *hot.* That is the subject of my next book. Here I just want to give you a little shove in the direction of hot. It is my desire, and has been for many years, to get people to start thinking about their salvation and stop assuming that it is already accomplished.

If one would take a realistic look at the one, holy, catholic and apostolic Church, I think we would all agree that we have fallen into a state of lukewarmness. It is time for someone to build a fire under Catholics. Guess who God chose to do the job? I'll bet you thought I was going to say it is me. Well, yes, that too, but He chose you! It is not reasonable to think that you could accomplish such an awesome job without first being on fire yourself.

The opening passage from the book of *Revelation* explains to us that the Church back then was lukewarm. We would be hard pressed to find something today to indicate that we have advanced beyond that state. Being vomited out of God's mouth is not something I want for you or me. So what do you say? Let's get out the Good Book, the manual, and build a fire in our hearts. Instead of helping Satan stoke the fires of hell, let's get fired up for Jesus. Let us put this life on the back burner and plunge headlong into consuming the word of God and putting it into practice. It is part of the fuel that will take us from the realm of *lukewarm* to that of *hot.*

In the above editorial I stated that I did not want to delve into all of the parameters of salvation. But here we are in that book mentioned above and here we can take as much time as we wish. I want to do a lot more here, so we can pass on to future generations a true and fire-filled faith.

I hope you can now see the jeopardy in which parents place their children when they pass on a lukewarm faith. In essence, it could be a ticket to hell. If parents do not place a desire in the hearts of their children to be saints, who is going to do it?

It is truly sad how many people simply assume that they are going to heaven. Scripture does not bear out their beliefs.

Mt 7:13-29 *"Enter through the narrow gate; for the gate is wide and the road broad that leads to destruction and those who enter through it are many. How narrow the gate and constricted the road that leads to life. And those who find it are few. "Beware of false prophets, who come to you in sheep's clothing, but underneath are ravenous wolves."*

By their fruits you will know them. Do people pick grapes from thorn bushes, or figs from thistles? Just so, every good tree bears good fruit, and a rotten tree bears bad fruit. A good tree cannot bear bad fruit, nor can a rotten tree bear good fruit. Every tree that does not bear good fruit will be cut down and thrown into the fire. So by their fruits you will know them.

"Not everyone who says to me, 'Lord, Lord,' will enter the kingdom of heaven, but only the one who does the will of my Father in heaven. Many will say to me on that day, 'Lord, Lord, did we not prophesy in your name? Did we not drive out demons in your name? Did we not do mighty deeds in your name?' Then I will declare to them solemnly, 'I never knew you. Depart from me, you evildoers.' "Everyone who listens to these words of mine and acts on them will be like a wise man who built his house on rock. The rain fell, the floods came, and the winds blew and buffeted the house. But it did not collapse; it had been set solidly on rock. And everyone who listens to these words of mine but does not act on them will be like a fool who built his house on sand. The rain fell, the floods came, and the winds blew and buffeted the house. And it collapsed and was completely ruined."

When Jesus finished these words, the crowds were astonished at his teaching, for he taught them as one having authority, and not as their scribes.

Not only for yourselves do you need to learn the Word of God and put it in practice, but for the salvation of your children, also. If you loved your children you would fight for their salvation. Hell is forever. Oh, how many times do I hear even theologians say, "God is too merciful to send people to hell." Inasmuch as they are being used as fools by Satan, they are partially correct. I don't believe God ever sends anyone to hell. I believe everyone who goes to hell makes the decision to go on their own.

You have to keep in mind that if you do not have a desire to be a saint you probably won't be a saint. How many times have I said that already? I say it many times because it is the entire point of this book. And if you are not going to be a saint there is only one other alternative, hell. I want you on the right side of the *Great Divide*.

If you are willing here and now to ask God for the desire to be a saint, to get on your knees and beg for that grace, you may proceed to Chapter Four. I am serious. Do it. Ask and you shall receive. What would be the point in finishing this book if you won't even ask? I cannot force you into heaven and God certainly won't, but I am not opposed to giving you a kick in that direction, nor is God. Ask! Get down on your knees and ask for the desire to be a saint. If you did that, move on. (It is probably not a good idea to do that if you are on a bus.)

NOTES

CHAPTER FOUR

WHO DOES NOT MAKE IT?

Before we even contemplate a list of the parameters for sainthood, let's take a look at those the Lord says may have a hard time in making it through the narrow gate and into heaven. Remember, these are not my judgments or condemnations, but those of our Lord. (In case you haven't noticed so far, the paragraphs in italics are Scripture quotes. When the paragraphs return to standard type it is my own reflection.)

Let's back track for a moment and contemplate a part of a Scripture that we used in the last chapter.

> Mt 7:21-23 *"Not everyone who says to me, 'Lord, Lord,' will enter the kingdom of heaven, but only the one who does the will of my Father in heaven. Many will say to me on that day, 'Lord, Lord, did we not prophesy in your name? Did we not drive out demons in your name? Did we not do mighty deeds in your name?' Then I will declare to them solemnly, 'I never knew you. Depart from me, you evildoers.'"*

Can you imagine someone being involved in such great works of the Lord and not making the cut? Who are these people? It is my true belief that God will not preclude your miracle just because I am a jerk. God wants to give you every chance to know Him in a personal way, so He will use also the falling and fallen to accomplish His deeds. He won't use evil, but he will use you and me in our non-saintly state. Let me explain.

If a person has what seems to be a gift from God, it could be from God, or it could be from Satan, himself. It could even be some of both. Unless you are involved in discernment, you could be taken by a religious fraud. God will allow good to come to you, although the good is wrought by someone who is intrinsically bad, to bring about your salvation.

Let's say someone has a sincere conversion. That person starts out on fire for the Lord, but becomes blinded by something – perhaps sex or money, two very popular allurements. He (or she) continues his ministry and you still believe in him, but he is in Satan's hands. Once there, Satan instills such tremendous pride that the convert justifies his actions. He begins to believe the end justifies the means and is convinced that he is a very good person in spite of his shortcomings. If that person told you about Jesus and you believed and converted to exactly the point that God wanted you to be converted, that is good.

I know speakers on the Christian circuit who have fallen prey to Satan's traps and have continued until caught, all the while fooling believers.

Outside of deception by certain Christian speakers, there is a proliferation of people who claim to have supernatural apparitions, some of which are true, but mostly not. The alleged visionaries of Scottsdale, Arizona became authors of a series of five books titled *My Jesus of Mercy.* They were accused of having plagiarized parts of those books from *Imitation of Christ* by Thomas a Kempis, a book to be quoted later in this effort.

One alleged Scottsdale visionary migrated to the Diocese of Baltimore, Maryland, specifically to the town of Emmitsburg. The diocese, while investigating the reported visionary, became aware of the possibility of this plagiarism. Eventually they shut down the would-be apparitions.

Things are not always as they appear and the number of apparition sites declared not supernatural by the Church proves that. Persons who falsely claim supernatural visits can cause the flock much harm. They will not make it to heaven unless they repent and are forgiven. It is possible that some could experience conversion from reported visionaries not supported by the Church, as mentioned above, but many times the conversion fails down the road because of the depression caused by the official Church rejection of the events in question.

God gives us parameters by which to live and fully expects us to abide by these laws. The problem begins when a person attempts to justify his actions by watering down the law to fit his own designs. Today this is called interpreting the spirit of the law. To an adulterer, the new *love* in which he is involved is too great to be wrong, so it is not adultery. You know the rest of the story from Chapter Two, but beware of people who speak of only the "spirit" of the law. Those who use this phrase are generally good people who are in the beginning of a tailspin.

Today we find many religious unwilling to follow the directives of the Magisterium. They make up their own laws and, yes, sometimes their own liturgies. It is hard to believe that someone who has given his life, even to the ultimate extent of the priesthood, can and does fall prey to Satan's traps. One would assume all priests are holy and going to heaven because of the tremendous sacrifice of their life, but it is not necessarily true. Judas was chosen not only as a priest, but a bishop and we are not so sure that he made it. We can only conclude that defiant priests such as we find in the diocese of Chicago, the one hundred plus pastors who dispense only general absolution in direct opposition to Canon law, will have a hard time making it into heaven. It has been made painfully obvious by the sex scandals of 2002 that not all priests and bishops are what they profess to be.

We must pray very hard for priests and all religious. After all, they are under the greatest satanic pressure. Satan, himself, is trying to kill them each and every day.

There are signs of failure for priests and lay people alike. Let's take a look at priestly failures first. The most innocent of all failures is when a priest relinquishes his priestly blessing at the end of Mass and puts in its place, "May God bless us." As I said, it is generally an innocent act. A priest somewhere along the line started using this corrupted phrase to be more equal, not so pushy, more like a layperson, reducing his profound blessing to "May God bless us." And so the progression began. Perhaps the first priest to use the phrase thought that "May God bless you," sounded rather presumptuous.

What the priests who are doing this seem to truly not understand is that the words they utter are *in persona Christi, (the person of Christ).* The priest, at that point, is standing in for

Christ. It is Christ giving us the blessing. So he then has God standing there and saying, "May God bless us." To take it to the furthest extent, the priest then has God calling on another god to bless him.

We all have to understand, (as much as we all would like to be equal), that there are differences, enormous differences, between lay people and priests.

Another example of a dangerous change that is coming about has to do with the breaking of the Bread at Mass. Some priests are now breaking the Bread when they speak the words, "and He took the Bread and broke it . . ." Although it sounds as though the Bread should be broken there, it is not the place designated by the rubrics of the Mass. Priests have no authority to change these rubrics of the Mass to align with their personal preferences. The priests' theology and actions have to align with the Magisterium. They cannot claim ignorance because it is their job to know what to do and say, and when to do and say it. It would be like a pilot deciding to land a 747 on a highway rather than at the airport.

A very dear priest friend of mine was doing that very thing and I was heartbroken to see him do it. I labored over how to tell him that he had to correct this error. Many times when you tell a priest about something he is doing wrong, he gets defensive, even if you do it with great love. This is true for most of us.

God arranged for a window to be opened for me to present the issue to my friend. When he heard what I had to say, he was shocked to know that he was doing something wrong and was very sorry that he altered the Mass in that way. He was profoundly grateful for the kindness bestowed upon him in bringing the matter to his attention. Wouldn't it be great if we could always get along like that?

If you notice that the kneelers are missing from a church, that the statues have disappeared, that the tabernacles have been moved from the center to some remote spot, that parishioners are ordered off their knees and directed to say his parts of the

Mass along with the priest (even at times while holding the Eucharist,) you have a priest who has moderate to bigger problems.

Although the Church now says it is permissible to position the tabernacle away from the center of the sanctuary, look at the effect - a great reduction in reverence for the Church and Christ. These advancing problems turn into full-blown failure indicated by homilies that are filled with heresies, changing the words of Scripture as the Gospel is read, and teaching in opposition to the Magisterium, e.g., contraception is not a sin. This priest has now breached the faith and may not make it into heaven if the sin goes unconfessed. Anyone who teaches that contraception and abortion are permissible in God's plan causes not only the destruction of his own soul, but may cause the person upon whom his false teaching falls, to inherit hell as well.

It is unconscionable for Catholics to be teaching and practicing contraception. Yet they do – even with the proven effectiveness of natural family planning.

The most despicable of all priestly failures is the priest who turns pedophile or gay and causes children to sin. If he practices that sin and dies with that sin on his soul he will not make it into heaven. Scripture says he would be better off tying a millstone around his neck and jumping into the ocean. Pedophiles are in a tiny minority in the priesthood but recent reports lead us to believe that the problem of gay priests may not be so small. Awareness of their existence by the general congregation is just now coming to public consciousness and is extremely troubling. It is hard to say which group causes more harm.

I praise the Lord that some of these issues are being addressed and pray we can get back to an authentic Catholic faith.

It is a shame that Pope John Paul II had to publicly read the riot act to priests. Recently the Holy Father strongly reiterated the Church's clear teaching on general absolution, which has been constant since the beginning. The practice of administering general absolution in place of personal, one-on-one confession (except in an extreme emergency) is a grave disobedience on the part of the priests involved, and it must be stopped.

The first place it should be stopped is in the Archdiocese of Chicago, where it is most out of control. The archbishop there inherited the problem, but he has an obligation and a direct order from the Holy Father to fix it. Regardless of these orders, the problem continues as it has for well over thirty years. The priests involved say it is a Catholic tradition there, but deliberate disobediance is never a Catholic tradition. The archbishop says some of the pastors who are involved are really good men. You cannot assign the words 'good' and 'disobedient' to the same person. And so these disobedient priests are not good, but can be again. They claim there is just no time to hear confessions and that flies in the face of all the good priests who do labor to hear confessions.

Why should a Pope ever have to demand that priests and bishops return to authentic Catholic teaching? Pride, or rather smoke, has entered the Church. How can a priest make it through the narrow gate when priestly vows are violated and go unconfessed? This is very serious stuff, but pride convinces them they are right and the Church is wrong.

> Mt 15:7-14 *"Hypocrites, well did Isaiah prophesy about you when he said, 'This people honors me with their lips, but their hearts are far from me; in vain do they worship me, teaching as doctrines human precepts.' He summoned the crowd and said to them, 'Hear and understand. It is not what enters a man's mouth that defiles him; but what comes out of the mouth is what defiles him.' Then his disciples approached and said to him, 'Do you know that the Pharisees took offense when they heard what you said?' He said in reply, 'Every plant that my heavenly Father has not planted will be uprooted. Let them alone; they are blind guides (of the blind). If a blind person leads a blind person, both will fall into a pit.'"*

I was told by one priest in my diocese, while in a meeting with him, "My theology and your theology, Thomas, are on opposite ends of the spectrum. You believe we should be obedient to the Magisterium, and I believe that we have to be disobedient so we can accomplish the changes that are needed in the Church." I told him that I could not continue a conversation like that and not only left, but left that parish.

It is not my purpose to beat up on priests or any religious, but only to point out how much we have to pray for them, because they will have to account for every act of disobedience. They need our prayers lest they become uprooted and cast into the fire. If we love them and our Church, we will fight for their immortal souls.

That having been said, one of the foremost dissenting Benedictine nun, Sr. Joan Chittister, was quoted as saying, "Today's heresies will be tomorrow's dogmas." This from a nun who champions women's ordination. What Sr. Chittister seems to be saying is that the heresies that she introduces now will soon be our authentic teachings, because she knows more than the Pope himself.

Knowing this and more, Catholic leadership invited her to be the keynote speaker at a national Catholic education conference. The reason catechists and educators attend this conference is to acquire continuing religious education credits. I know of only two bishops that stood up to her contempt for obedience by refusing to grant the credits the attendees were seeking - Bishop Donald W. Wuerl of Pittsburgh and past bishop of Peoria, Illinois, Most Reverend John J. Myers. In recognition of all the criticism that these brave bishops received for this, my hat goes off to them.

Sr. Joan will not know the damage she has caused by her dissent until a moment after her death. She needs us now or she will suffer forever.

If we want to claim that we know love, if we want to lay hold of sainthood, we must pray and fast much for those who serve and fail. They, after all, were serving us until their fall. Just as God is merciful to us in our falls, we must now reach out to them.

If you are not in this race for *God alone*, as advised by none other than St. Louis de Montfort, you risk hearing the Scripture that commanded, *"Depart from me, you evildoers,"* recited to you on judgment day.

Try to live the law of God to its fullest and spare yourself the nightmare of judgment. It is better to err on the side of caution rather than to risk the one time you might liberalize God's law to the point of failure.

On top of our own failures, we lay people are, often times, the cause of failure for many religious. With our tongues, we convince our priests to do things they would never have done on their own. It was, in part, the laity who encouraged and influenced priests to neuter Scripture. The radical feminist movement demanded that the Bible be changed so as not to offend women. Rather than recreating my point here, let me simply plug in an editorial I wrote on the subject recently.

Man, oh, Man, oh, Man!

> It is not that it was a New Year's resolution or anything, but I did state to my staff that I was going to try to write a very positive editorial for this issue. I realize that I tend to go off a bit because of all of the disturbing news that seems to permeate the Church these days. It would be nice to have a week or so without some ridiculous altering of the way Church rituals are prescribed to be done. It is quite obvious that people, in general, do not like change, especially when something is changed that we hold very dear. But this month I was going to be uplifting.
>
> And then I went to Mass. You would think that going to Mass in a Catholic church would be the last place on earth that one would be infuriated. So much for a positive editorial.
>
> What in the world is the Church thinking when it kowtows to extreme feminism? A handful of women who do not have a clue to who God is, start beating a drum against the word man and the Catholic publishers cannot bow to their demands quickly enough. The Bibles are being

changed, the lectionaries, the missalettes and songbooks, all to the dismay of the Magisterium and the Holy Father himself. Soon you will not be able to find the word man or men anywhere.

I guess the next place from where they will strike the word men is on the doors to the toilets in all of the churches. After all, these feminists want to be in the men's locker room while the guys are standing there almost naked, if not completely so. Why not use the same toilets? Let's just forget that there is a difference in equipment and discard all modesty for the sake of tolerance. (That is tongue-in-cheek for you feminists who are out there nodding and saying, "That's a great idea!")

Satan has not dispensed a bigger dose of pride in centuries. Think of it. A "progressive" woman reads the Bible and sees the words "Our Father" and she takes offense at that. If this is not Satan, then who is it that convinces a woman to object to Scripture? And worse than that, what fool would actually want to change Scripture to please any human being?

But the best part of these foolhardy demands is what they actually demand. "I want the word mankind changed to humankind." Don't you get it? Hu-man-kind. The word that they find so offensive, man, is still there! I find that change, full of nothing, quite disgusting. Let's take this stupidity to the ultimate laugh. Remember, we must get rid of man. But what is this, woman or wo-man? Take out the man and you are left with wo. Woe is me. Isn't that a hoot? I am sure that God is not laughing, but saying, "Woe to all you who are involved in changing My WORD."

Then there is that "female" word. But what is this? Isn't the word male in there, also? The feminists say, "We demand that you eliminate that male reference right this instant." They obviously do this with some foot stomping included. Let's drop the male from female to make the feminists happy.

Uh oh, look at what we have left - a simple fe. He made them male and fe. I would imagine that there is a fee associated with demanding that you want God's Word to be changed. That price you do not want to pay. He made them man and wo. Am I making my point?

This is how stupid changing what amounts to nothing really is. But because I was not willing to bow to this kind of arrogance, I was advised to leave my former parish, by the pastor, no less, and I did. I also left the dust from my shoes (sandals) behind.

God's Word is not enough for feminists to attack, they have to attack His songs, also. That is exactly what put me on this tangent in the first place, the changes made in Christmas songs at Mass this year. You see we got new songbooks at the beginning of Advent and everything is different. I don't think the word man is to be found. Today we actually sang *It Came Upon a Midnight Clear* with the words "Peace on the earth, good will to all." It used to be "Good will to men." Truthfully, it makes me ill, not because of the tremendous amount of pride displayed in these demands, but because they must weary my God. I certainly can forgive them their huge failure, but God will not, until the prideful ones go to confession. And for those who support these dastardly changes, shame on you. In actuality, the feminist sin becomes the sin of the changers and supporters.

Well, that is about as uplifting as I can get right now. Wait! Can you hear that? Can you hear the feminists? They seem to be saying, "Boy, oh boy, oh boy." Stop that right now! You must change that immediately to "Girl, oh girl, oh girl." Anytime you see something that is rather bewildering, let's all start saying "Girl, oh girl, oh girl."

I don't know about you, but now that I think about it, this editorial *is* uplifting. It is good for a laugh.

P.S. I wonder if the feminists will allow me into their locker room while they are in their skivvies? Guess what.

I don't want to. Let me finish with a head shake and a "Man, oh Man, oh Man!" Take that, Gloria Steinem. I feel better now.

So remember that the laity chartered a large part of this ego trip into changing Scripture.

Too many times the laity tries to lead the Church with their uneducated ventures into the supernatural. Thanks be to God that most of the Church is cautious in this area. We, as lay people, see someone perform a miracle and instantly want to proclaim them saints. Remember what the Lord said many times when someone was healed by *His* loving touch, "It was your faith that healed you." It is not always the seemingly pious person doing the praying who brings about your gift from God. So do not put people with healing ministries, or any kind of gift from God, up on some kind of pedestal. You just may help set them up for the big fall. If a person believes he is special because of spiritual gifts and that problem goes uncorrected, he, more than likely, will have a difficult time making it into heaven.

I can remember a rather famous lay Catholic author saying to me, when I would not bow to her demands on a certain subject, "God gets even with people who do not cooperate with me." On the outside the person performed as a very holy individual, but the key word here is *performed.* It would be very difficult to enter the narrow gate by dictating to others what God will and will not do.

In this case, the concept of loving your neighbor would have been good to implement. I pray my response was appropriate. I said, "I am sorry but I can't get involved in a conversation like that. I have to go." Maybe there was a better way to say it.

If you do not fight to be humble you will eventually eat humble pie. The best rule is to follow all of the rules. Read the Book, the Good Book, the Rulebook, the Bible.

The Ten Commandments

Exodus 20:1-17 *And God spoke all these words, saying,*

1: "I am the Lord your God, who brought you out of the land of Egypt, out of the house of bondage. "You shall have no other gods before me.

2: "You shall not make for yourself a graven image, or any likeness of anything that is in heaven above, or that is in the earth beneath, or that is in the water under the earth; you shall not bow down to them or serve them; for I the Lord your God am a jealous God, visiting the iniquity of the fathers upon the children to the third and the fourth generation of those who hate me, but showing steadfast love to thousands of those who love me and keep my commandments.

3: "You shall not take the name of the Lord your God in vain; for the Lord will not hold him guiltless who takes his name in vain.

4: "Remember the Sabbath day, to keep it holy. Six days you shall labor, and do all your work; but the seventh day is a Sabbath to the Lord your God; in it you shall not do any work, you, or your son, or your daughter, your manservant, or your maidservant, or your cattle, or the sojourner who is within your gates; for in six days the Lord made heaven and earth, the sea, and all that is in them, and rested the seventh day; therefore the Lord blessed the Sabbath day and hallowed it.

5: "Honor your father and your mother, that your days may be long in the land which the Lord your God gives you.

6: "You shall not kill.

7: "You shall not commit adultery.

8: "You shall not steal.

9: "You shall not bear false witness against your neighbor.

10: "You shall not covet your neighbor's house; you shall not covet your neighbor's wife, or his manservant, or his maidservant, or his ox, or his ass, or anything that is your neighbor's."

Violate any of these Ten Commandments - that is, commit what the Church deems as grave sin and die with that sin on your soul unforgiven, and you, more than likely, will not be a candidate for heaven.

I did mention abortion and contraception previously, but it is so important that you understand: you will go to hell if you die with those sins on your soul. Cafeteria Catholics like to develop their own theology and grant themselves immunity from God's law that states, "Thou shall not kill." Sorry, the only entity on earth that can make laws that will be bound in heaven is the Catholic Church. Opt for life and live. Opt for natural family planning and live. Opt for the easy way out and go to hell. Can I make it clearer than that? Anyone who tells you differently, religious or not, is lying to you.

Not only do those who break God's laws become jeopardized, but also those who come after them. Take a close look at commandment number two. You could not only lose your salvation, but cause great harm to your children, grandchildren, great grandchildren and very possibly your great, great grandchildren. The pressure and burden of your sin placed on them could cause their failure.

The following Scripture quotes shed some light on the subject also:

> Mt 12:30 *Whoever is not with me is against me, and whoever does not gather with me scatters.*

It sounds like we should be increasing the flock and not moving from one to another. Well then, can we gather into 37,000 different flocks? That is how many different denominations of Christianity there were at the printing of this book. The Lord asks us to be in one flock. As divided Christians, we do more bickering among ourselves and consume far more energy there than we ever thought of expelling in the direction of evangelizing the seventy percent of the world's population that does not know Jesus as Savior. It will be a miracle if any of us make it.

> Mt 12:31-50 *Therefore, I say to you, every sin and blasphemy will be forgiven people, but blasphemy against the Spirit will not be forgiven. And whoever speaks a word against the Son of Man will be forgiven; but whoever speaks against the Holy Spirit will not be forgiven, either in this age or in the age to come.*

Speak against the Holy Spirit, insult the Holy Spirit, claim you work through the Holy Spirit when you don't and you fall into the realm of those who do not make it. Example: "The Holy Spirit told me to start a new denomination because all of the others have fallen into sin." Or, "Not even the Holy Spirit can save me. My sin is too great." You cannot speak for the Holy Spirit.

> Mt 12:33-37 "*Either declare the tree good and its fruit is good, or declare the tree rotten and its fruit is rotten, for a tree is known by its fruit. You brood of vipers, how can you say good things when you are evil? For from the fullness of the heart the mouth speaks. A good person brings forth good out of a store of goodness, but an evil person brings forth evil out of a store of evil. I tell you; on the Day of Judgment people will render an account for every careless word they speak. By your words you will be acquitted, and by your words you will be condemned.*"

If you do not want to be among those going down into the pit, those who do not make it to heaven, guard your tongue. We are to be temples of God, and so if we want to inherit eternal life, we must defend ourselves against the evil that wants to dwell within us.

A great example of someone not guarding his tongue would be William P. Barker, author of *Everyone in the Bible*. As he lists the Bible characters and gives his own "personal opinion" of each, he makes some possibly deadly mistakes. In the case of the Blessed Mother, the mother of Jesus Christ, he states that at the wedding at Cana, she appeared anxious and bossy. Because of being in a denomination that has little respect for Mary, he finds it easy to gossip and make false assumptions about the Mother of God.

Mary obviously was led by the Holy Spirit to say what she did and so William does not attack Mary, he attacks the Holy Spirit. What a shame to be so lost. He also lists six possible other children that Mary had, four by name. One of the problems with that is the four he lists by name have other mothers listed somewhere else in the Bible.

I wonder how Mr. Barker would feel if I stated that at his own wedding, his mother appeared fat and old? When the shoe is on the other foot, all does not seem as good as it first did.

I would not want to ever be caught assigning negative adjectives to the mother of Jesus Christ or any mother, for that matter. I only used them in the case of Barker's mother as an example to show how foolish we can allow ourselves to become.

For your enlightenment, Mr. Barker, this Mary was placed prominently in the Bible so we all could see a perfect example of how we should live out our lives. She did her job perfectly well and was the most faithful of all of Christ's disciples. She is the one who never failed Him.

It is quite unintelligent to pick on the spouse of the Holy Spirit and the Mother of God. I personally would not want to be in his shoes on judgment day, as I would not want to be in the shoes of Judas. If you do not know something for a fact, it would be best to say nothing at all.

All of the statements made by dissenters that do not align with the Magisterium are caused by demons. They do not consider themselves possessed, but something caused them to drift from the truth.

> Mt 12:38–45 *Then some of the scribes and Pharisees said to him, "Teacher, we wish to see a sign from you." He said to them in reply, "An evil and unfaithful generation seeks a sign, but no sign will be given it except the sign of Jonah the prophet. Just as Jonah was in*

the belly of the whale three days and three nights, so will the Son of Man be in the heart (bowels) of the earth three days and three nights. At the judgment, the men of Nineveh will arise with this generation and condemn it, because they repented at the preaching of Jonah; and there is something greater than Jonah here. At the judgment the queen of the south will arise with this generation and condemn it, because she came from the ends of the earth to hear the wisdom of Solomon; and there is something greater than Solomon here. "When an unclean spirit goes out of a person it roams through arid regions searching for rest but finds none. Then it says, 'I will return to my home from which I came.' But upon returning, it finds it empty, swept clean, and put in order. Then it goes and brings back with itself seven other spirits more evil than itself, and they move in and dwell there; and the last condition of that person is worse than the first. Thus it will be with this evil generation.

Another group that will have a much harder time making it is the rich.

Luke 18:18-30 *And a ruler asked him, "Good Teacher, what shall I do to inherit eternal life?" And Jesus said to him, "Why do you call me good? No one is good but God alone. You know the commandments: `Do not commit adultery, Do not kill, Do not steal, Do not bear false witness, Honor your father and mother." And he said, "All these I have observed from my youth." And when Jesus heard it, he said to him, "One thing you still lack. Sell all that you have and distribute to the poor, and you will have treasure in heaven; and come, follow me." But when he heard this he became sad, for he was very rich. Jesus looking at him said, "How hard it is for those who have riches to enter the kingdom of God! For it is easier for a camel to go through the eye of a needle than for a rich man to enter the kingdom of God." Those who heard it said, "Then who can be saved?" But he said, "What is impossible with men is possible with God." And Peter said, "Lo, we have left our homes and followed you." And he said to them, "Truly, I say to you, there is* *no man who has left house or wife or brothers or parents or children, for the sake of the kingdom of God, who will not receive manifold more in this time, and in the age to come, eternal life."*

We have become so tight when it comes to giving that it will be almost impossible to get in the narrow gate. We have lowered the bar so much that we just expect God to make it all possible without any help from us. We find it extremely difficult to understand our financial relationship with the Lord and, thus, we shortchange our salvation and ourselves. If only we could do with less and see that the starving receive more. Then we may stand a better chance of being assumed into heaven. There is a lot more on this subject in Chapter Ten. Here I just want those who still are holding on to their First Holy Communion money to know that it is time to share it.

> 1 Tim 6:11-2 *But as for you, man of God, shun all this; aim at righteousness, godliness, faith, love, steadfastness, and gentleness. Fight the good fight of the faith; take hold of the eternal life to which you were called when you made the good confession in the presence of many witnesses. In the presence of God who gives life to all things, and of Christ Jesus who in His testimony before Pontius Pilate made the good confession, I charge you to keep the commandment unstained and free from reproach until the appearing of our Lord Jesus Christ; and this will be made manifest at the proper time by the blessed and only Sovereign, the King of kings and Lord of lords, who alone has immortality and dwells in unapproachable light, whom no man has ever seen or can see. To him be honor and eternal dominion. Amen. As for the rich in this world, charge them not to be haughty, nor to set their hopes on uncertain riches but on God who richly furnishes us with everything to enjoy. They are to do good, to be rich in good deeds, liberal and generous, thus laying up for themselves a good foundation for the future, so that they may take hold of the life which is life indeed. O Timothy, guard what has been entrusted to you. Avoid the godless chatter and contradictions of what is falsely*

called knowledge, for by professing it some have missed the mark as regards the faith. Grace be with you.

How could we get better advice than this? If we want not to fall into the pit we must sharpen our conversions to a razor's edge. It is best to be ablaze for the Lord, occupy our time with Him and suffer here rather than failing the final test.

The list is long that could cause our demise. Taking God's name in vain has become so popular that when called to task about it, some say, "Oh, I don't mean to insult God; it is a small 'god' that I use." The Lord says to not have other gods before Him. You cannot make up your own rulebook. If God tells us not to use His name for any reason but a holy one, we cannot alter His word or ignore His command.

I want to be a saint, so I will try to do as the Lord asks. Will you? I will make mistakes as will you, but if the Lord sees us trying He will send the grace to bring our sainthood to fruition.

Are you getting the drift of what God is trying to get accomplished here? It is like we are hardly trying to stay afloat yet we all believe we are going to heaven. Christ said that He suffered and died to save at least some. Every one is not going to heaven. Get that into your head, everyone is not going. We have to get that premise ingrained in our minds. And if every one is not going to get in, what is it that I am doing that makes me one of the chosen? We all need to ponder that more. No! We all have to ponder only that. If we do not, how can we begin to understand all that God wants us to accomplish?

I read an article recently in *Our Sunday Visitor*, a Catholic paper. It was by a religious, who said that there was nothing we could do about our salvation; it was in God's hands and we needed to stop trying to accomplish it. I could think of a few expletives from my past that would sum up my thoughts on that theology. Let's just leave it at hogwash and say, "Get thee behind me, Satan."

Luke 13:23-28 *Someone asked him, "Lord, will only a few people be saved?" He answered them, "Strive to enter through the narrow gate, for many, I tell you, will attempt to enter but will not be strong enough. After the master of the house has arisen and locked the door, then will you stand outside knocking and saying, 'Lord, open the door for us.' He will say to you in reply, 'I do not know where you are from.' And you will say, 'We ate and drank in your company and you taught in our streets.' Then he will say to you, 'I do not know where (you) are from. Depart from me, all you evildoers!' And there will be wailing and grinding of teeth when you see Abraham, Isaac, and Jacob and all the prophets in the kingdom of God and you yourselves cast out.*

The poor, pathetic individual who authors such material, and the poor, misguided editors who allow the heresies in their papers may be a fulfillment of this Scripture. I would not want to be in their shoes.

The very same Catholic paper published an article delivering the message that Harry Potter was a harmless fantasy. My response to *Our Sunday Visitor* was found in my editorial the following month. I have included it here so you will know the truth.

Potter's Mystical Attraction

> On the surface, for the extremely naïve, *Harry Potter* seems to be a simple, innocent fantasy. And what child would not be attracted to fantasy? After all, fantasy is fun, a delicate slip from the pressure of life. Fantasy is to dream, to desire; it is the flight of the imagination, a mystical escape from reality. What could be wrong with that?
>
> But therein lies the problem. Is Harry Potter an escape from reality into the imaginative? The answer for anyone who has done his homework is NO, NO, a thousand times NO! Harry Potter deals with the occult and is an intrinsically evil reality. There is no escape here; it is reality. Harry Potter is a highly polished, well-orchestrated and magnificently marketed attack against

God Himself. It is witchcraft. It is alluring. And it is all too easy to slip supernaturally right on into the dark side. And they have for their champions Coca Cola, Mattel, Warner Brothers, Our Sunday Visitor and the list goes on. Disney must be pulling its hair out or at least casting a few spells. They do not have a piece of this pie.

It is so easy for the deceived to say that I am making something out of nothing, but foolhardy is the person who cannot see the big picture here. Satan's onslaught of late has been through *Dungeons and Dragons, Pokemon, Potter* and the like. Satan is laughing out loud, "I am killing your children and you can't even see it."

Let me clue you into the theology of the subject at hand. Scripture says:

> Deu 18:10-12 *Let there not be found among you anyone who immolates his son or daughter in the fire, nor a fortune-teller, soothsayer, charmer, diviner, or caster of spells, nor one who consults ghosts and spirits or seeks oracles from the dead. Anyone who does such things is an abomination to the LORD, and because of such abominations the LORD, your God, is driving these nations out of your way.*

Check also 2 Kings 9:12, 17:17, 21:6, and Jer 14:14 (NAB.) Scripture is clear on the subject and the prognosis for those involved in witchcraft is not good. So why, I ask you, subject your little ones to the tempter? Is it just fun?

> Mark 13:22-23 *False messiahs and false prophets will arise and will perform signs and wonders in order to mislead (if that were possible) the elect. Be watchful! I have told it all to you beforehand.*

God warns us that even the elect will be deceived, and so we see *Our Sunday Visitor* and many Catholic papers promoting the Potter path to hell. The very name Potter, a female goddess, reflects the trap. The scenario is mother goddess, the woman as the creator. We see this attraction to evil theology in many Catholic circles through Wicca, enneagrams and the promotion of woman as goddess, even if we have to trample on Scripture itself.

Watch and you will see. The ones who promote the demasculinization of Holy Scripture will be high among the promoters of Harry Potter. Having our children sucked into the vortex of cultism and having parents and religious alike cheering them on is a classic case of the elect being deceived.

God and His prayers are not allowed in the schools, but Potter, witchcraft and the like are not only allowed, they are heralded as solid teaching. Thirty-five different magazines distributed through all American secular schools by *Scholastic Publishers*, promote Potter. Even though the government has classified witchcraft as a religion and given it nonprofit status as a religion (to the point of having witchcraft chaplains in the military), we now see the embracing of this religion by almost everyone, especially in the schools. It is mother goddess worship that makes the male subservient to the female god. The Catholic Church has a name for it. It is called anti-christ. It is everything that stands against God. It is the opposite of God at work here. Let there be no doubt about that.

Oh, you cannot see this in Harry Potter? You'd better look again. You can tell a tree by its fruit. I admit you cannot see mother goddess in the forefront of the Potter trap; Harry is just the bait for the trap. What happens next is that natural inquisitiveness embarks the child on a journey for a more fulfilling, hands-on excitement. And where does he find that? On the web. Most every child is familiar with the web. You will find witchcraft and all that Satan has to offer on the web. Go to "search" on the web and type in "witchcraft" and now you will find mother goddess. The trap is sprung. Hands on? Excitement? It is all there, from the very basic spells to the blackest of black magic.

Start asking children what they think about *Harry Potter*. The answers? "I want the power that Harry has." This is not the power that saints have, the power that comes from God. Oh, no, they want Harry's evil power. Yes, Harry has power and in the books and the movie, he uses his power for "good," does he not? He uses his power for revenge and spell casting is what he does. Is that good? "Yes," some say, "it is against his more evil enemy." But that does not make it good. It is the one and the same power at work in Harry Potter and his archenemy, Voldemort. We need a disclaimer on the *Potter* book covers that says: CAUTION: SATAN AT WORK - possibility of possession high.

"Can I go to the Hogwart School?" That is another popular question children have. This school, just like our schools, teaches evil, but a hundred times greater. Hogwart is the next step in being a full-blown wizard or witch. You can call this a fantasy all you want - that is the lie they want you to believe. The fact is, it is a reality and children are casting spells on each other, just for practice. Through practice, just like Harry, they develop their power.

The books are provocative, humorous and beautifully written. The author, J. K. Rowling, majored in mythology in college. She has brought forth, in this box-office smash, all that history has stored up in that seemingly harmless mythology. The books and the first movie (several more are to come) teach children about the other side - sorcerers and the like - and they find solace in that. Distant from the far-too-often boring faith we teach children about *the* God, this new attack by Satan is slick and well presented. Your children find much fun in the tapes, books and sorcerers' games you buy them. And isn't it wonderful to see them read so much? It is reported that kids read these books three and four times. Is it not wonderful how quiet they are as you place them serenely in Satan's lap and he lulls them off to dream dreams of him?

Think about it. Our children's souls are at stake. Talk to them. Ask them what it makes them think about. You can bet it is not Jesus. It is about Harry Potter's mystical attraction and they want to be like him. Your children just may be casting spells on you because of your attempt at discipline. Getting any migraines lately? Wake up and smell something other than roses. *God* is really the "Potter" and *we* are the clay.

Still think I am off base? This just in: Rome's official exorcist, Father Gabriele Amorth, warns parents against the *Harry Potter* book series. This priest, who is also the president of the International Association of Exorcists, says, "Satan is behind the works. Behind Harry Potter hides the signature of the king of the darkness, the devil."

You want to go to the Internet and check what I'm saying for yourself? Start with scholastic.com. Search on *Harry Potter.* As you can see, the schools promote him and so the schools promote Satan over God.

A copy of the above editorial was sent to *Our Sunday Visitor* and they replied that no official church statement was ever made against the Potter series. How could they miss my editorial's quoting the Vatican exorcist? They also made light of people like myself who believe Potter is evil. Does this sound like people who are completely on the side of God?

Do you see that there are many traps and many ravenous wolves that are trying to steal your gift of salvation? Be very careful what you read and be very careful whom you trust. Every article claiming to be Catholic is not from God. Every Catholic priest is not working for God. And for sure, every Catholic lay person is not working for God. It is a shame it has come down to the point that we cannot trust just any Catholic paper, priest or layman. But that is a fact and God has warned us about these very things.

So no matter who tries to convince you otherwise, just try to live life God's way *and try hard.* And no matter what God sends in the way of tests, or Satan sends as stumbling blocks, keep trying to be a saint. God will bless your trying. It is when you stop trying that you fall into the pit. *Our Sunday Visitor* did all Catholics a grave disservice when they printed a story by a priest who said we do not have to work on our salvation. Stop trying and you may find yourself one of the many who does not make it through the narrow gate.

> Phil 2:12-16 *So then, my beloved, obedient as you have always been, not only when I am present but all the more now when I am absent, work out your salvation with fear and trembling. For God is the one who, for his good purpose, works in you both to desire and to work. Do everything without grumbling or questioning, that you may be blameless and innocent, children of God without blemish in the midst of a crooked and perverse generation, among whom you shine like lights in the world, as you hold on to the word of life, so that my boast for the day of Christ may be that I did not run in vain or labor in vain.*

You do have to be aware of scrupulosity. You cannot be so concerned with doing it God's way that you go overboard and destroy the faith of others in your wake.

Believe me when I say that this is in no way a complete list of failures that could cost us our salvation. The Lord told us to run the race to the end. It is only a misguided individual who thinks he does not have to try in running the race. Those who do not try are called losers. If you get the drift of it all, if you understand this chapter and the premise that you have to devote your whole life to the goal of heaven, and that everyone is not going to make it, continue on to Chapter Five.

NOTES

CHAPTER FIVE

SOME OF THOSE WHO MADE IT

The apostles were mean and contemptible in the eyes of the world, neither recommended by birth, riches, friends, learning, nor abilities. Yet totally destitute as they were, of all those advantages on which men here set so high a price, they were chosen by Christ, made His friends, replenished with His graces and holy charity, and exalted to the dignity of spirit princes of His kingdom, and judges of the world.

Blind and foolish are all men who overrate and eagerly pursue the goods of this life; or who so enjoy them as to suffer their hearts to be wedded to them. Worldly pleasures, riches, or honors, if they become the object of our affections, are, as it were, fetters which fasten us to the earth, and clog our souls; and it is so hard to enjoy them with perfect indifference, to consider them barely as a dangerous stewardship, and to employ them only for the advancement of virtue in ourselves and others, that many saints thought it safer utterly to renounce them, and others rejoiced to see themselves removed from what it is difficult to possess, and not be entangled by. Are not the maxims of the gospel, and the example of Christ, our king and leader, and of all his saints, sufficient to inspire those who enjoy the advantages of this world with a saving fear, and to make them study the various obligations of their stewardship, and by watchfulness, voluntary humiliations, mortification, compunction, assiduous prayer, and conversing on heavenly things by holy meditation or reading, to stand infinitely upon their guard, lest the love of the world, or the infection of its pride, vanity, or pleasures, seize their hearts?

Faith must be extremely weak and inactive in us, if we look upon the things of this world in any other light than that in which the gospel places them; if we regard any other goods as truly valuable but those of divine grace and charity, or if we set not ourselves with our whole strength to pursue them by the road of humility, patience, meekness, and piety, in imitation of the saints. The apostles are herein the objects of our veneration, and our guides and models. We honor them as the doctors of the law of Christ, after Him the foundation stones of His church, the twelve gates, and the twelve precious stones of the heavenly Jerusalem, and as the leaders and princes of the saints. They also challenge our gratitude, inasmuch as it is by their ardent charity for our souls, and by their labors and sufferings that we enjoy the happiness of holy faith, and are ourselves Christians: through them we have received the gospel.

—Author unknown

The fortunate eleven original apostles and the replacement Matthias knew well how to do the will of God. Oh, they made their share of mistakes, but unlike Judas, they repented of their sin and became saints. Learn well what you have to do to become saints lest you end up like Judas. Hell is forever and do not ever forget that!

In the world today, you are not often considered worthy of service unless you hold a degree. It is getting to the point in some places that you have to have a master's degree to be a director of music for a parish. It was not this way when the Lord chose His leaders. In fact, we are on a head-trip to the point of detriment. The music in Catholic churches used to be quite profound and now it is getting hard to find a Mass that is not like a funeral Mass or a folk festival. Often the music is played in such a slow tempo that it is hard to see the celebration in the celebrating of Mass. Scripture says to praise the Lord with high cymbals and to make a joyful noise. Maybe if we look at how the Lord chose His saints, we would improve our miserable track record, that of losing seventy-three percent of the Catholic Church in the last forty years.

It is not those with the biggest brains, but the biggest hearts who make saints. So don't try so hard to be smart as try to be good and good to those who have the least. Learn to be good at the things at which God wants you to be good. Do not associate with those who are killers of the faith, but work hard at knowing what is required of you to please the Lord.

Knowledge of Scriptural Requirements

Deu 6:4-25 "*Hear, O Israel! The Lord is our God, the Lord alone! Therefore, you shall love the Lord, your God, with all your heart, and with all your soul, and with all your strength. Take to heart these words, which I enjoin on you today. Drill them into your children. Speak of them at home and abroad, whether you are busy or at rest. Bind them at your wrist as a sign and let them be as a pendant on your forehead. Write them on the doorposts of your houses and on your gates.*

"When the Lord, your God, brings you into the land which he swore to your fathers, Abraham, Isaac and Jacob, that he would give you, a land with fine, large cities that you did not build, with houses full of goods of all sorts that you did not garner, with cisterns that you did not dig, with vineyards and olive groves that you did not plant; and when, therefore, you eat your fill, take care not to forget the Lord, who brought you out of the land of Egypt, that place of slavery.

The Lord, your God, shall you fear; him shall you serve, and by his name shall you swear. You shall not follow other gods, such as those of the surrounding nations, lest the wrath of the Lord, your God, flare up against you and he destroy you from the face of the land; for the Lord, your God, who is in your midst, is a jealous God.

"You shall not put the Lord, your God, to the test, as you did at Massah. But keep the commandments of the Lord, your God, and the ordinances and statutes he has enjoined on you. Do what is right and good in the sight of the Lord, that you may, according to his word, prosper, and may enter in and possess the good land which

the Lord promised on oath to your fathers, thrusting all your enemies out of your way.

"Later on, when your son asks you what these ordinances, statutes and decrees mean which the Lord, our God, has enjoined on you, you shall say to your son, 'We were once slaves of Pharaoh in Egypt, but the Lord brought us out of Egypt with his strong hand and wrought before our eyes signs and wonders, great and dire, against Egypt and against Pharaoh and his whole house. He brought us from there to lead us into the land he promised on oath to our fathers, and to give it to us. Therefore, the Lord commanded us to observe all these statutes in fear of the Lord, our God, that we may always have as prosperous and happy a life as we have today; and our justice before the Lord, our God, is to consist in carefully observing all these commandments he has enjoined on us.'

All who follow the good advice of God "Our Father" will be led to advance on to bigger and greater endeavors. Chart a sound course, lest you miss your homeport. Know the rules and play by them always, if you want to be like the following, those who made it into the Kingdom of God.

Saints

In the following pages are just a few saints I have selected from thousands to illustrate attributes for which we should strive. I did not spend hundreds of hours or even dozens of hours in the selection process. I believe the Lord selected them for us, but in no way does this selection attempt to diminish the ability of any saint to help us in this treacherous endeavor towards sainthood.

The first three are child saints. I used three to impress on children and young adults the tremendous ability that they have at their finger tips if they just choose to follow the path of righteousness. These three are young people who stood above the crowd and elected to not follow the masses, but to lead the masses and to show the way to sainthood.

SAINT MARIA GORETTI

(October 16, 1890 - July 6, 1902)

I use Maria Goretti to exemplify purity. The body is only ours to give to the person to whom God chooses to espouse us. Far too many times do we, as youngsters, believe we have reached maturity and can make all decisions on our own? Even as adults, it is a wise person who seeks the counsel of the experienced before making a decision. We believe we can decide, at an early age, whom we love and to whom we give our bodies and in the process, exclude God from the loop. We had better ask God to help in our decision in choosing a mate, lest we fall from grace. Many children take talk like this as a joke, but Maria Goretti took the gift of chastity very seriously and defended it with her life. Now she is called saint and we are not. She will live in heaven forever, but will we? In her case, heaven was as close as a No! If you can mirror Maria and say no to anyone who asks for your body before you are married, you may inherit heaven, as she did. The yeses are for those who want to dwell with Satan in hell for all eternity.

St. Maria Goretti - as introduced by her brother

"My name is Angelo Goretti. I joined the Apostolate of Our Lady of Fatima only a few years after it became organized in the United States. I had moved to America from Italy. I was living in New Jersey, only seven miles from the Ave Maria Institute, headquarters for a Fatima Apostolate. Monsignor Harold V. Colgan was a priest in that area. He had been cured suddenly of a serious heart attack in the hospital through the intercession of Our Lady of Fatima. He had not been given long to live. Then a magazine explaining the message of Our Lady of Fatima fell into his hands in the hospital. He promised Our Blessed Lady that if she obtained for him his health again, that he would spend the rest of his days on earth spreading devotion to her. It was this priest who came to see me when I moved to New Jersey. He asked if I would come to his parish and speak to the children about my sister Maria, who had preferred death rather than commit a mortal sin. I was the one who found my sister, who has been declared a saint by the Church. I found her bleeding to death after she had been stabbed fourteen times by the young man with whom she refused to commit a sin.

Maria was only six years old when our mother and father moved and became tenant farmers on the marshes of Nettuna. Nettuna is very close to Rome. Maria had to walk many miles for each one of her First Holy Communion instructions.

Our parish priest was a very holy man. Over and over he would say, "Keep your soul pure! It is better to die a thousand times than to commit one mortal sin."

Maria and I grew up knowing that one shares in the very life of God when one is in the state of sanctifying grace. We learned very young how priceless and beautiful a soul is if it is in the state of grace. Our parish priest taught us that the most terrible thing that could ever happen in the world would be to fall into mortal sin. That would be a great offense against God. The guilty one would be separated from God, would lose Christ, the Light of the world, as grace in the soul. The Blessed Trinity would no longer live in a soul blackened by deadly sin.

My sister, Maria Goretti, determined that she would live all her life upon earth without ever once committing any kind of deadly sin.

Our father became very ill. Before he died, Father arranged to share the farm with the Serenelli family. This worried my sister, Maria. She knew that their son, Alexander, was a bad boy. Even our mother found out that Alexander read bad books.

No one can read dirty books, look at bad pictures and entertain bad thoughts deliberately without falling into temptation. Impurity is not the only kind of sin. There are

Ten Commandments. But many souls have gone to hell because they sinned first by bad thoughts, then by bad actions.

The Sixth Commandment, which demands that we be pure in thoughts, words and actions, can often be the most difficult to obey. But with God's help, no temptation will ever be too great. Jesus has promised us that He will always give us enough grace to overcome every temptation. Both Mother and our parish priest taught us the importance of having a deep devotion to God's Mother in order to keep pure. My mother did all she could to protect her family from Alexander. Every night Maria would pray three Hail Marys to Our Lady so as always to keep the gift of holy purity.

Frequent confession and Holy Communion are also very important to keep close to God. We never missed Mass, even though it meant a two-hour walk to get there. Maria went to confession as often as she could. We were taught that the Sacrament of Reconciliation not only takes away sin for which we are sorry but gives grace to the soul as well. We did not fear to talk to our holy priest when we went to confession, asking such things as how to avoid sin. The Sacrament would give the soul that special help to overcome temptations. And then in Holy Communion, the soul receives Jesus, who is God and Life itself, all holy, all good, all pure and the promise of future resurrection.

When the young man named Alexander tried a few times, when Maria was only twelve years old, to make her sin, she absolutely refused. She did her best to avoid him from then on. She was practicing what we had been taught: one must avoid those who are an occasion of sin. Maria did not tell Mother that Alexander tried to sin with her, for he threatened to kill her if she ever said anything.

My sister Maria would help on the farm after Father died. Mother appreciated that. Maria never complained because we were poor and did not have much. She knew we should be happy with whatever God had given us. She helped in the house and took care of the other children. She would pray to God every day. She used to look forward to participating in the Sacrifice of the Mass and receiving Jesus into her soul in Holy Communion. In our family, Sunday was considered the best part of the week.

One day when Mother was working in the fields and I was away, too, Alexander came home. He locked the door. He came toward Maria. She said, "Alexander, I would rather die than sin." He became angry and stabbed her again and again with a knife. Then he ran and locked himself in his room. One serious sin can lead to another when one deadens his conscience. Alexander did not hesitate to commit murder as well as be impure. Mother heard Maria's screams as she worked in the field. She came with a neighbor. I arrived first. We found her in a pool of blood. When Mother saw her she asked, "Who did this?" Maria still had enough strength to say, "Alexander wanted me to sin, but I would not."

The ambulance was called, and it took Maria to the hospital. The police came to arrest Alexander. He pretended that he was insane, but he was judged sane and sent to jail. His only insanity came from deadening his conscience by reading bad books, looking at bad pictures and thinking bad thoughts. He was not sorry for his serious sins and refused to repent and go to confession.

For a long, long time, Alexander lived in prison and did not repent of his terrible crime and sins, including murdering my sister because she would not sin, too.

Maria lived for about twenty-four hours after she was stabbed fourteen times. Just as Jesus hung dying on the Cross and forgave those who put Him to death, so as she lay dying, she forgave Alexander. She promised to pray for him in heaven.

What was important to my sister as she lay dying was that Alexander be sorry and make a good confession. She wanted him to get back into the state of grace so as to permit Jesus to save his soul.

The priest anointed Maria and gave her Jesus again in Holy Communion as Holy Viaticum. Maria suffered terribly that last day from the many wounds. She offered up that suffering for the conversion of sinners. She died on July 6, 1902.

Eight years later, my sister appeared to Alexander in prison. She offered him flowers. At that moment Alexander was converted. He called for a priest. He made a good confession and became a good Catholic. Alexander spent the rest of his life doing penance for his sins. You see, even though our sins be as scarlet, God can make them white as snow; that is, our soul can be forgiven of any sin, no matter how serious, if we repent, confess and come back to God humbly.

Pope Pius XII proclaimed my sister, Maria Goretti, a saint of the Universal Church. She was named the new patroness of Catholic youth in the Holy Year 1950.

My mother, still living, my brothers and other sister — all of us were together in Rome that day when my sister Maria was canonized. I did not have enough money to go to Rome for it, but then devotees of my sister paid my way so that all of us could be there for that great day.

After I came back to America, many years passed and I was finally growing old, trying to live the Blue Army Pledge. Once in a while a leader of the Blue Army would stop at my house to chat with me. Suddenly one day a Blue Army leader drove into my yard. I was sitting on the porch. He came up and put his arms around me and said that he wanted to offer me special congratulations on my sister's feast day. It was July. I was old and had forgotten the Feast of St. Maria Goretti, my own sister. How happy I was that he reminded me.

Then my joy increased when he surprised me and said, "When have you been back to see how they have turned your old farmhouse into a shrine, and to see the big new church with your sister's tomb in Nettuna?" I was surprised and answered, "I have never been back." "Well, then, as a feast day gift from your sister, the Blue Army will take you back there next month, because we are having a pilgrimage and it will be stopping in Nettuna." It came true. The next month I was on my way to Europe after all those years. I got to see my sister, who is a nun in Taorminia. I saw my brother too, who was not too well at his farm near Naples. But above all, I had the joy of going back to the farmhouse, where now an iron grille is around the spot where I found my sister bleeding to death, where she spoke those words of forgiveness to the boy who had stabbed her and where Maria gave an example to all young people of the world, "It is better to die than commit a mortal sin."

I did not realize how much I had missed my dear family in all those years, even though I had reared a family of my own in America. It was with a heavy heart that I was once again to say good-bye knowing that I would never see my family in Italy again.

But something wonderful happened. While I was waiting in Genoa for the ship to go back to America, I was sitting in the kitchen with some cousins, and the feeling came over me that here is where I was going to remain.

Death came to me quickly but it came at the moment of joy of having been with those I love. God called me to join my dear mother, who had been with us all in Rome for the canonization of St. Maria Goretti.

Maria Goretti, my sister, is canonized. I lived on earth many years after it took place; I lived as a member of the Apostolate of Our Lady of Fatima. The Fatima Apostolate members who keep their pledge believe that Our Lady will come at the time of their death with all the graces they need for salvation. It is a reward for wearing the Brown Scapular of Our Lady of Mt. Carmel and for making the First Saturdays of reparation while striving, day by day, to live a good Catholic Christian life.

St. Maria Goretti has inspired many youth in the 20th century in which she died. This patroness of youth for purity is indeed important when there is so much impurity around us on every side. Television, the movies, magazines, most every kind of media that should rather serve God are instrumental in leading souls to hell when it is controlled by bad people.

Many have been brainwashed by the media without realizing it. They try to say that one could be a good Catholic and still be impure in action alone or with others. The use of sexual powers before marriage is seriously sinful. Pope Paul VI, in 1976, issued a Vatican declaration on sexual morality. The Pope, speaking as the Vicar of Christ on earth, reminded the world that homosexual practices, premarital sex and masturbation are intrinsically and seriously disordered acts. Objectively, they are serious sins. They are sins against purity, such as Alexander's sin from which St. Maria Goretti died rather than commit.

On August 6, 1993, Pope John Paul II issued the Encyclical Letter *The Splendor of Truth (Veritatis Splendor).* Because the world was becoming so confused the Pope saw it was necessary to explain the true teachings of the Catholic Church on moral actions in this one hundred and fifty-four page encyclical. He wrote:

71. "Human acts are moral acts because they express and determine the goodness or evil of the individual who performs them. They do not produce a change merely in the state of affairs outside of man but, to the extent that they are deliberate choices, they give moral definition to the very person who performs them, determining his profound spiritual traits...

72. "The morality of acts is defined by the relationship of man's freedom with the authentic good. This good is established, as the eternal law, by Divine Wisdom which orders every being towards its end; this eternal law is known both by man's natural reason (hence it is 'natural law'), and - in an integral and perfect way - by God's supernatural Revelation (hence it is called 'divine law.')" The universal *Catechism of the Catholic Church* talks about "The Battle for Purity."

2520 "Baptism confers on its recipient the grace of purification from all sins. But the baptized must continue to struggle against concupiscence of the flesh and disordered desires. With God's grace he will prevail.

—By virtue and gift of chastity, for chastity lets us love with upright and undivided heart.

—By purity of intention, which consists in seeking the true end of man; with simplicity of vision, the baptized person seeks to find and to fulfill God's will in everything.

—By purity of vision, external and internal; by discipline of feelings and imagination; by refusing all complicity in impure thoughts that incline us to turn aside from the path of God's commandments: 'Appearance arouses yearning in fools.' (*Wis. 15:5*)

—By prayer . . .

2521 "Purity requires modesty, an integral part of temperance. Modesty protects the intimate center of the person . . .

2526 "So-called moral permissiveness rests on an erroneous conception of human freedom; the necessary precondition for the development of true freedom is to let oneself be educated in the moral law. Those in charge of education can reasonably be expected to give young people instruction respectful of the truth, the qualities of the heart, and the moral and spiritual dignity of man."

Alexander, as told in this chapter, thought he could engage in pornography of the media and get by with it. He did not. Thanks be to God, he was finally converted through the prayers and sufferings of St. Maria Goretti.

Suggested Actions to Imitate St. Maria Goretti

✔Resolve to pray three Hail Marys each day for the gift of purity.
✔If news and magazine racks in the community display immoral literature, join with others in requesting that the same be removed and no longer sold.

✔Keep open with your confessor in learning how to avoid sin and overcome temptations.
✔Seek a priest confessor who is most helpful to demand strong and high standards of morality.
✔Dress yourself modestly at all times, but also alert others who may not be mindful that their dress or attitude is an occasion of sin to others.

I, as your author, would like to add: if you go to a confessor and even in your uneducated state, detect that the theology being taught you is tainted, find another confessor immediately. Do not stake your sainthood on someone whom you suspect is in failure himself. Here a few responses to confessed sins that should alert you to your need to change confessors:

"Masturbation is not a sin."
"Using contraceptives is not a sin."
"Only confess one sin and I will absolve all."
"You do not need to come to confession so often."
"Anger is never a sin, it is only an emotion."

Let me not be too simplistic with the last two. We have to be careful with scrupulosity and not be running to a priest every time we think we have offended God in the slightest way. And remember that blessing yourself with holy water can take away venial sins, if you ask for that grace from God while you are making the sign of the cross.

You should also know that there are two kinds of anger, and two ways of dealing with anger. Yes, anger is an emotion but it can still be a sin. Sinful anger is that on which you allow the sun to set. Do not brood over injury. I can remember some good advice that I received from someone when I first got married: "Never go to bed angry with your wife. Always settle your differences before you retire." I never realized how scriptural that was.

In fact, Scripture says in Ps 4:4 *"Be angry, but sin not; commune with your own hearts on your beds, and be silent."* David could never say this if anger was automatically a sin.

St. Paul quotes David also in Eph 4:26-27 "*Be angry, but do not sin; do not let the sun go down on your anger, and give no opportunity to the devil.*"

Jesus was angry several times, but didn't sin. He must have been angry when he drove the money changers from the temple, but He didn't sin! Lk 19:45-46 says "*And he entered the temple and began to drive out those who sold, saying to them, "It is written, 'My house shall be a house of prayer'; but you have made it a den of robbers.*"

Mark 3:5 says Jesus was angry. "*. . . and he [Jesus] looked around at them with anger, grieved at their hardness of heart, and said to the man, 'Stretch out your hand.' He stretched it out, and his hand was restored.*"

But yes, it is also a sin under certain circumstances as the *Catechism of the Catholic Church* clearly states:

(2302) By recalling the commandment, "You shall not kill," our Lord asked for peace of heart and denounced murderous anger and hatred as immoral.

Anger is a desire for revenge. "To desire vengeance in order to do evil to someone who should be punished is illicit," but it is praiseworthy to impose restitution "to correct vices and maintain justice." If anger reaches the point of a deliberate desire to kill or seriously wound a neighbor, it is gravely against charity; it is a mortal sin. The Lord says, "Everyone who is angry with his brother shall be liable to judgment."

Do not allow yourself to be lulled into not listing your sins and the number of times you have committed each offense. If you had an abortion and never confessed it out loud, but accepted general absolution from a priest, the sin of abortion is still with you. Please get to a confessional as soon as possible and tell the priest what happened and any good priest will fix the problem. God loves you and wants you in heaven and this could be His way of telling you.

Saint Dominic Savio

(1842 - 1857)

In this section you are going to meet another teenage saint - a young man who died at the age of fifteen. It is well known that when we become teenagers, many new temptations explode upon us and within us. Dominic Savio, the subject of this section, was no different from any other teenager in having temptations. He was different in the way he handled them. He was different from many teenagers in having the courage to lead other teenagers away from sin and toward Jesus Christ.

Dominic was a teenager who was more teacher than he was student. Placing himself in harm's way just long enough to represent Christ when Satan was on the prowl made him one of the youngest saints. In our day and age we find far too few Dominics, but one thing is for sure - if more children tried to be like him there would be a lot more child saints.

Before we let Dominic Savio tell his story as he might tell it today, as the Church starts the march into the Third Millennium of Christianity, the editor of these saint volumes wants to ask you a question or two. "What do you think is the biggest temptation of teenagers? Where do you think many teenagers go wrong? How do you think many teenagers begin to lose their faith and stop practicing it openly?"

Here is how I would answer these questions. The biggest temptation for teenagers concerns temptations of the flesh in one form or another. Temptations against holy purity, the misuse of the body and of the new sexual powers developing within the body are an all too common serious sin for many teenagers. It sets them on the way to immorality. Already in early centuries of Christianity, great saints made statement like this: "More souls go to hell because of sins against the flesh than for any other reason." Our Lady of Fatima said that very thing to the little shepherd girl, Jacinta.

How does one get started with sins against the holy virtue of purity? It starts with impure thoughts that go uncorrected.

Often impure thoughts are stimulated and brought to the explosion stage by looking at impure pictures, listening to or reading impure stories. This can be through bad magazines, movies or television. That is known as pornography.

Teenagers, sometimes even at a younger age, get caught up in the use of alcoholic drinks and the use of other drugs of various kinds. Young people may think such is exciting. They get a thrill, a high. They lose control of their judgment. They may hallucinate. Their will power is greatly weakened. They can fall into all kinds of sins under the use of alcoholic drinks and other drugs. To deliberately take such things, which seriously affect the human body and disturb the right use of our faculties of intellect and will, is to take upon oneself responsibility for whatever mortal sins by act, word or deed may be committed while under such influences.

How would you feel if you were a priest and you were called to the side of a young man or woman who had just committed suicide or been killed in a serious accident while under the influence of such stimulants? How would you feel if you were the parent of such a youngster? You may have know of something similar that happened to one of your peers. Did you think of what might have been the condition of his or her soul at the moment of death? Where is that soul now?

Why do some people stop practicing their faith? Sometimes it is because they never learned to love Jesus in a deep and personal way. Some never discover that the Catholic Church is the fullness of true faith. It is the mystical Body of Jesus Christ. Some never discover the true face of Catholicism. They are "Catholic" in name only.

If one does not know that the Mass is the Sacrifice of the Cross perpetuated, will it bother her to miss it? If one has never learned that the Catholic faith is receiving the Body, Blood, Soul and Divinity of Jesus Christ Himself in Holy Communion, will it bother him to not receive Holy Communion? Perhaps some do not know what the Holy Eucharist is — and go to Communion in the state of mortal sin. The *Catechism of the Catholic Church* makes it very clear, it is a mortal sin of sacrilege to receive Jesus in Holy Communion without first repenting and having the mortal sin forgiven by a priest in the Sacrament of Reconciliation (Confession).

The *Catechism of the Catholic Church* tells us we are all called to holiness, to perfection:

2013 "All Christians in any state or walk of life are called to the fullness of Christian life and to the perfection of charity." All are called to holiness: 'Be perfect, as your heavenly Father is perfect.'

In order to reach this perfection the faithful should use the strength dealt out to them by Christ's gift, so that . . . doing the will of the Father in everything, they may wholeheartedly devote themselves to the glory of God and to the service of their neighbor. Thus the holiness of the People of God will grow in fruitful abundance, as is clearly shown in the history of the Church through the lives of so many saints.

2015 "The way of perfection passes by way of the Cross. There is no holiness without renunciation and spiritual battle . . ."

Did you notice that the *Catechism of the Catholic Church* says that all are called to holiness, to the fullness of Christian life, to perfection, "in any state or walk of life." That includes teenagers.

There are many holy teenagers. I've known many. I've taken many on pilgrimages to Fatima, Portugal, where the Mother of God appeared to three little children. It is possible to be holy even in these sinful times.

Now I want you to meet St. Dominic Savio who was born in Italy in 1842. Here is his story as he might tell it.

"My father was a blacksmith and I lived with my parents in the small town of Rira, in northern Italy. When I was only four years old my mother noticed I had disappeared. She went looking for me. She found me in a corner praying with my hands folded and my head bowed. At that tender age I already knew the basic Catholic prayers by heart. I had heard them prayed often in the home and learned them spontaneously from others.

I became an altar boy, serving Mass, when I was only five years old. I would get up at five o'clock with my father and go to the church to serve Mass. Then at an early age, almost unheard of then, I received Jesus in Holy Communion for the very first time when I was only seven. I chose for my motto that day: "Death, but not sin!" I always kept it. My soul was never tarnished with mortal sin.

I was an ordinary boy, normal in every way. But even before I began school I had a special love for God. That love grew as I grew in age, even as I grew into the age when young people find temptations more attractive and hard to control.

When I was twelve years old I knew already I wanted to be a priest more than anything else in the world. I was so eager to begin the studies to prepare me for this that I went to see Father John Bosco [later canonized a saint also] . . . I entered the school known as a Salesian Oratory which Father Bosco had founded for boys who wanted to better their lives. That great and holy priest examined me first before he admitted me to the school.

"What do you think of me?" I asked Father Bosco. "I think you're good material," answered the priest with a big smile.

"Well, then," I said, "you are a good tailor, so if the material is good, take me and make a new suit out of me for our Lord Jesus." One time I said to Father John Bosco, "I have to become a saint, Father!"

Other boys at the school, and the teachers noticed from the way I prayed that I was different from the average boy in my love for God. I loved all the other boys very much. Even though I was younger, I worried about the other boys at the school. I knew what they would do and say sometimes it worried me that they would lose the grace of God by sinning.

One day one of the boys brought a bad magazine full of dirty pictures to school. He was flashing it around but Father Bosco and other teachers did not see this. In a minute a group of boys gathered around that boy to see the magazine. Then I came along.

"What's up?" I asked as I went to take a look. One glance was too much for me. I grabbed the magazine and tore it to pieces!

"Poor us!" I cried aloud. "Did God give us eyes to look at such things as this? Are you not ashamed?"

"Oh, we were just looking at these pictures for the fun of it," said one older boy.

"Sure, for fun," I replied, "and in the meantime you are preparing yourselves to go to hell!"

"Oh, what is so wrong about looking at these pictures anyway?" demanded another boy.

The answer came quick to me: "If you don't see anything wrong, this is even worse. It means you're used to looking at shameful things!" No one answered me after that. They all knew that what I said was right.

I got the boys to burn any dirty magazines they had. Then I got them to go to the priest to make a good confession of what they had done.

There was another time I came across a terrific stone-throwing fight between two angry boys. I held up a little crucifix between them and said, "Before you fight, look at this and say, 'Jesus Christ was innocent and He died forgiving His murderers. I am a sinner, and I am going to hurt Him by not forgiving my enemies.' Then you can start and throw your first stone at me!"

Those two boys were so ashamed of themselves that they made up and promised to go to confession.

You see, I had the greatest respect for the Sacraments. I knew one must be in the state of sanctifying grace to receive Jesus in Holy Communion worthily. That is why I'd get the boys to be sorry and make good confessions.

Now it was not easy for me to do these things when sometimes I was so outnumbered. But, my love for God and the souls of my fellow teenagers made me forget about any fears of being criticized. I did what the love of God prompted me to do. The other boys came to respect me for it.

You can understand then why the great priest who is today the patron saint of spiritual fathers (Father John Bosco) is also a very dear friend. I went to confession to him often, even every week. I founded a club among the boys called the Sodality of the Immaculate Conception, to encourage frequent reception of Holy Communion.

One day when I was fourteen years old, I began to feel very sick. I was sent home to get better with a change of climate. But I grew worse. The parish priest came to see me. I received the last Sacraments: Viaticum and the Anointing of the Sick. I knew I was going to die. I kept praying, "Jesus, Mary and Joseph, assist me in my last agony!" I was overjoyed at the thought of going to heaven soon.

Just before I died, I tried to sit up. "Goodbye," I murmured to the good father. Suddenly my face lit up and I said to Fr. Bosco, "Oh! Father what I am seeing is so beautiful!" I spoke no more. I had left for heaven. Not long afterwards boys in the dormitory were awakened at night by a light. They knew I was in heaven and was remembering them.

I died when I was only fifteen years old. It was Pope St. Pius X who canonized me, declaring me to be a saint in heaven.

"A teenager such as Dominic, who bravely struggled to keep his innocence from Baptism to the end of his life, is really a saint," said St. Pius X.

Summary: Young Catholics today must get the true spirit of Catholicism and be fearless so that they do not hesitate to be different. To be different is not to be peculiar or unlike what Jesus wants you to be. The important thing for happiness in this life and the next life is not acceptance by one's peers. To be pleasing to God within our souls — that is what counts.

Modern youth are very mixed up and misled when they think their values and actions should be based on acceptance by other youth who have not resisted the world but followed the urgings of every passion.

In addition to "Death rather than mortal sin" one could use the motto, "Fear not to be different." Don't follow the crowd. Follow Jesus. Influence others to follow Jesus Christ, and live in His grace.

Suggested Actions to Imitate St. Dominic Savio:

✔Make the resolution never to gaze upon pornographic literature or pictures of any kind.
✔Make the resolution, "I'll dare to be different" when it means not following others in sinful ways or into occasions of sin. "I'll dare to be different by living a holy life even if others think I'm odd."
✔Encourage others whom you know may be neglecting the sacraments to go to Confession.

Your author's comments:

It is becoming very difficult to stay away from pornography. It is everywhere. Television is almost impossible to watch without being subjected to it. And the Internet delivers it to your eyes without your ever seeking it out unless you install filters. At the stores, you can't approach the magazine racks without seeing it. Satan is trying with all of his might to take each of us to hell with him. We must fight hard to keep away from his grasp. The Scripture that commands us to be hot or cold or the Lord will begin to vomit us from His mouth, is in full play these days. You can see our release from the grace of days gone by and our tree is starting to rot. We must double and triple our efforts. We must not listen to any advice that tells us not to try. These are Satan- influenced teachers who want only to lower the bar. The Lord warned us that they would come.

Saint Joan of Arc

(January 6, 1412 - May 30, 1431)

Perhaps my favorite saint of all time is this young girl. She risked the loss of her family to do the will of God. I have viewed both motion pictures dealing with her life and I am overwhelmed at the heroism and courage of this child-saint. I believe all children and all parents should watch one of these movies to begin to comprehend the power that God can exert in inspiring ordinary human beings to do extraordinary deeds.

The Maid of Lorain

Saint Michael the Archangel, the patron of my country, started it all for me in a bright light one day. I was working in my father's garden when it happened. He said to me: "Daughter of God, go save France!"

I was only 19 years old when I died. But my short life was full of excitement and sorrow. At 13 years of age I talked with an archangel and saints. At 16 I led an army to victory. I am considered the savior of France and its national heroine. I have become an inspiration to young people and a symbol of those willing to die for what they believe is true.

My name is Joan of Arc, and I was born in Domremy, France. It was January 6, 1412, the feast of the Epiphany. Both my parents were good Catholics who taught me very early to pronounce with reverence the holy names of Jesus and Mary. My father's name was Jacques d'Arc. There were five children. My mother taught me sewing and spinning. I was a country girl, and like most children of my time I never learned to read or write.

As a child I had a love of prayer. I was faithful in attendance at the Holy Sacrifice of the Mass and made frequent use of the Sacraments of Reconciliation and Holy Communion. I tried to be kind to sick people. I had a special sympathy for poor wayfarers. Sometimes I gave up my own bed for them. People of the village loved me.

My country was in a sorry state, however. There was the Hundred Years War between England and France. Whole provinces of my country were being lost to the English and the Burgundians. The government of France was then weak and offered them little resistance. One time I had to escape from my town of Domremy with my parents as the Burgundians, who set fire to the church near my home, were raiding it.

I was only three years old when in 1415 King Henry V of England invaded Normandy and claimed the crown of the insane King Charles VI. My country of France was then already in civil war. King Henry and King Charles both died in 1422, but the war continued. One town after another fell to the English or to Burgundian allies. Charles VII, called the Dauphin, considered the matter hopeless. He was supposed to be crowned King in Rheims, but the enemy occupied that city. So the Dauphin spent his time in ridiculous pastimes, acting as if he didn't care about his country.

I was in my early teens when I first heard the unearthly voices. I believe they brought me messages from God. There was a blaze of light one day as I worked in the garden. That is how it all started. From that light I heard the voice of St. Michael the Archangel, who identified himself. The archangel gave me some wise advice to help me lead a good life. He finished by saying that God wanted to save France through me. I was thrilled and yet frightened to think that God wanted to save my country through me.

The archangel came again. St. Catherine of Alexandria and St. Margaret accompanied him. The images of these three saints stood in my parish church at Domremy. I was told to take Charles to Rheims to be crowned and then drive out the English. I did not mention any of this at home. I feared my father's disapproval.

By May, 1428, the voices had become so clear and insistent that I knew I must go to see Robert de Baudricourt, who commanded the Dauphin's forces. I was now sixteen years old and had been hearing the voices for at least three years. My uncle went with me to tell him that I was appointed to lead the Dauphin to his crowning. This I did, and Baudricourt laughed and said that my father should give me a whipping. I went back home to Domremy, but the voices came again. I told the voices that I was only a poor country girl and that I could neither ride nor fight. They answered, "It is God who commands it."

When I went to Baudricourt again, he was more inclined to believe me. News had just reached him telling of the serious French defeat, which I had predicted. Orleans seemed destined to fall as well. Baudricourt now agreed to send me to the Dauphin and gave me an escort of three soldiers. For protection, I put on male clothing. On March 6, 1429, we reached Chinon, where the Dauphin was staying. Charles VII, to test me, disguised himself as one of his courtiers. I knew him and pointed him out without hesitation. I gave a sign that only he and I understood. This convinced him that my mission was true.

It was not so easy to convince other authorities, as it was Charles. They regarded me as a crazy visionary or an impostor. They sent me to Poitiers to be questioned by a committee of theologians. The questioning was a long ordeal. It lasted three weeks. They found me honest, good and virtuous. They told Charles, the Dauphin, to make prudent use of my services.

I resumed to Chinon and was given a small force. I had a banner made which contained the words "Jesus, Mary." On it was also a figure of God the Father, to whom two kneeling angels were presenting the royal emblem of France. I put on dazzling white armor, and my troops called me "the Maid." I appeared handsome, healthy and with a smiling face and dark hair, which had been cut short on April 27, when I led forth the army. I had learned to ride well but had no knowledge of military tactics.

The soldiers admired my gallantry, and we broke through the English line and entered Orleans on April 29. Our presence inside the city greatly strengthened the spirits of the French people. By May 8, the English fort outside Orleans was captured. In the attack I was slightly wounded by an arrow in the shoulder. There were further successes.

I next urged the coronation of the Dauphin because the road to Rheims was almost cleared. The French leaders, still disorganized and fearful, delayed. Finally they followed me to Rheims. There, on July 17, 1429, when Charles VII was crowned King, I proudly stood behind him with my banner of Jesus and Mary, God the Father and the Angels.

But the mission given to me by the heavenly voices was not yet completed. The English were still in France. King Charles VII was weak and did not follow up these happenings with strength, as he should have. The attack on Paris failed because of lack of his promised support and presence. I was again wounded in this attack and had to be dragged to safety. There followed a winter's truce.

In spring, May 23, 1430, I renewed the battle to help Compiegne, which was besieged by the Burgundians. Through a miscalculation, as my forces were going over a drawbridge, it was lifted too soon, and I fell into the hands of the enemy. I became the prisoner of the Duke of Burgundy and was held in a high tower of the castle of the Luxembourgs. I finally tried to escape, leaping from the tower and landing on soft turf. It was considered a miracle that I was not killed, but I was sorely bruised and stunned and did not succeed.

King Charles made no effort to have me released during the time I was a prisoner. Whenever I was in trouble, no matter what I had done for my country, he did not come to my aid. The English were anxious to have me. On November 21, the Burgundians accepted a large indemnity and gave me into English hands.

The English knew that I was responsible for their defeat in war against the French. They decided to have me condemned as a sorceress and a heretic. They considered me to have given the devil's own courage to the French. The English and Burgundian soldiers said that their losses were due to my diabolical spells over the French.

I was taken to a cell in the castle of Rouen. I was chained to a plank bed. Guards watched over me night and day. On February 21, 1431, I was brought before a court of the Inquisition. The Church was to decide twenty-five years later that the trial was unjust. But that did not help me now. A ruthless, ambitious man, who was also Bishop of Beauvais, presided at the trial. He hoped through English influence to become Archbishop of Rouen. That ambitious Bishop Cauchon had carefully chosen his own judges whom he knew would favor his side, giving the English the decision they wanted.

I was now only nineteen years old. I stood alone and undefended before that unfair court which pretended to be interested in protecting the true faith. My fearless conduct, my honesty, piety and accurate memory proved embarrassing to these hardened men.

During the trial I admitted that at the age of thirteen I had received a voice from God to help and guide me. I admitted that almost always the voice came with a light. I admitted that I believed the voice came from God. I said the voice protected me well. When I was asked what instruction the voice gave for the salvation of my soul, I answered that it taught me to be good and to go to church often. I admitted how the voice told me to save France. I said that I recognized King Charles by the counsel of the voice when I entered his room.

One time during the trial I was asked if I was in God's grace. I answered, "If I am not, may God put me there; and if I am, may God so keep me. I should be the saddest creature in the world if I knew I was not in His grace."

I told the court that other saints besides St. Michael spoke to me, but it was St. Michael who came first. I said that St. Michael, whom I saw before my eyes, was not alone. He was accompanied by many angels from heaven. "I saw them with my bodily eyes as well as I see you; and when they left me, I wept and I wished that they would have taken me with them, too." That is what I said to the court.

During the trial, I was asked if I would submit my deeds and words to the decision of the Church. I answered, "I commit myself to Our Lord who sent me, to Our Lady, and to all the blessed saints of paradise." I asked them why they made it so difficult. Our Lord and the Church are all one. I had a clear understanding of the Church as Christ's Mystical Body and the Communion of Saints binding the Church on earth with that in heaven. The court had tried to separate the Church Triumphant in heaven from the Church Militant on earth.

I was human, and the court got me fearful at times. Only when I was led out into the churchyard of St. Quen before a large crowd, and I heard the sentence committing me to the flames, did I kneel down and blurt out I had been speaking falsely. Then I was taken back to prison. When Bishop Cauchon, with some witnesses, visited me in the cell to question me further, I recovered from my weakness. Once more I said that God had truly sent me and that the voices came from God.

On May 28, I was asked whether I had heard the voices of St. Catherine and St. Margaret since Thursday, when I had said I had not told the truth. I answered, "Yes." When asked what they told me, I answered that they told me God had sent me word through St. Catherine and St. Margaret of the great pity of this treason, by which I had consented to renounce and recant in order to save my life. The voices said that I had damned myself to save my life. I told them that if I now declared God had not sent me, I would damn myself, for in truth, I was sent from God. I told them that my voices told me that I had done very wrong to say what I did. I said I had stated that only for fear of the fire. I added that I did not deny or intend to deny my visions. All that I had said was said for fear of the fire.

On May 29, 1431, the judges condemned me as a relapsed heretic and delivered me to the English. The next morning, at 8 a.m. I was led out into the marketplace of Rouen to be burned at the stake. At my request, a Dominican priest held up a cross before my eyes. As the flames leapt higher and higher, I called out the name of Jesus.

At the moment of my death some said they saw my soul leave my body under the form of a dove. John Tressart, one of King Henry's secretaries, viewed the scene of my death with horror. He said with great sorrow: "We are lost! We have burned a saint!" They threw my ashes into the Seine.

Twenty-five years later when the English had been driven out and the Pope was living at Avignon, he ordered a rehearing of my case. By that time I was already being considered the savior of France. The first trial was judged improper. I was formally reinstated as a true and faithful daughter of the Church.

I was beatified in 1909 and canonized a saint by Pope Benedict XV in the year 1919.

Summary: The life of the teenager Joan of Arc, who from the ages of thirteen to nineteen became the savior and national hero of France, has inspired millions of young people in their love for God and country. If anyone thinks being a Christian means excluding oneself from the needs of mankind, not being involved in any way in political ventures, the life of Joan of Arc says otherwise. If anyone thinks that only when one reaches the age of mature adulthood should they be interested in the social dimension, the life of the sainted Maid of France declares otherwise. So does the Church, by canonizing her at the beginning of our present 20th century.

The genuine Catholic is committed to restore all things in Christ, including the world and his own country. The Church on earth is called the Church Militant, not a passive body of believers. This means Christians must go over to the attack. St. Joan of Arc can serve as a model. The voices of heaven, led by St. Michael the Archangel, told Joan to go and save France. Christians today must work to establish a Christian social order working in a system of Christian states throughout the world.

The Second Vatican Council in its "Decree on the Apostolate of the Laity" called on lay Christians to carry the message of Christ to the world, to Christianize the laws, the structures, institutions and customs of the civil society in which they live. We have all heard expressions like "dirty politics" or "dirty tricks." Too often good Christian people have been sleeping, thinking that their role was only to pray; to look for miracles, and that somehow God would step in and solve everything. Even the miraculous life of Joan of Arc, when the heavenly voices from the blaze of light instructed and encouraged her, still did not simply tell her to pray. St. Michael, the messenger of God and the patron of her country, told her, "Daughter of God, go save France!"

St. Michael the Archangel is the general of the Blue Army Cadets of Our Lady of Fatima. Catholic liturgy applies to this archangel the name "Angel of Peace." There is an axiom, "If you want peace, prepare for war." A major objective is to fight Satan for the conversion of sinners and peace of the world by living our consecration to the Immaculate Heart of Mary. The badge of consecration is the Brown Scapular of Our Lady of Mt. Carmel. The daily food for strength in the battle to Christianize the world, beginning at home, is Our Lord in the Holy Eucharist.

Christian action is social action for Christian living. The lives of the saints, and that of St. Joan of Arc, give us that message over and over. We must pray for peace and for a Christian social order in a system of Christian states, yes. But we must also work for it. St. Michael the Archangel instructed Joan of Arc to strengthen herself by prayer, by the Sacrifice of the Mass, by frequenting the Sacraments.

The good Catholic cannot live in isolation. He is part of a community. How the community thinks, acts and lives, affects whether each of us can live the full Christian life. If pagan mentalities, if the principles of atheism, best represented by Communism, which spreads the "errors of Russia" throughout the world, continue to form our laws, our community ideas, it will become more and more difficult, if not morally impossible, to live the full Catholic life. If God occasionally grants miracles, as in the light and voices of St. Joan of Arc and the voices to the Fatima children and the spinning of the sun witnessed by 100,000 spectators, it is not to entertain the curious bystanders, but to tell them "Go, work. Do something about renewing the face of the earth in Christ."

Pornography, those dirty newsstands, those X-rated movies and some others: abortion, contraception, the killing of the innocent unborn, indecency in dress, disrespect for the Lord's Day, failure to worship on Sundays and holy days, drugs and alcoholic abuse, the abuse of the powers of sex before marriage — are all examples of where we can start in the community at home to Christianize the social order. Young people should be interested in politics if there is going to be a Christian social order in America and elsewhere. If Christians in America had been really active Christians there would have been no black Monday on January 22, 1973, when the highest court in the U.S.A. made it legal to murder the unborn. Some at this very moment work to make it legal to murder the hopelessly sick, the crippled, the retarded. It will happen if Christians only pray but do not work.

Suggested Actions in Imitation of St. Joan of Arc:

✔Develop an awareness of all the things in your community that are not Christian.
✔Organize with others to correct them.

Your author's comments:

Joan flies in the face of all those who do less and lower the bar. They are Satan's drones who prowl the world seeking the ruin of souls. We see here that God will get children to do the job if we, as adults, refuse. There is a price to be paid for those who teach a lax faith and convince the children of God to revert. Joan led thousands of men into battle in the name of the Lord and was burned at the stake because of the pride of a bishop. She persevered in trials and is called a saint and that bishop - where is he now?

Blessed Padre Miguel Pro

Martyr of Joy
(January 13, 1891 - November 23, 1926)

I choose Blessed Padre Miguel Pro as a pillar of truth and of endurance for all who have chosen the life of a priest. We see in Father Pro a man who was willing to suffer all for Christ and with a great sense of humor in the midst of profound pain and mental stress. I guess the message here is, many before you have suffered through much to bring the faith to you and now hand that baton over expecting that you will do no less than they. Represent your priesthood well with a great commitment to authentic Catholic teaching and uphold the rubrics of the Mass so we all can worship as one.

Pride tries to convince all of us, and especially priests, to demand that our way is the right way. Pride tries to get us to turn against the Magisterium and we have suffered greatly because of pride's success. We have lost seventy three percent of the once faithful and loyal in the Catholic Church in the last forty years. That is pride's success.

If we all were more like Father Pro, willing to die for the faith, our faith would grow.

Blessed Padre Miguel Pro

> I died for the Catholic faith in my native land of Mexico when I was a young priest of thirty-six years of age. Today the pilgrims form a continuous procession. They pass my tomb and remember the long years of persecution of the Church in Mexico. They make the Sign of the Cross reverently and bestow a kiss. They touch their rosaries and medals to this place they consider holy. The silence is broken only by the photographs of my execution, which speak again of the atrocities committed by the anti-Catholic government in Mexico. Written above this humble little shrine are the words:
>
> Blessed Padre Miguel Augustin Pro
> Apostle, Martyr and Model of Joy.

I was born on January 13, 1891, in a small mining town called Guadalupe and given the name Miguel Augustin Pro. I was the third of eleven children. Senor Miguel, my father, was a successful mining engineer. My mother, Josefa, while attending to the needs of the family, also founded the San Jose Hospital for the poor. The Catholic faith was the center of our family life. This was verified with our home being filled with many beautiful and sacred traditions.

When I was only three years old, I became violently ill shortly after the family had moved to Mexico City. I was left with a continuous stupor with my head hanging and my mouth open and with no ability to speak. I remained in this state for a year, until a series of convulsions left me near death. My father, Miguel, overcome with grief, snatched my lifeless body and lifting his son on outstretched arms before an image of Our Lady of Guadalupe cried, "Mama Mia, give me back my son!"

All present, including the doctors, were astounded at what happened next. They witnessed my sudden and miraculous transformation! My first words were clearly articulated, "Mama! I want a cocol." I was asking for my favorite sweet roll. Years later, during the religious persecution, I frequently signed perilous letters to my Jesuit brothers "cocol" in order not to give away my identity to the Mexican authorities.

On August 15, 1911, at twenty years of age, I received the habit of the Society of Jesus. I began my studies in the novitiate of El Liano. I prayed and studied so diligently that my classmates and professors began to call me "the brother who is convinced that God wants him to be a saint."

Three years after receiving the religious habit, my classmates and I were ordered to don civilian clothes and flee. The Jesuit Fathers had already concealed the books. They hid the chalices, crucifixes and other religious objects to prevent their destruction. Mexican authorities were approaching to arrest, torture and even kill the priests, religious and loyal Catholics. The terror of the religious persecution had finally reached the doors of El Liano.

Together with my classmates we escaped to the city of Zamora, which was soon engulfed by the same terrible nightmare! All roads were barricaded and any attempt to leave the city was extremely dangerous. This was exactly the sort of challenge that gave me an opportunity to use the talents God had given me. Disguised as a peasant with "serape" and "sombrero", I rubbed stain and mud to darken my face. Then I shuffled toward the police as a decoy for my fellow seminarians. This threw attention away from them.

Safely outside the city, we boarded a train for Guadalajara, and still dressed as a peasant, I amused them all by elaborating my role. I juggled our skimpy hand luggage and waited on them, assuming the attitude of a servant. This was fun and useful for our purposes at the same time. At first it was difficult to hold their composure, but after some time, my classmates actually forgot that their "amigo" under the enormous sombrero was not a genuine servant.

The Mexican government was more and more bringing persecution upon the Catholic Church. Soon my companions and I were forced to flee our beloved country altogether in order to prepare for the holy priesthood, with the hope of returning to our people one day.

As a seminarian I never lost hope nor my joyful spirit. Even though I experienced severe attacks of excruciating stomach pain and continuous headaches, I managed to lift the spirits of all those around me. By being human and creative I could brighten the darkest moments. My songs played on the guitar brought forth a burst of laughter and they found my impersonations irresistible. I acted out one-man skits. Father Portas writes, "It was impossible for anyone, no matter how solemn by nature or however bowed down he might be, to restrain laughter in those unforgettable moments when Miguel called upon all his ingenuity." These gifts would later serve me well as a priest in persecuted Mexico.

The exile first led us to California and then to Granada, Spain. I progressed in my studies, but others recognized success in the lively way I would teach the catechism. The simple folk and the gypsies named me "Father Delightful." As soon as my presence in a village was known the entire population locked their houses and followed me through the winding streets!

On August 31, 1925, after fourteen years of study and apostolic work, I, Miguel Augustin Pro, was ordained a Jesuit priest in Enghien, Belgium. "I could not keep back the tears on the day of my ordination," I later wrote.

Now known as Padre Pro, I immediately began apostolic work among the miners experiencing firsthand their problems and working conditions. I rode the worker's trains, seizing opportunities to evangelize. On one occasion, I was surrounded by angry socialist and communist workers who threatened me, demanding to see my secret "weapon." I rummaged through my pockets. Then I smiled and pulled out a crucifix and said, "With this along, I have no fear of anyone!" Shocked at my response, they permitted me to speak of the effectiveness of my "weapon!"

My apostolic work came to an abrupt end, as I could no longer conceal my illness. I was taken to Saint-Remi Clinic in Brussels for three stomach operations. Prior to my second operation, the surgeon informed me that they could not risk using an anesthetic. "In that case," I calmly replied, "I would like to be given my Code of Canon Law to read!" To the amazement of the doctors, I closed my mind to the pain and quietly read the Code, giving no evidence of pain while they cut and stitched my body.

A third and final operation left me dangerously weak and debilitated. I was sent to an infirmary for priests in southern France. Instead of resting, I arose each morning to say the first Mass. I attended to the dying, administered the last Sacraments and heard Confessions. I was even instrumental in converting the gardener.

My recovery was not rapid with all this activity, so my Jesuit superiors decided that if they returned me to Mexico it might work the necessary miracle. If not, it would at least give me the consolation of dying among my loved ones. First I went to Lourdes and received the necessary strength for the long journey home. From Saint-Nazaire on June 24, 1926, I embarked for Mexico on The Cuba.

I was on my way back to my native land of Mexico where it was against the law for Catholic priests to enter. No one suspected that I was not the well-dressed young playboy that I had disguised myself to be. I disembarked from The Cuba and entered the customs hall.

"It was by an extraordinary concession of God that I was admitted into my country," I later wrote. They did not even open my bags. The chalice and vestments in those bags, which I had received at my recent ordination in Belgium, would certainly have cost me my life. Arriving in Mexico City, I knew that I was now in more danger of dying by the political conditions than by poor health.

I made my way through the crowded streets, still wearing the disguise of a playboy. It had been twelve years since I and my fellow seminarians had been forced to flee from our homeland. I remembered the way to our Jesuit provincial house. The provincial superior greeted me warmly and secretly. "You certainly don't look like a newly ordained Jesuit priest, Padre Pro," laughed the superior. "What guardian angel warned you to come so well-disguised?"

"There were Mexican travelers visiting our house in Belgium shortly before I left. They filled us in on the thirty-three articles regarding religious practices in the new constitutions. Is it true that President Calles has closed the schools?"

"Not only are the schools closed," said the superior, "but orphanages also. All Catholic institutions had to either close or turn themselves over to the State. What will happen to the poor people? Calles says he is for the poor working people, but without education there will be no future for our country. On July 31, the feast of our patron, St. Ignatius, the churches also will be officially closed." The older priest had heard of my intelligence and saintly life. He was impressed with the young priest before him. "Father Miguel, are you prepared to go underground? To risk your very life to bring the Sacraments and the Gospel to our people?"

I paused before responding. Then I answered, "Yes, Father, I have offered my life to God through my vows as a religious. And through my priestly ordination, I have committed all my energy to preaching the Gospel and to celebrating the Sacraments with my fellow Mexicans. I am prepared to do whatever is necessary."

"I thought you would say that. Que bien! Tomorrow, go visit your family in Mexico City. In the meantime, Fr Miguel, don't let anyone know your true identity. The people are flocking to Confession by the hundreds, trying to receive the Sacraments one last time before July 31. Go in and out of the church at night."

Later I wrote, "Most priests are unable to minister on account of being known. As I am unknown, I am substituting for many. I have set up something I call Eucharistic stations where I go each day to give Holy Communion."

Since priests were hunted people by the anti-Catholic government, I would sport a new disguise each day. I'd race my bicycle up streets and down alleys, passing unsuspecting police officers in order to administer the Sacraments to hundreds and sometimes a thousand people a day. It was said that my ability to outwit the police seemed to know no limits.

With a sense of humor I fooled the police more than once. "I went to a rather eccentric part of the city to say Mass,"

I once wrote to a friend. "Imagine my surprise when I found two police guarding the door! 'This time you are in for it,' I said to myself. But I pulled myself together and walked straight up to the officers. With an air of being in on the secret, I jotted down the number of the house, drew back my lapel as if to show my detective's badge, and said in a low voice, 'There is an eel here under the rock.' The two gave me a military salute and let me go by, convinced I was an agent."

I then celebrated the Sacrifice of the Mass that day with the two police officers guarding the door, not realizing that Mass was being offered inside.

On another occasion the police had been pursuing me. I managed to get into the guise of a police uniform just as police caught up with me and asked if I had seen Padre Pro. I answered, "Yes. I saw the rascal go that way" and I pointed in an opposite direction of my own intent, which sent the police away with haste.

One way the Catholic people kept up their courage was distributing leaflets with parts of the Gospel, catechism and prayers. Anyone caught distributing them could be shot with no trial. One day a police officer spotted me when I was disguised as a street cleaner. He picked me up for questioning. My pockets were filled with Catholic leaflets.

Maintaining my disguise as a street cleaner, I began to entertain the officer with stories of all the crazy things I had done as a youngster. I got the officer laughing uncontrollably. As he drove along toward the police station, I was tossing the leaflets out the car window. This was also good Catholic publicity for whoever found them. By the time we reached the police station the officer let his delightful young prisoner go without questioning.

The city officials gradually became aware of my clever disguises. So far I had always managed to slip by the security officers posted throughout the city. On the Feast of Christ the King, 1926, the people organized a peaceful procession to the shrine of Our Lady of Guadalupe. Thousands took part. Armed police were everywhere, looking for an excuse to begin shooting at the crowd. But there was no trouble. The people simply sang hymns and prayed the Rosary. Disguised as a worker, I marched proudly with my people. Every so often we'd shout, *"Viva Cristo Rey!"* - Long live Christ the King!

It had become the rally motto of the persecuted Church of Mexico. As the people did not give up their faith, President Calles became more corrupt. He ran the country as a military state with his sidekick, General Obregon. Among the most active opponents of Calles were Humberto and Roberto Pro, my two younger brothers.

On December 4, 1926, they stuffed six hundred balloons with anti-Calles leaflets. They filled the balloons with helium and released them over Mexico City. When the balloons reached a certain height, they burst and anti-government propaganda rained down over the streets of Mexico City.

I continued my underground church work among thousands of Mexicans, bringing them Jesus in the Holy Eucharist, hearing Confessions. I was much loved by the people and so persecuted by the government.

On November 17, 1927, I was awakened by twenty-four soldiers bashing in the doors of the house. I was arrested with my brothers, Humberto and Roberto, leaders of the underground Catholic Defense League. We were subjected to four days of interrogations and spent our last days in the dark stench of dungeon Number One which was beneath the police station. We divided our food among the prisoners, prayed the rosary and sang hymns. Triumphantly, we wrote on the prison wall *Viva Cristo Rey!* and *Viva La Virgen de Guadalupe!* (Long live the Virgin of Guadalupe). Soon the spirits of all the inmates were lifted and the entire prison echoed with prayer and song.

The innocence of the Pro brothers was obvious. Yet, the government wanted to silence another priest and so the police issued a false report. They claimed that the Pros planned an assassination on President-elect General Obregon. The notorious Plutarco Calles ordered "a big show" at the execution. Invitations were quickly sent to all government officials, dignitaries and press agencies.

At 10:00 A.M. on November 23, 1927, a guard came to escort me to the execution place. The prison yard was lined with news reporters, photographers and city officials.

The inspector approached me and said, "Padre, I ask your pardon for my part in this."

"You not only have my pardon, but my gratitude. I give you thanks," I replied.

A soldier then led me to the far end of the courtyard. "Is there anything you wish?" he asked me.

"That I may be permitted to pray." I knelt, slowly made the sign of the cross and prayed with my arms folded over my chest. I then rose, kissed a crucifix I was holding, and with outstretched arms in the form of a cross, I confidently and affectionately said "*Viva Cristo Rey!*" A sharp explosion launched and the lights of cameras flickered as my body fell to the ground. It was reported that I was still retaining the form of a cross!

My brother, Humberto Pro, was executed that same morning but Roberto Pro was spared and expelled from the country.

A multitude of more than fifteen thousand people joined in our funeral procession. It was a joyful celebration. Cheering from both sides of the streets could be heard – *"Viva Cristo Rey!"* Flowers were dropped from the balconies, carpeting the streets and people knelt as the coffins passed by.

The result of the murder of their favorite priest was a strengthening of the faith in the Catholic people. The reaction was not what the government wanted or expected. Thousands took to the streets, shouting, *"Viva Cristo Rey!"* and "Long live the Pope!" and "Long live the Catholic Church!" Leading the crowds was my seventy-five-year-old father, Señor Pro. At the graves of his two sons the next day, he led the huge crowd in singing the *Te Deum*—a traditional hymn of praise sung on the most solemn and joyful of feast days.

Pope John Paul II beatified me on September 25, 1989. My feast day is celebrated on November 23, the anniversary of my death. I am now known as "Blessed Padre Miguel Augustin Pro" or simply "Blessed Pro."

Summary: The 20th century has been so full of wars and revolutions and attacks against Catholicism. When Communism was making inroads in Russia and from there to nations of the world, Mexico, too, was in revolution from anti-Catholic forces. Social problems, political unrest and government opposition, which practically outlawed the Church in Mexico, climaxed in the constitution of 1917. The year 1917 was the exact year of the Bolshevik Revolution in Russia, resulting in Communism taking over and spreading out from there to the nations of the world. The Bolshevik Revolution was the very same year and months when our Blessed Mother was appearing in Fatima, Portugal with a message for the world to turn back to her Son, Jesus Christ, or persecutions would spread to all the nations of the world. What was happening was that even in countries considered Christian, there was no longer the recognition of Jesus Christ as King.

God always raises up great saints and heroes in times of need. Blessed Miguel Pro was just such a person.

Pope John Paul II, in his Apostolic Letter, *Tertio Millennio Adveniente*, on Preparation for the Jubilee of the Year 2000, took note of this. He wrote:

22. Special tasks and responsibilities with regard to the Great Jubilee of the Year 2000 belong to the ministry of the Bishop of Rome. In a certain sense, all the popes of the past century have prepared for this Jubilee. With his program to renew all things in Christ, Saint Pius X tried to forestall the tragic developments which arose from the international situation at the beginning of this century. The Church was aware of her duty to act decisively to promote and defend the tendencies in our time. The popes of the period before the Council acted with firm commitment, each in his own way: Benedict XV found himself faced with the tragedy of the First World War; Pius XI had to contend with the threats of totalitarian systems or systems which did not respect human freedom in Germany, in Russia, in Italy, in Spain and even earlier still, in Mexico. Pius XII took steps to counter the very grave injustice brought about by a total contempt for human dignity at the time of the Second World War. He also provided enlightened guidelines for the birth of a new world order after the fall of the previous political systems. Furthermore, in the course of this century, the popes, following in the footsteps of Leo XIII, systematically developed the themes of Catholic social doctrine, expounding the characteristics of a just system in the area of relations between labor and capital.

Pope John Paul II then recalled the great encyclicals of the popes of the past century, including his own, which dealt with world situations and the justice required in the social issues for peace and advancement of society and the Christian life. Pope John Paul II in his Apostolic Letter on the Advent of the Third Millennium wrote:

23. In fact, preparing for the Year 2000 has become, as it were, a hermeneutical (interpretive) key of my Pontificate.

There is justification for concluding, that in the 21st century, we can expect a new Golden Age for the Church. The world has been in turmoil in the 20th. There have been millions of martyrs, if we consider all those who died under the injustice of communism, Nazism, etc., as outlined by Pope John Paul II in *Tertio Millennio Adveniente.* The blood of martyrs is the seed of Christianity with the intercession of the powerful martyrs, such as Blessed Miguel Pro and countless others, who have now passed into the Church Triumphant from the Church Suffering, and as the extraordinary guidance of the teachings of popes of the 20th century become absorbed gradually by the masses, we can expect the "new dawn of Christianity" which Pope John Paul II anticipates.

While the persecution of the Church in Mexico was mitigated later in the century, yet, as late as 1988, when I entered Mexico City, it was still the law of the land that clerics were not to be dressed in clerical clothing. Nonetheless, I walked the streets of Mexico in my black suit and Roman collar with no bother. Had a priest done that earlier in the century it would have meant sudden death. I had never gone into the public without being identified as a priest and felt by now the sufferings of good Catholics in Mexico, such as Padre Pro, had brought greater freedoms. I did the same each year after my initial pilgrimage to Our Lady of Guadalupe. I wore the black suit and Roman collar, even meeting the police along the way. No one said a word. Into the 1990s, the restriction was officially lifted. Still, I sense among the native clergy a reluctance to go out into the public identified as priests outside their parish property.

There can be little doubt that what the 20th century has been through has been the fruit of diabolic endeavors and mankind, in general, not being open to the good holy angels, in short, not being open to the Holy Spirit. I saw evidence of this the first time I visited the tomb of Blessed Miguel Pro in February of 1995. A group of young people with Satanic symbols on their persons had gathered outside the Holy Family Church which contains the shrine-tomb of Blessed Miguel Pro. They then made their way into the Church, went up to the Tabernacle which contained our Eucharistic Lord and attempted to grab the contents. An aged priest, with cane in hand, assisted by a young man, drove them from the sanctuary.

There always are those who, in times of persecution, give in easily and follow the least course of resistance. But such is not the true Christian and Catholic way. The true Catholic way is to be willing to die rather than ever deny Jesus Christ or the Catholic Church. The true Catholic spirit is to evangelize the Truth who is Jesus Christ. *Viva Cristo Rey!*

Padre Pro made catechetics exciting. We now have the *Catechism of the Catholic Church* to guide us. That catechism is exciting.

Even in times of persecution the spirit of Christian joy should permeate our very beings. This spirit of joy, even the joy with which Jesus Christ went to His own execution, reigned in Padre Pro. He knew that love is stronger than death, and that death for Jesus Christ and His holy Catholic Church and for the welfare of souls, would lead to eternal happiness.

Suggested Actions in Imitation of Blessed Pro:

✔Place a picture of Christ the King in your home to remind you who is it who should govern the home and society.
✔Tell your friends about Padre Pro (Blessed Miguel of Mexico) to inspire them how to live their faith in the face of opposition.
✔Form a firm resolution that you'd die before denying the fullness of true faith.
✔Have a discussion with friends on how all of us should be willing to suffer martyrdom if need be.

Your author's comments:

Blessed Pro is a real pro; he is the epitome of what every priest should strive to be. But because of wolves in sheep's clothing, many men who stood up to be counted were rejected from the seminaries while the wolves brought in their own kind, and we now see the tragic results. But there is still hope for the poorly taught and failing priest. Pray to Blessed Pro and you may help in his canonization and save yourself in the process.

Any good men who were unjustly rejected from studying the priesthood should try again and again and know that there are wolves in charge in places. We must show God that we can drink their deadly poison and live. Call on Miguel Pro for help.

And for all of you men who want to be priests and saints, play their evil game. During your entrance process, give the answers that the admissions wolves want to hear. Please do your seminary time as passively as you can and do not disclose your faithful heart until you are ordained. Then come out of your liberal closet and be the best holy priest you can be. Ask Blessed Padre Pro for help and possibly you will turn out like him.

Saint Teresa of Avila

March 28, 1515 - October 15, 1582

I chose beloved Saint Teresa as an example in this book for all of us, but mostly for female religious. Obedience, obedience, obedience is everything. In these days of many women religious leaving their habits behind and abandoning their orders in droves, we see in Saint Teresa a role model of the sort that made all of the now dissident nuns choose religious life in the first place. Satan is powerful and we need to be on guard always, lest we fall prey to his traps.

St. Teresa of Avila

Don Alonso Sanchez y Cepeda, my father, wrote this: "On Wednesday, the twenty-eighth day of the month of March of the year 1515, about half an hour after five o'clock in the morning, with the first glimmers of the light of day, Teresa, my daughter, was born."

The very day I was baptized, April 4, marked also the beginning of the Convent of the Incarnation, a house of Carmelite nuns in my town. My life was to go down in history as deeply influencing the Carmelite Order.

My father was a man who believed in deep respect for the traditions that had gone before him. He also believed in progress, moving with the times. Being devoted to the study of books himself, he insisted that his children should learn to spell and read from their youngest years.

My father was a man highly respected. He had great respect for manners and obeying God's Commandments. He had a very understanding nature. Even though in my time it was considered proper to have slaves, my father refused to have any. Noble in character, his sword at his side, his rosary always within hand's reach, my father was considered important in Avila, Spain, and passed for a very rich man.

My father's first wife died and he became very sad. When he was nearly thirty, he married Dona Beatriz de Ahumada, a beautiful lady, much younger than my father. This second wife was to become my mother. She was a tender mother, compassionate to her children's needs. There were twelve children in my parents' family; nine were born to my mother and there were three children of my father's first marriage.

My parents reared us piously in the holy Catholic faith. Both I and my brother Rodrigo loved to read the lives of saints and martyrs. Rodrigo was near my age and my partner in young adventures. It seemed that martyrs got to heaven the easy way. When I was only seven, my brother and I made a plan to run away to Africa. There we might be beheaded by the faithless Moors.

Rodrigo and I set out secretly. We would beg our way like the poor Franciscans. We only got a short distance when; found by an uncle, we were taken home to our mother, who was much worried. She already had servants searching the streets of Avila for us.

Next we decided to become hermits. We tried to build small cells in the garden. However, we quickly ran out of stones from the garden and had to give up the idea of building a hut for a hermitage.

I was only fourteen years old when mother died. As soon as I began to understand how great a loss I had sustained by losing her, I was very much afflicted; and so I went before an image of Our Blessed Lady and besought her with many tears that she would agree to be my mother.

About this time, a girl cousin started visiting me. She was most welcome, but it led me to become interested in worldly things. I read, as a teen-ager, so many foolish romances in novels, that I began to lose the love for prayer that I had at a very young age. It became so important to me to look beautiful and dress well.

These tales did not fail to cool my good desires and were the cause of my falling insensibly into other defects. I was so enchanted that I could not be happy without some new tale in my hands. I began to imitate the fashions, to enjoy being well dressed, to take great care of my hands, to use perfumes and wear all the vain ornaments which my position in the world allowed.

My father noticed the change coming over me. He placed me in a convent of Augustinian nuns in Avila. There other young women of my class were being educated. I became aware to what great danger my soul had been exposed.

One and a half years after entering the convent school, I became ill and my father brought me home. I began to read the *Letters of St. Jerome*. This helped me reach a decision about entering the religious life. St. Jerome was both idealistic and practical and had a great effect on me. I decided to enter the religious life as a nun. My father refused, saying that I would have to wait until he died.

Secretly, I left home, even though I loved my father dearly. It pained me to do this. I remember while I was going out of my father's house, I believed the sharpness of sense would not be greater in the very instant of the agony of my death than it was then. It seemed as if all the bones in my body were wrenched asunder. There was no such love of God in me then as was able to quench the love I felt for my father and my friends.

A year later, I made my profession in the religious life. Later, I again became so ill it was thought I would die. Gradually I began to improve. My pious Uncle Peter gave me a little book, which instructed me on prayers of recollection and quiet. I began to concentrate on mental prayer. I eventually learned the "prayer of quiet." This means the soul rests in God, forgetting all earthly things. Sometimes I would briefly be gifted with the "prayer of union." No particular words are needed in the prayer of quiet, and when one attains the prayer of union, all the powers of the soul become absorbed in God.

After three years, I was able to go back to my convent. In those days it was a custom in Spain for young nuns to receive friends in the convent parlor. I had a long way to go to grow in union with God, for I would spend much time chatting with friends. I gave up my habit of mental prayer. I excused myself, thinking my health permitted that. This excuse of bodily weakness was not a sufficient reason why I should abandon so good a thing, which required no physical strength, but only love and habit. In the midst of sickness the best prayer may be offered, and it is a mistake to think it can only be offered in solitude.

I went back to the habit of daily mental prayer. I never gave it up again. One needs time in quiet with God every day. I did not yet have the courage, however, to follow God completely. I still wasted time and talent. But gradually my soul was being formed in the Lord.

When I would remember my own unworthiness, I would turn to the intercession of St. Mary Magdalen and St. Augustine. This would give strength to my will. After all, they had at one time been great sinners. St. Augustine's *Confessions* helped me. Also, I would look at a picture of the suffering Jesus, and this would encourage me to do penance.

I felt St. Mary Magdalen come to my assistance. From the day I felt her assistance, I went on improving in my spiritual life. When I withdrew from the pleasures of social life, I found myself able to pray the "prayer of quiet" and the "prayer of union."

I began to have mystical experiences, visions, and to hear inner voices. I became very worried about these, especially when one priest told me that a life full of such imperfections as mine would not receive such divine favors. Then I made a general confession to another priest. He told me that I was experiencing special divine graces. At the same time, he advised me that I was in need of penance in my life so as to have a true, solid spiritual life.

One day when I was praying the great hymn of St. Gregory the Great, *Veni, Creator Spiritu* (Come, Holy Spirit), I was overtaken by the love of God and heard the words: "I will not have you hold conversation with men, but with angels." I had to suffer much from others around me. They did not approve of my penances and spirituality. I was called a hypocrite. I felt sad in my soul for these reasons. It appears God wanted me rejected by others, so that I could give my heart entirely to Him.

I obeyed my superiors. When my confessor told me to treat any vision as if it were an evil spirit, and to make the sign of the cross, I did so. But it became more obvious to me that my visions were truly from God and not a trick of the devil. I continued to be slandered by others, but the Holy Spirit continued to work in my soul. God then filled me with His sweetness, even though others persecuted me. Sometimes I was lifted from the ground. God seemed not content with drawing my soul to Himself, but He wanted to draw up the very body, too. God did this to my body even though it was of unclean clay, as I had made it by my sins.

At this time the great experience of my life took place - a mystical marriage to Jesus Christ. My heart was pierced with the love of God. I saw an angel very near me, towards my left side, in bodily form, which is not usual with me, for though angels were often represented to me, it was only by mental vision. This angel appeared rather small, not large, and very beautiful. His face was so shining that he seemed to be one of those highest angels called seraphs, who look as if they are all on fire with divine love.

The angel had in his hands a long golden dart; at the end of the point I thought there was a little fire. And I felt him thrust it several times through my heart in such a way that it passed through my very bowels. And when he drew it out, I thought it pulled them out with it and left me wholly on fire with a great love of God.

The pain in my soul spread to my body. At the same time there was great delight. I was transformed. I did not care either to see or to speak but only to be on fire with the mingled pain and happiness.

Like St. Paul who wrote in the Bible that he had mixed desires, so I longed to die that I might be united with God forever in heaven. Still I desired to suffer more for Jesus upon earth.

I respected those who persecuted me. I saw them as true servants of God.

During the time, about fifteen years, when I was working to found new convents of Carmelite nuns to live a stricter religious life, I also wrote books. These included *The Way of Perfection* as guidance to my nuns, and *Foundations* to further help them. *The Interior Castle* is a book I wrote on the spiritual life, which can be of value to everyone. I became known as a teacher of mystical theology. The Church has, therefore, declared me a doctor of theology.

Unfortunately many nuns in my time had become undisciplined in not living a community life as religious. The nuns easily left the enclosure of the Carmelites. This had happened so gradually that the religious themselves did not realize how careless they had become in following their religious profession.

One of the nuns began talking about founding a new and stricter community. It seemed to me like an inspiration from heaven. I decided to undertake the task myself. Peter of Alcantara and Father Angelo de Salazar, the provincial of the Carmelite Order, approved of my plans. However, some nuns, the local nobility and others united to stop my project, and so Father Angelo withdrew his permission.

A Dominican, Father Ibanez, privately encouraged me in my plan to found a convent of stricter observance. One of my married sisters, together with her husband, began to build a small convent at Avila in 1561. People thought they were building another family house. My little nephew was crushed by a wall of the new building as it fell on him while playing. He seemed lifeless and was carried to me. I held the child in my arms and prayed. After some minutes he was restored to life.

Another seemingly solid wall of the proposed convent fell during the night. My brother-in-law did not want to pay the bricklayers. I told him that it was not their fault but that the evil spirits did not want the convent built.

I was given time to write my ideas for a reform of convent life when a woman of Toledo, Countess Louis de la Cerda, who was mourning the death of her husband, asked the Carmelite provincial to order me to come to her assistance. For six months, I lived with her, using part of the time to write. While at Toledo, I met Maria of Jesus, of the Carmelite convent at Granada. She had had messages from heaven about a reform of the Carmelite Order. This gave me strength about my plans.

When I arrived back in Avila, a letter from the Pope was presented to me the very evening of my arrival. It authorized the new reformed convent. The Bishop of Avila agreed. The convent, dedicated to St. Joseph, was opened quietly. In 1562, on St. Bartholomew's Day, the Real Presence of Jesus came to our little chapel by way of the Most Blessed Sacrament. Four novices took the habit.

An uproar broke out in the city when the news spread of my new convent. The prioress of the Incarnation convent sent for me and demanded an explanation. City authorities joined in the protest. How could the city support an unendowed convent? Don Francis sent a priest to Madrid to beg the King's Council for permission for me to continue. I was permitted to return to my convent, and shortly the bishop appointed me prioress. The noisy protests settled down.

My nuns were strictly cloistered, shut out from the outside world. Strict poverty was required, and almost complete silence, as the nuns engaged in mental prayer. We were poor, without regular revenues. We wore habits of coarse serge and no shoes. Because we wore sandals and were shoeless, we were called "discalced," or shoeless Carmelites.

I thought that too many women under one roof would lead to laxity in discipline. That is why I had worked for a reform: to get nuns back to a stricter form of religious life according to Carmelite profession. At first I allowed only thirteen women under one roof but later increased the number to permit twenty-one.

John Baptist Rubeo of Ravenna, the prior general of the Carmelites, visited Avila in 1567. He was impressed with our sincerity and rule. He gave permission for other convents to be established according to the same plan.

I had spent five peaceful years with the thirteen nuns in St. Joseph Convent. The sisters engaged in all kinds of useful work such as spinning, while keeping strictly to contemplation and religious exercises. When August, 1567, came, it was time to found a second convent at Medina del Campo.

Convents, which I founded according to my reformed rule, began to appear, but only with much hard work on my part, even though my health was frail. A third was founded in Malagon; one at Valladolid. A fifth was established at Toledo.

On beginning my work of establishing new convents, I had no more than four or five ducats (which amounted to only a few dollars). I said, "Teresa and this money are nothing; but God, Teresa, and these ducats suffice."

It was at Medina del Campo that I met two friars who wished to adopt my reform - Antony de Heredia, prior of the Carmelite monastery there, and John of the Cross. With their help, and under the authority of the prior general, we established a reformed house for men at Durelo and in 1569, another at Pastrana. The men's reformed monasteries also required great poverty and strictness of spiritual life.

I placed John of the Cross, only in his late twenties, in charge of these reformed monasteries and others that I hoped would be started. John of the Cross ran into difficulties similar to my own beginnings with the reformed Carmel for women. His provincial ordered him to return to Medina. When he would not, he was imprisoned for nine months at Toledo. He escaped to become vicar-general of Andalusia and to work for papal recognition of the reform for men.

A great spiritual friendship in Christ developed between me and John of the Cross. He was much younger than I, but he was made director and confessor in the motherhouse at Avila. He later won fame as a poet, mystic, confessor, and was finally to be canonized a saint by the Church.

There were many hardships involved in my work of founding new convents. The first furniture I provided, wherever I founded convents, was straw. Having that, I had beds to sleep on. One time I was given a vision of hell and shown my place there; that is, if I would not have cooperated with the graces God was giving me.

One time as I was crossing a stream and my cart was upset. When I flew out and settled in the water and mud, I cried out in a moment of disgust. "Oh, God, why do you treat me this way?" He answered, "I treat all my friends that way." I answered, "No wonder you have so few."

Pope Pius V assigned a number of apostolic visitors to look into the relaxation of discipline in religious orders everywhere. Great fault was found with the Incarnation convent, and I was sent for and told to direct a reform of the abuses there. This was a difficult situation for me. Here I was, returned to the old house that had been opposing my reforms. Likewise, I had to leave my beloved spiritual daughters.

At first these nuns refused to obey me. They laughed wildly at my ideas. I told them I did not intend to force them, but that I had come to serve and learn from the least among them. By gentleness and love, mixed with prudence, I gradually won the affection of the community. Discipline was reestablished. I forbade the frequent callers. Religious exercises were organized. After three years, these nuns wished that I would stay longer. I was directed to return to my own convent.

The difficulties of my life were not over. I was even reported to the Spanish Inquisition when I attempted to found a convent at Seville. An unhappy novice reported my nuns to the Inquisition, saying we were Illuminati who claimed that salvation came through the enlightenment of each individual by his own vision of God. This falsehood claimed we did not depend on the Church.

My reform seemed in trouble when Italian Carmelite friars, learning of the reforms in Spain, thought they might one day be forced to reform themselves. There were those among the Spanish Brothers, still unreformed, who shared that thought. A general chapter was held at Piacenza and decrees were passed restricting the reform. I was told to retire and not found any more convents.

King Philip II, who was a devout champion of the faith, in protection from the Protestant movement, joined my cause. The King called the nuncio and scolded him for severity toward the discalced friars and nuns.

An order came from Rome in 1580 separating the authority over the unreformed Carmelites and those, which were reformed. We were each given our own provincial. Father Gratian was elected our provincial. It was sad in many ways to see this separation, but it ended the dissension. At this time, I was already sixty-five years of age, and my health was broken.

Still, in the next two years, I found the strength to establish three more convents. These were in the north, at Burgos, in the far south, at Granada and also in Portugal at Soria. I had founded sixteen convents in all, while traveling in mule-drawn carts over poor roads, crossing mountains, rivers and dry plateaus. Little food and difficult climates added to the discomfort.

You know, this body has one fault - that the more people pamper it, the more its wants are made known. It is strange how much it likes to be indulged. How well it finds some good pretext to deceive the poor soul. You, who are free from the great troubles of the world, learn to suffer a little for the love of God without everyone's knowing it.

God deliver us from anybody who wishes to serve Him, thinks about her own dignity and fears to be disgraced. No poison in the world so slays perfection as these things do.

There are persons, it seems, who are ready to ask God for favors as a matter of justice. A fine sort of humility. Hence, He who knows all does well in giving it to them hardly ever. He sees plainly they are not fit to drink the chalice.

Sometimes the devil proposes to us great desires, so that we shall not put our hand to what we have to do and serve our Lord in possible things, but stay content with having desired impossible ones. Granting that you can help much by prayer, don't try to benefit all the world, but those who are in your company, and so the work will be better, for you are much bounder to them. In short, what I would conclude with is that we must not build towers without foundations. The Lord does not look so much to the grandeur of our works as to the love with which they are done. If we do all we can, His Majesty will see to it that we are able to do more and more every day, if we do not then grow weary. And during the little that this life lasts—and perhaps it will be shorter than each one thinks— we must offer to Christ, inwardly and outwardly, what sacrifice we can. Then His Majesty will join it with the one He made to the Father for us on the

Cross, that it may have the value which our will would have merited, even though our works may be small.

I submit in all things to the teachings of the holy Roman Catholic Church, of which I am now a member, as I protest and promise both to live and die. May Our Lord God be forever praised and blessed, Amen. Amen. Such in summary describes my spirituality.

It was autumn of 1582 when I set out for Alva de Tormez, even though I was ill. An old friend was expecting a visit from me. I grew worse on the road. There were very few dwelling places along the way. The only food we could get along the way was figs.

When we arrived at the convent, I was exhausted. I never recovered. Three days later, I said to my friend, Anna, who had accompanied me on the journey, "At last, my daughter, I have reached the house of death." Father Antony de Heredia anointed me. He asked me where I wished to be buried. I answered, "Will they deny me a little ground for my body here?"

I sat up to receive the Sacrament, saying, "O, my Lord, now is the time that we shall see each other!" I then died in Anna's arms.

Summary: St. Teresa of Avila reached the highest degrees of mystical life. Her writings earned for her, already in the times of Popes Gregory XV and Urban VII, the title of Doctor of the Church. The Catholic Church, since Vatican II, has recognized that same title in St. Teresa. It was during the night of the 4th to the 15th of October that she died. Pope Gregory XIII had just ordered the suppression of ten days, in order to reform the calendar and so her feast day is celebrated October 15.

The heart of St. Teresa was miraculously inflamed with divine love. She made the difficult vow of always doing what she judged most perfect. This saint is still a model, much needed to inspire modern times. The way she showed to reform religious life, without any compromise to the true Catholic faith, can inspire all religious orders in our times. With modem youth becoming very interested in mysticism, the life of St. Teresa points out that authentic mysticism is to be found in the Catholic Church.

With those who might become unbalanced in our day, with a valid devotion to the Holy Spirit, but think they need no authority of the Church, St. Teresa's experience with defending her position in regard to the Illuminati reminds us that whereas God may deal directly at times with individual souls, yet never must any individual Catholic consider his spiritual guidance and way to God in Christ as being independent of the Church, Christ's Mystical Body on earth.

It is significant that whereas Teresa had inclinations toward spirituality, yet for real progress, she had to learn the need for penance and reparation in her life. St. Peter of Alcantara, who entered into the life of Teresa, died in 1562. Appearing to St. Teresa, he said, "O blessed penance which has earned for me such great glory."

The need for penance, making reparation for one's own sins, and those of others, is most necessary in the spiritual life, and the modern era has all but forgotten this doctrine of the Church, taught us by Christ Jesus.

Silence is necessary for growth in union with God. Constant occupation in useless chatter and the many noises of the world do not leave time or vacuum to be filled with divine love. St. Teresa can teach modern youth and adults the need to return to prayer and give themselves to silence at times for mental prayer.

Memorized formal prayers are good and often needed. Prayer life is needed that constantly strives to remove oneself from the life of sin and inclinations to worldly satisfactions. But, if we earnestly strive to love God and grow in holiness, we must also move on, not simply to avoiding sinful attractions, but to real growth in the knowledge of love for things divine. Finally, we should achieve and may achieve at times, with proper environment and asking it of God, union with God — even occasional profound union.

St. Teresa of Avila can do much to teach us the real meaning of the life of prayer. With growth in holiness, definite words are not always needed. Mental prayer is interior, coming from the mind and will. Meditation, affective prayer and contemplation are forms of mental prayer. Mental prayer is recommended for all, not just for priests and religious.

St. Teresa of Avila gave the name "prayer of quiet" to a type of prayer which other writers have called a prayer of silence. It has three distinct phases: 1) Passive recollection. Here there is an action of grace upon the faculties of the soul, which creates a gentle and affectionate absorption of mind and heart in God. 2) The soul passes in a supernatural state, which causes the soul to experience God present within it. Every soul in the state of grace has God dwelling in it, but now the soul relishes God's presence within. 3) Finally, the soul reaches a state of the sleep of the faculties in which it is marked by a total abandonment into the hands of God.

There is also a "prayer of simplicity" for those advancing in the spiritual life. The soul's life becomes more like the life of God. Long processes of reasoning in meditation are no longer needed. The various steps, which are necessary for beginners of growth in spirituality, are now simplified. It is really contemplation, simplifying affections into a simple act of trust and abandonment to God.

The "prayer of union" is when a soul reaches real and habitual intimate union with God. Great mystics have experienced this and some souls may occasionally experience it.

There is an old saying, "Don't get ahead of your graces." Inexperienced souls beginning in the spiritual life may imagine themselves to have a greater degree of growth in spirituality than they really do. Those who think they have reached such high states, but are lacking in obedience and the life of penance and suffering, are deceiving themselves. The guidance of a prudent, wise and holy director and confessor is needed for those who advance to great degrees of spirituality.

At the same time, God calls most souls to a much higher union with Himself than these souls are often willing to respond in their prayer life. Some with mere curiosity may read even this book. Others will read it in a spirit of prayer and be inspired to give their hearts to God more fully.

Our life in Christ upon this earth must always be centered in the Eucharistic Christ. Apart from the Sacrifice of the Mass and the Sacraments, together with the lawful authority of Christ in the Church, especially of the Pope and the world's bishops in union with the Vicar of Christ on earth, we cannot authentically reach a spirituality rooted in Christ. St. Teresa insisted that one must build first on solid foundations.

St. Teresa of Avila, being shown her place in hell if she did not correspond with God's graces, reminds us of the vision Our Lady of Fatima showed the three shepherd children in our own century. The fear of hell had a profound effect on Jacinta in particular. All of the children were moved to pray and make sacrifices for the conversion of sinners. Contrary to modernistic theories, the knowledge of hell and its horrors did not remove these children from closer union with God. It brought them to a much closer union with God, and the strong desire that other souls love God and be saved. Centuries earlier, Teresa of Avila had a similar experience.

Fortunately, Teresa of Avila woke up in time to the dangerous threats that worldly attractions, such as romantic novels, fine clothes and perfumes, were posing for her soul. Today, in addition, soap operas on television and movies pose the same threats. At the same time it should be clear that there is really "nothing new under the sun" and youth of centuries ago experienced the same basic dangers as today. But where sin abounds, grace can more abound to those who open their hearts and respond to God's love.

Suggested Actions in Imitation of St. Teresa of Avila:

✔Develop a sense of humor when you meet opposition to live and lead others to a deeper spiritual life in Christ.
✔Spend some minutes each day in silence, engaged in mental prayer.
✔Perform an act of mortification and penance each day and offer it in reparation for sin.
✔Strive to reform the attitudes of others where their thinking and activities have been influenced by modernistic thinking, which is opposed to Church authority and teachings.
✔Form a resolution, and keep it, to give up unnecessary romantic worldly novels, television, and movies.
✔Dress not only modestly, but not according to extreme worldly fashion.

Your author's comments:

We see that there were dissident nuns through all of history. Your choice should be to emulate the best of the best like Saint Teresa and in the following of her lead, find sainthood, as she did. You holy ladies will find many convents falling apart and holy orders disintegrating. God is allowing this to weed out the bad convents and open the door for new ones. Only the good survive. If you cannot find a holy order that suits your strong, well-disciplined faith, then pray to Saint Teresa to help you start a new one.

Saint Juan Diego

(c. 1476 - May 30, 1548)

This want-to-be-saint waited almost five hundred years to be canonized on July 31, 2002. I chose him as a model for adult laity. How many times do we offer excuses as to why we cannot fast or go to Mass? We see here a man willing to walk fourteen miles to go to Mass every Saturday and Sunday and fourteen miles back home. His effort was so well- observed by God that the Lord sent the Blessed Virgin Mary to visit Juan Diego. As a result of Juan's yes, millions of people have had their lives changed.

You might argue with me that I am trying to get you to go to Mass every day and Juan Diego only went two times a week - and he made it to sainthood. Why is this? It is the fifty-six miles he chalked up walking those two days for love of the Eucharist that weighed heavily in Juan's favor. Most of us will not *drive* fourteen miles each way to Mass to touch God Himself, and that weighs heavily against us.

Saint Juan Diego

> The Bible, God's own Word, informs us that there were prophecies and incidents which happened to God's People foreshadowing the Birth of Jesus Christ, when God first came to this earth as man. What many do not know is that there are many incidents in ancient Mexican history foreshadowing the coming of Christ through His holy mother to this new western continent.
>
> I am Juan Diego, an Indian convert to the holy Catholic faith. This is my story and how I fit into a plan from heaven that helped shape the new world for Christ through Mary. Most of the world, indeed America itself, now approaching the fifth century since it happened, is first learning the real meaning of the greatest continuous supernatural manifestation that the Mother of God ever produced.

I was the person who received a letter from heaven, from the Mother of God. So powerful was that letter that within seven years, eight million pagans joined the Catholic Church and fell deeply in love with the Son of God made Man and the woman whom God chose to bear the Savior of the world.

For centuries many people thought that heaven had given the people of Mexico just a beautiful picture. Now it is known that it was more than a picture but a letter, obviously supernatural. The Indian people of Mexico recognized almost immediately what it has taken many in the rest of the world hundreds of years to realize - that it was in fact picture writing (hieroglyphics.)

Being of a noble character, I enjoyed the greatest prestige in all levels of society of my time, from the highest nobility to the lowliest servant. Not only did the Mother of God give me a picture writing of herself, but also I was included in the picture. Only in 1962 - that's a long time from 1531 when heaven first gave me the picture-writing - was it discovered, from greatly enlarged photographs of the eyes of the sacred image known as "Our Lady of Guadalupe," that they contained the reflections of three persons. It was concluded that the middle figure was myself.

More than four hundred years after the Mother of God played such a tremendous role of bringing her Son to the newly discovered continent of the world, the Americas, it was learned that my likeness was contained and perpetuated as an integral part of the image of God's Mother, painted by heaven, as a written message for the New World.

Many people are now asking this question. "Could it be that the plan of Divine Providence was to withhold the glorification of Juan Diego until Vatican II declared the Lay Apostolate a formal branch of the Church, so as to have him designated as its patron?"

For too long, Catholics have looked upon the reported miracles connected with the Mother of God, such as at Lourdes and Fatima, only as heaven directly intervening to convert. All of this is true. But too often it is forgotten the role that each one of us is likewise to play as lay apostles for the salvation of souls and the Christianizing of society.

The past century has been called the "Marian Century." At its conclusion, it was discovered that as a lay apostle, I played a significant role in the work of Jesus and as a coworker with His Mother.

Mexico City was founded in 1325. Its eight million people make it the second largest city in the western hemisphere. For centuries, it was the largest city in the new world.

About five miles north of the center of the city is located the Basilica of Our Lady of Guadalupe, which contains the greatest treasure in the world, (with perhaps the exception of the Holy Shroud of Turin.) The treasure I speak of here is a present that God gave the world more than four centuries ago in the form of the image of the Most Blessed Virgin Mary.

The image appeared suddenly in colors on my blanket after Our Lady had appeared to me four different times, talking with me in my native language which was *Nahuatl*. That was the language of the Aztecs, who were the original Mexicans, of which I was one.

Hernando Cortes, the conqueror of Mexico, established Christianity after conquering our land. He ordered the destruction of the pagan temples. They would be replaced with Christian churches. The Mexican Empire fell to Cortes in 1521. The first Christian church built was that of Santiago, and one year later my wife and I were baptized there. The baptismal font where I was baptized still stands.

I spent most of my life in pagan civilization, but I was one of the first to be converted to Christianity after the Spanish conquered the Mexican Empire. By 1531, which was ten years after the conquest, my people were on the verge of revolting against the Spanish because of conflicts and tensions. It was through Our Blessed Mother herself, who especially loved my people, that the revolt was prevented by the great miracle of December, 1531.

I became the human instrument, the lay apostle, in establishing Christianity in a pagan society and thus starting a great growth of the true religion in the western hemisphere. The Blessed Virgin Mary had promised to pay me well for my services, and that she did. The Mother of God transformed part of the clothing I was wearing into a continuous miracle that is still thrilling the world as it learns about it for the first time and discovers deeper and deeper messages.

You see, God uses men to save other men. God used me to initiate the conversion of eight million Mexicans in seven years and this has continued to grow. We are to pray, and we are to work for the salvation of others and ourselves. *Ora et Labora* (pray and work.) God used me to intervene, and His divine intervention, it is said, was as great as anything in the Old Testament preparing for the New Covenant of mankind with God in Christ.

The Blessed Virgin's words to me made it clear that I, and no one else, was to be Our Lady's special messenger with a special mission. When the Spaniards came to conquer Mexico, they were exceedingly surprised to find such a highly developed civilization. They were surprised greatly also to see how the Mexicans could so rapidly adapt to and accept the Christian religion.

Mexicans are not the same as Indians, but Mexican and Aztec are originally the same. The word "Mexico" comes from the name of the Aztec god of war, "Mexitili." God must have had a special love and purpose for the Mexican people to give them one of the world's greatest treasures.

In 1754, Pope Benedict XIV wrote: "To no other nation has this been done." It was at the time of my birth that the majestic Aztec or Mexican Empire included all the territory of Mexico's present boundaries.

The origin of my people is not known. They were different from all other peoples of the western hemisphere. Generally accepted is a theory that my people were originally tribes, perhaps from Egypt, that came across the Bering Straits from Asia and worked their way to the south. You see, the only two civilizations of the world that have pyramids and the sphinx were my people and the Egyptians. Also, we both had picture-writing languages, although other nations also used hieroglyphics.

Around 1200 A.D., my people entered the Valley of Mexico from the north. We did not settle down but kept moving from place to place. Our pagan priests had told my people they were to keep moving until they discovered an island where they would see an eagle devouring a snake. Finally they stopped on the southwest border of Lake Texcoco where they saw just such a sight on an island in the lake. They then started to build their city in the year 1325 A.D. The eagle clutching the snake became the emblem of Mexico.

My Mexican people spoke *Nahuatl*, which means, "clear-speaking people." *Nahuatl* is spoken as a second language in central Mexico to the present day. Mexico City grew to become a bustling metropolis, and in its midst, I spent fifty-one years of my life as a citizen. People meeting me on the street in those days could not have guessed that I, as a gentle, mild type of person, was to become a lay apostle God would use to convert millions from paganism to Christianity in such a short time, conversions such as the world has never known on such a wide and rapid scale.

And now, since 1962, just when Vatican Council II was getting under way, through the eye-image of the Mother of God, suddenly again, I come into your times. There must be a message. There must be a divine purpose.

On February 2, 1974, on the "Right Ordering and Development of Devotion to the Blessed Virgin Mary," sec. 37, Pope Paul VI wrote:

"The Blessed Virgin does not disillusion any of the profound expectations of the men and women of our time but offers them the perfect model of the disciple of the Lord; the disciple who builds up the earthly and temporal city while being a diligent pilgrim towards the heavenly and eternal city; the disciple who works for that justice which sets free the oppressed and for that charity which assists the needy; but above all, the disciple who is the active witness of that love which builds up Christ in people's hearts" (*Marialis Cultus*).

Pope Paul was not necessarily thinking of me when he wrote the above. But it certainly applies to the way God and His Mother used me. The Pope wrote that after Vatican Council II had said of the Apostolate of the Laity, "The apostolate of the social milieu, that is, the effort to infuse a Christian spirit into the mentality, customs, laws, and structures of the community in which a person lives, is so much the duty and responsibility of the laity that it can never be properly performed by others" (chapter 3, sec. 13).

The same Council said, "It is the task of the whole Church to labor vigorously so that men may become capable of constructing the temporal order [world] rightly and directing it to God through Christ . . . The laity must take on the renewal of the temporal order as their own special obligation . . . The temporal order must be renewed in such a way that . . . it can be brought into conformity with the higher principles of the Christian life . . . Outstanding among the works of this type of apostolate is that of Christian social action" (chapter 2, sec. 7).

Discovering my image in the eye of the image of God's Mother, who is the Mother of the Church and the model of everything the Christians should be, at the very time of the opening year of Vatican Council II, reminded many that I may well be a powerful intercessor in heaven, especially for all the laity engaged in the work of the Church for the salvation of all peoples and the Christianizing of society, such as had to take place in Mexico City through my willing service as a lay Mexican.

A strong caste system existed in my day. There was the emperor. I was twenty-four years old when Montezuma became emperor. There were the kings of the twenty-nine larger states. There were high nobles and lower nobles, the priesthood, the merchants and the large middle class to which I belonged. There were also the laboring and servant classes, the lowest being the slaves. But really, according to the condition of life of my family, our life-style was hardly better than that of the slaves.

I was a citizen, obliged to vote in elections. I was a landowner. I was educated for the times. Under the empire it was required to go to school. After my marriage, I farmed the land next to my house in *Cuautitlan*. I grew corn, beans and various vegetables. I would hunt turkey and deer. Gradually, I worked up a business of making mats and furniture. These I made out of the reeds growing along the shores of Lake Texcoco.

It is said that God gives special revelations to persons whom He has fitted to receive them. This would especially be true when the revelations were not just for oneself, but for others and for hundreds of years to come. In my own time God had selected me to lead my fellow Mexicans to accept the Catholic religion.

The true God had prepared my people, something like the people of the Old Testament, for revelations of the one true God. In 1464, God had sent His angel to *Nezahualcoyotl*, the king of Texcoco. The king then gave up the pagan religion and built temples to the true God. He prayed before altars containing offerings of flowers and incense. *Nezahualcoyotl* shortly before his death made a great speech. He said, "How deeply I regret that I am not able to understand the will of the great God, but I believe the time will come when He will be known and adored by all the inhabitants of this land."

The son of this King of Texcoco was just like his father. He (*Nezahualpilli*) continued the great devotion to the true God and became known as the wisest man of his time. He died in 1515. Before he died, he told the emperor Montezuma that he had had a dream a few days before. The dream said that Montezuma was soon to lose his throne to invaders from across the sea who were going to bring the true religion.

You can see then why Montezuma surrendered so easily to Cortes in 1521. It has often confused worldly historians why Montezuma would surrender his great Aztec empire without much resistance. Prophecies had also been made to his sister, the Princess *Papantzin*, in 1509.

Being aware of such events, I was disposed from the very first to accept the true faith brought by the Catholic Spaniards. Princess *Papantzin* was included with wife, my uncle, among the very first group to be baptized into the true religion and me.

I, and my wife, Maria Lucia, continued to receive instructions in the Catholic faith every Sunday, walking fourteen miles to *Tiatelolco* for Holy Mass. I and my wife were very happy in our new religion. However, Maria Lucia became sick and died in 1529.

Because I was so very sad and lonely after the death of my wife, I became even closer to my converted uncle, Juan Bernardino. He lived in the village of *Tolpetlac*, and I built a house not far from his.

With the loss of my wife, my devotion to the Blessed Virgin Mary became very strong. Very early every Saturday morning I would rise and go to participate in the holy Mass in honor of the Blessed Virgin Mary. Saturday has long been dedicated by the Church in a special way to the Mother of God. Aztecs were strengthened from a very early age to walk long distances, and so the nine miles from *Tolpetlac* to *Tlaltelolco* was not too big a sacrifice. I made the journeys even as I was getting somewhat older, on both Saturday and Sunday.

During my time, the Feast of the Immaculate Conception was celebrated on December 9th rather than the 8th. It was on a cold morning, December 9, 1531, as I was walking around Tepeyac Hill to participate in Holy Mass for the great feast day, that I heard strange music coming from the top of the hill. I went to investigate. As I came close to the top of the hill I was struck with awe at the sight of a most beautiful lady calling to me.

All of the appearances of the Virgin of Guadalupe were during the octave of the Feast of the Immaculate Conception. There were two appearances on December 9, one on December 10, and two on December 12. I was fifty-seven years old at the time.

The beautiful lady called me with a sweet voice and affectionately said, "Juanito, least of my sons, where art thou going?" I answered, "My Lady and my Child, I must go to the church at *Tlatelolco* to study divine mysteries which are taught us by our priests, the emissaries of Our Lord and Savior."

The Lady said to me, "Know and take heed, thou, the least of my sons, that I am Holy Mary ever Virgin, Mother of the true God, for whom we live, the Creator of the world, Maker of heaven and earth. I urgently desire that a temple be built to me here, to bear witness to my love, my compassion, my aid and protection . . . Go to the palace of the bishop in Mexico and say that I sent thee to make manifest to him my great desire."

After going to the Bishop's residence, I had to return sorrowfully to meet the good Lady on Tepeyac Hill again. "My littlest daughter, and my Lady, I went where you sent me and obeyed your orders. I entered into the palace, which is the seat of the bishop, though I did this with difficulty. I saw him and delivered your message exactly as you told me. He received me kindly and listened to me with attention, but when he answered me, it seemed as if he did not believe me . . . So I beg you most earnestly, my Lady and my Child, to send someone well known, respected, and esteemed, to entrust such a person with the delivery of your message, in order that he may be believed."

The Lady looked kindly at me, but she was determined that I was the one to do this work requested by heaven. I was supposed to meet the Lady on Tepeyac Hill on December 11, but missed my assignment. I was caring for my very sick uncle Juan Bernardino. On the morning of December 12, I was hurrying to get the priest to come and administer the anointing to my uncle. Approaching the hill, I remembered my broken appointment. I feared the beautiful lady's disapproval and delay, so I changed my route and started to walk around the hill.

The Lady was very wise. She came over to my side of the hill and asked, "What is the matter, least of my sons? Where art thou going?" You know, I tried to change the subject, for I was very childlike in many ways. I asked the Mother of God how she found the morning and said, "I hope that you are well." I begged to be excused, as I must hurry to get the priest for my uncle. "If I first succeed in doing this duty, I will return here later to go and deliver your message. Forgive me, my Lady and my Child. Be patient with me for the moment. I am not deceiving you, my littlest daughter: Tomorrow I will come in good season.

The beautiful Lady told me not to worry, my uncle would get well. I was to gather flowers at the top of the hill. I went to the cold December hilltop, usually without growth of anything, and found there beautiful Castilian roses. I came back to the Blessed Virgin, and with her delicate hand she arranged the roses in the tilma I was wearing. I was not to show the roses to anyone as I took them to the bishop.

I had more trouble than usual getting through those gates to see the bishop. The servants tried to see what I had and take them from me. Finally, I was admitted to Bishop Zumarraga's presence.

First, let me tell you something special about Bishop Zumarraga. At this time, the Mexicans, being treated badly, had conspired and were planning to attack and destroy the Spaniards. Bishop Zumarraga realized that things had become so serious that only a miracle could save the uprising and destruction. He was very devoted to the Blessed Virgin and had begged her for help. He had secretly asked Mary for Castilian roses as a sign that she would help. That in itself would have to be a miracle, for Castilian roses did not grow in Mexico.

Coming into the bishop's presence, I fell to my knees and began to tell all that I had seen. "My Lord, I have done what you asked of me; I went to tell the Lady from heaven, Holy Mary, precious Mother of God, that you asked for a sign so that you might believe me that you should build a temple where she asked that it should be erected; also I told her that I had given you my word that I would bring some sign and proof, which you requested, of her wish. She condescended to your request and graciously granted your request, some sign and proof to complement her wish . . ." I continued to tell the bishop about the roses and opening my white cloth tilma to permit them to fall to the floor. I said, "Behold! Receive them!"

Suddenly there appeared the precious image of the Virgin, Holy Mary, Mother of God, just as it can be seen now in her temple at Tepeyac, in Mexico City. The bishop and all who were with him were not now so struck by the roses. They fell to their knees admiring in awe the image of the Mother of God.

The bishop, with sorrowful tears, prayed and begged forgiveness for not having been more prompt to answer the will of the Mother of God. He arose to his feet to untie from my neck the cloth, which the Mother of God had tied to me. He took it and placed it in his chapel. I stayed with the bishop one more day. Then the bishop said to me, "Come, show us the place where the Queen of Heaven wants her temple built."

A group of people accompanied me to see my uncle Bernardino, who had been sick and for whom I was going to fetch a priest to hear his confession and give him the other sacraments. We found my uncle well and happy. It was then that my uncle told us that he, too, had seen the Lady in the same manner. Also the same lady had told my uncle that he should go to see the bishop and tell him that he, too, had seen the lady, had been miraculously cured, and how the lady wished to be known through her image on the cloth.

Uncle Bernardino said, so it was at first thought, that she should be properly known as *The Entirely Perfect Virgin Mary of Guadalupe Her Precious Image.* However, a mistake was made and is now properly understood. Neither Bishop Zumarraga nor other Spaniards could understand why the Mother of God wanted to be known by the same name as her shrine in Spain. But Our Lady had not spoken in Spanish. She spoke in *Nahuatl* and used the combination of the words *"te coatlaxopseuh"* which must have sounded like "Guadalupe" to the Spaniards.

Scholars now recognize that translating the words of the Blessed Virgin in their proper order in the *Nahuatl* language, the correct meaning of her message is, "Her precious image will be thus known (by the name of) *The Entirely Perfect Virgin, Holy Mary,* and it will crush, stamp out, or eradicate (the religion of) The Stone Serpent."

In recent years people now know that the title Our Lady gave to her image means that through her Sacred Image there will be brought about the elimination of the pagan religion.

"Te" means "stone"; *"coa"* means "serpent"; *"Tla"* is the noun ending which can be interpreted as "the," while *"xopeuh"* means "crush" or "stamp out." Our Lady's message to uncle Juan Bernardine has to be rearranged so as to give its true meaning: *'The Entirely Perfect Virgin, Holy Mary,* and it will crush (stamp out, abolish or eradicate) the stone serpent.'

Until the time of the Spanish conquest, the Aztec or *Nahuatl* language was written in a form of hieroglyphics (picture writing). The native Mexicans saw the sacred image not simply as a miraculous picture but as a pictograph with a message from heaven, the true God, for them. It served to teach them the fundamentals of the true Christian religion.

Shortly after this miracle, the Aztec language was no longer written in hieroglyphs. The Spanish converted it into letters of our alphabet. But still, the powerful miraculous message was there for all the native Mexicans at that time to read.

The picture writing from heaven told the Mexicans that their former religion was wrong and was being replaced by a true religion of the true God. They had believed in idol worship from the king down to the lowliest peasant.

Quetzalcoatl was one of several Aztec gods to whom the native Mexicans each year sacrificed over 20,000 men, women and children. This god represented Venus. *Quetzalcoatl*-Venus was a terrible god to whom thousands of bloody human sacrifices were offered annually.

There is now evidence that Venus was not always earth's beautiful morning and evening star. Thousands of years ago Venus was a comet that appeared at intervals for over a thousand years. It looked like a terrible serpent of fire. Coming close to earth it caused panic. At any rate, native Mexicans did worship a serpent-like comet in very ancient times. They called it *Quetzalcoatl*—the Serpent with

Feathers, the flying serpent. It became identified with Venus.

The likeness of this pagan god was carved out of stone. It can still be seen in ancient pyramids in Mexico.

The dead comet in the Guadalupe image is now recognized in the black, burned-out crescent on which the Virgin Mary stands. It is not a new moon of bright light, but in this picture it is black.

This gave a message to the pagan Mexicans. Quetzalcoatl, the god they had worshipped, the crooked serpent that flew through space, and which they decorated with feathers to show its flight, was now dead. The true God, invisible God, had written that message into what others have seen as just a beautiful picture of His Mother.

The Mexicans had also adored the sun. They would offer it the heart of a man, and men would lay down their lives to the sun, as a great honor. A pagan priest would open the chest and offer the still beating heart to the sun on its altar.

What were the native Mexicans told about the sun god? The Blessed Virgin stood in front of the sun. Her human body covers the sun and blots it out while its rays are visible. This means a human being is greater than the sun. The sun is no god.

The Mexicans had also worshipped stars, like Mars. The Blessed Virgin's blue mantle was covered with stars. This told them that the invisible true God had made the stars, and they were to serve intelligent creatures and the true God and not to be worshipped.

The brooch with a black cross at the neck of the Lady's tunic reminded the Mexicans of the Cross, which was a sign of the religion of the Spaniards. The Mexicans asked Juan Diego for a meaning for the Cross. He told them that the true God who was invisible had become a man.

His name was Jesus, and He had died on a Cross. The Son of God made Man had offered His life to God the Father for the salvation of the entire world.

There was no longer the need for the twenty thousand bloody human sacrifices the pagan Mexicans had been offering to a false god each year. No human sacrifice could equal the sacrifice of the one true God become Man being offered on the Cross. They ended their pagan form of sacrifices and turned to the Holy Eucharist.

By the time the Mother of God, to whom I was very devoted, appeared to me and gave the miraculous image, I already knew well the Christian doctrines. Immediately I saw the message from heaven written into the picture. I had no difficulty explaining it to my fellow countrymen. They had no trouble understanding it.

Almost at once the natives wanted to embrace the true Christian faith. In great numbers they went to the Catholic missionaries to be baptized. I was able to explain to the natives that Mary's words in picture writing told that the stone serpent is really the fallen Satan. She had come to destroy the powers of the devil through her Son. With the angel beneath her feet, God's Mother is Queen, above angels and saints, Her Son is King, ruler of all.

The miracle of Our Lady of Guadalupe is witness that God uses the laity too, in the apostolate of the Church. It tells too how the apostolate of the laity depends upon Mary for the fruitfulness of Christianity — to give birth to Christ in souls.

Bishop Zumarraga put me in complete charge of the little chapel, 15 by 15 feet in size and built at the foot of Tepeyac Hill. There the image was brought. More and more Mexicans came to see the message from heaven, and I explained the true religion of the white man. When my people went to the priests for baptism, God had already used me in partnership with His holy Mother to instruct and to convert them. Then too, the Mexican converts in turn influenced others toward conversion.

In 1548, Bishop Zumarraga was appointed the first Archbishop of the New World. That same year he made a trip to the town of *Tepetlaoztoc.* In four days he baptized, confirmed and married about fourteen thousand natives. He worked so hard that he died a few days later at the age of seventy-two.

Bishop Zumarraga and I gave evidence and still give evidence to the modern Catholic world, now becoming more aware of the duties of the apostolate of the laity, of how a priest-bishop and a baptized layman, also confirmed in the Sacrament of the lay apostolate, can and should work together for the common cause of the Church, the glory of God and the salvation of souls. The work of the lay apostolate is to Christianize society and thus glorify God and save souls.

So closely did our lives serve a common purpose after my conversion and the great miracle, that the next sixteen and a half years were to end almost at the same time for both of us. I lived just three more days after the death of Bishop Zumarraga.

I went to my eternal reward on May 30, 1548.

Addendum: Before my presenting the summary of this chapter, it is important for readers to appreciate the very high approbation given this miraculous image by heaven and God's own divinely protected Church. Secular historians say that Hernando Cortes, an explorer with a military force of between seven hundred and thirteen hundred men conquered a great empire that stretched for about two thousand miles and comprised about nine million people, highly civilized and with a fully developed society. In reality, Our Lady conquered this people for her Son.

The shrine containing the miraculous image of Our Lady of Guadalupe is a center of Eucharistic devotion, like all major Marian shrines. Pope John XXIII declared the year from October 12, 1960, to October 12, 1961, a Marian Year of Our Lady of Guadalupe.

The same Pope Paul who sent a golden rose to Fatima sent also a golden rose to Guadalupe on March 25, 1966. Already in the 16th and 17th centuries, approvals of the Holy See were given in the form of popes granting indulgences to encourage devotion to Our Lady of Guadalupe. In the 18th century, Benedict XIV approved a special Mass and Office in her honor. In the 19th century Leo XIII ordered the sacred image to be crowned in his name. This was done in 1895. Pius XII renewed this coronation in 1945.

Suggested Actions in Imitation of Saint Juan Diego of Guadalupe:

✔Explain the true meaning of the miraculous image of Guadalupe to others as a means of communicating the fullness of the true faith.
✔Organize prayer cells of holiness to pray, study and work to Christianize society.
✔Study the Vatican II decree on the Apostolate of the Laity.

Your author's comment:

After almost five centuries, Juan Diego became a canonized saint in our time. Our Lady of Guadalupe has become Our Lady of the Americas. She has become the banner of the pro-life movement and we all should find the grace sufficient to bring about our sainthood if we simply listen to our Mother and do as she says.

Now for this chapter's *coup de grace*, the elite of those who became saints, the Incorruptibles. These are not just people who made it; they lived this life so completely according to the will of God that even in death, they proclaim God's mercy. Their bodies refuse to rot. Many Incorruptibles look as they did the day they were put into the ground and others like Saint Anthony were found with only a tongue intact. Incorruptibles are only found in the one, holy, Catholic and apostolic Church. This amazing profession of authenticity should be enough for anyone to understand that the Catholic Church is the true Church. So before anyone can teach or preach against the Catholic Church, they should show the world comparable profound supernatural events that involve their particular faith (outside of healing the sick,) but the truth is, they can't do it.

My best advice is, along with the Bible, Canon Law, the Study Guide on Vatican II and the *Catechism of the Catholic Church,* you add reading about the early Church Fathers, most assuredly *Butler's Lives of the Saints* and *The Incorruptibles* to your list of books to help you get into heaven.

After making a commitment to be more like the saints above or any of the saints, for that matter, you can claim passing the test of Chapter Five and go on to Chapter Six. Congratulations for making it this far. If you have attempted to neuter God, I am sorry; you have to go back to the beginning of the book, not to mention confession.

NOTES

CHAPTER SIX

SUFFERING

I remember getting a call from a man a year or so ago. He asked if I was Tom Rutkoski, the Catholic evangelist. I confirmed that I was and he proceeded to make a statement. "I'm looking for a church to join and I would like you to convince me that your church is the right one to join." I told him I wasn't really in the business of convincing people from other faiths to join the Catholic Church, not that I didn't believe that was a good thing. I told him my specific assignment by the Lord was to retrieve lukewarm Catholics.

He told me he had tried several other denominations and had not found one he really cared to join. I said to the man, "If I were to give you any advice whatsoever, it would be to ferret out the most persecuted, suffering church on earth and join that church, knowing that Satan would be trying to destroy the authentic church." He chuckled a bit and said, "Everybody in the world knows that's the Catholic Church. Everybody picks on Catholics." I responded with, "Then I rest my case." The man called me back some time later and related that he had joined the Catholic Church. Praise the Lord!

It is hard to find people willing to capitalize on suffering these days, for these are the days of kicking back, relaxing and having a good time. More entertainment is what we crave, and even demand. Any kind of suffering, no matter how slight, is to be avoided at all costs. I can't recall reading about the life of even one saint that would even come close to a lifestyle like that. All the saints I've read about suffered immensely at some point. There were people in the early church who would travel long distances just so they could be in a place where there was a possibility of being martyred. Today, people travel long distances just to stay alive a little longer. Some will travel halfway around the world to find a cure or relief for their physical ailments. We don't want to suffer and God does not want us to suffer so how do we come to a meeting of the minds?

I, like most people, have bad thoughts at times. Satan is trying to kill us all. St. Francis of Assisi was no different than the rest of us. He had bad thoughts. When I get bad thoughts, I call on the name of Jesus to help me and rebuke the evil that is attempting to steal my salvation. Saint Francis, on the other hand, was a little more creative than I. When he would get bad thoughts, he surely called on the Lord to rebuke the evil, but he threw in a little something extra. In one particular case, when he experienced a little more temptation than he believed he could deal with, Francis jumped into the rose bushes; and the bushes, being full of thorns, cut and scraped him and caused a lot of pain. Francis knew that the suffering would get his mind away from the bad thoughts. St. Francis knew and welcomed suffering as a good friend. Testament to the validity of his thinking is in those same rose bushes in Assisi. After Francis, and still today, they no longer grow with thorns. If per chance the rose bushes are transplanted somewhere else, they again grow thorns.

I want to look at capitalizing on suffering as a good thing. Suffering in itself is a struggle with evil, a battle with Satan in some form or another. In this present day, we do not have to look any further than Pope John Paul II. Surely the Holy Father would find it much easier to sit in a soft chair inside the Vatican walls and kick back a bit in his old age and his infirmity, but not this Pope. He knows the value of suffering well and rising above Satan's attack. He knows our Church is in deep trouble. He knows what evil the dissenters and liberals have caused. So he, rather than rejecting suffering, embraces it, to do battle with evil, and bring glory to God through it. He is definitely a hero in our day.

Father Philip Pavic kindly points out to me that when one perseveres and stays faithful through suffering, it is a great victory for a soul. But God never draws good out of evil. That is a false and immoral principle. God can never use evil to do good. For those who are faithful to God in the midst of suffering and evil, God pours on more grace. It is as in Rom 5:20, *"Where sin abounded, grace did more abound."* God just pours on more grace in the midst of evil and temptation for those who are faithful to Him.

Saint Therese of Lisieux suffered and died an early death in her service to God. If we want to be saints, we have to understand the value of suffering well. Too many people waste valuable suffering by complaining about it. The best possible posture when one is suffering is to praise the Lord. Thank God in all things. A whiner's path leads to destruction.

If you are a Roman Catholic today, more than likely you are suffering. The dissenting liberals in the Church cause more pain, suffering and anguish than they can even imagine. They are crucifying Our Lord all over again. But we can capitalize on this suffering by offering reparation for their and our sins. Loving our enemies, praying for them and fasting for them is what the Lord expects from us. No sense whining and complaining about it. That will accomplish nothing. But if we fast, pray and do battle against evil, with God on our side, how can we lose?

If any form of suffering comes your way, do not rebel against it. Embrace it, give it a saint's embrace and use it for the salvation of mankind. If you would like to read more about what suffering well accomplishes and who the great sufferers in the world were, *Butler's Lives of the Saints* is an excellent place to begin.

Notes

CHAPTER SEVEN

FAITH

What is faith? The *Catholic Encyclopedia* states: The assent given to a truth and the first of three theological virtues; the virtue by which one, through grace, adheres in intellect to a truth revealed by God because of the authority of God rather than of the evidence given.

My explanation? Faith is the ability to believe in the existence of God when the world says not to. I believe faith is directly proportional to grace. Grace is the spiritual bonanza that God sends, in various ways, to help us believe in Him. Grace is not something deserved, but freely given by God. The more grace you have, the more faith you have, and if you respond to that grace in a positive way, more may come. Exit this life in grace and you are guaranteed sainthood. One of my jobs in this book is to get you in touch with as many things as I can that have the ability to generate grace and, thus faith; but I can only introduce you to them to the point that grace is given to me. Store up grace, develop faith and you will not only enter heaven yourself, but you will then discover the enormous joy in helping others to get there as well.

> Mt 6:19-34 *"Do not store up for yourselves treasures on earth, where moth and decay destroy, and thieves break in and steal. But store up treasures in heaven, where neither moth nor decay destroys, nor thieves break in and steal. For where your treasure is, there also will your heart be."*

How hard we work at making Scripture's words of truth into worthlessness. For if we do not take the time to absorb Scripture, then it is worthless to us. If we do not hear the Word of God and put it into practice, we, ourselves, render the Word worthless. If the Lord took the time to put in place the universe and all of its amenities for our edification and salvation, and we turn our backs to it, then we are Godless. We can show up at a church every Sunday, call on the name of the Lord all we want, purport to be holy and go straight to hell the moment after judgment.

It is not a great faith that we have, for if we look at the lives of the saints and compare their faith to what we want to call faith, we will soon see that our faith is something less than sad. We can only rationalize our actions so many times before we cannot even fool a child. Faith is something that defies the senses and challenges the mind. Faith is not earthly. It is the ability to trust that all will be well when all say it will not. You cannot touch faith, but you can feel it in your heart.

Weak faith is full of whys and assorted questions. But when all of human reality fails and you have God as your friend, faith kicks in and you continue on. That is true faith. Have faith and you have a true companion. Have it not and you have nothing, though you have the entire world.

> Mt 6:22-34 *The lamp of the body is the eye. If your eye is sound, your whole body will be filled with light, but if your eye is bad, your whole body will be in darkness. And if the light in you is darkness, how great will the darkness be.*
>
> *No one can serve two masters. He will either hate one and love the other, or be devoted to one and despise the other. You cannot serve God and mammon. "Therefore I tell you, do not worry about your life, what you will eat (or drink), or about your body, what you will wear. Is not life more than food and the body more than clothing?*
>
> *Look at the birds in the sky; they do not sow or reap, they gather nothing into barns, yet your heavenly Father feeds them. Are not you more important than they?*
>
> *Can any of you, by worrying, add a single moment to your life span? Why are you anxious about clothes? Learn from the way the wild flowers grow. They do not work or spin. But I tell you that not even Solomon in all his splendor was clothed like one of them. If God so clothes the grass of the field, which grows today and is thrown into the oven tomorrow, will he not much more provide for you, O you of little faith?*
>
> *So do not worry and say, 'What are we to eat?' or 'What are we to drink?' or 'What are we to wear?' All these things*

the pagans seek. Your heavenly Father knows that you need them all. But seek first the kingdom (of God) and his righteousness, and all these things will be given you besides. Do not worry about tomorrow; tomorrow will take care of itself. Sufficient for a day is its own evil.

How much more can the Lord do for us than give His life and sound teaching such as the above? But who is going to take the advice? The answer is the one who desires not what is vain, but the Lord, Himself. If the Scriptures we have just read were also read at last Sunday's Mass, ask yourself, "Would I have put that teaching into practice after hearing it?"

Who is it that leaves church with the Word implanted in their consciousness? How many depart the Mass with a firm conviction to more fully understand the Scriptures that were used that day and implement them into their lives? Do you walk out the back door of the church, glad hand the pastor, jump into your car with the family and say, "Now, what do we want to do today?"

I am here to tell you, if it is not your desire to be a leader and see to it that the discussion that Sunday, in the car, and at home is about the Word you just heard, then you have little faith. You are not advancing towards heaven. You will not pass "Go" and you will not collect $200 worth of grace. Get a life. Do what God asks. It takes a lifetime to develop enough faith to face death, and at the moment of death you can use it all up in an instant. You do not want to run out of grace at death's door, for you would then not have the faith to pass through fire and on into heaven.

There are many theories and theologies circulating about what it takes to get into heaven. Sadly enough, most of them are false or half-truths. The truth is that it takes the whole package to be a champion on God's team. It may sound impossible to do everything this book will strongly suggest. Only fools will claim that it is impossible. For me, my household and all true followers of Christ know full well that it is in trying you succeed. It is in trying that grace comes, and with that comes success. That is faith. Know this: Jesus Christ is the only portal into heaven, but He cannot bestow the ultimate gift on you without your help or your acceptance.

Try to cut corners and you meet not your Maker at the end of the journey, but the one who deceived you. Faith alone is something taught by many splinter denominations and the truth is that they are quite right; it is faith alone, except they do not know what faith is. They believe and teach that you simply claim Jesus Christ as your Savior and you're in. They call that faith. They claim that you do not need works. You do not need to stop sinning. You just claim Jesus as your Savior and you're in. The only problem with that is the following Scripture. I used it before and I will use it here and again in the chapter on works, because it is a matter of life and death.

> James 2:14-26 *What good is it, my brothers, if someone says he has faith but does not have works? Can that faith save him? If a brother or sister has nothing to wear and has no food for the day, and one of you says to them, "Go in peace, keep warm, and eat well," but you do not give them the necessities of the body, what good is it? So also faith of itself, if it does not have works, is dead. Indeed someone might say, "You have faith and I have works." Demonstrate your faith to me without works, and I will demonstrate my faith to you from my works. You believe that God is one. You do well. Even the demons believe that and tremble. Do you want proof, you ignoramus, that faith without works is useless? Was not Abraham our father justified by works when he offered his son Isaac upon the altar? You see that faith was active along with his works, and faith was completed by the works. Thus the Scripture was fulfilled that says, "Abraham believed God, and it was credited to him as righteousness," and he was called "the friend of God."*

Do you see how a person is justified by works and not by faith alone? And in the same way, was not Rahab, the harlot, also justified by works when she welcomed the messengers and sent them out by a different route? For just as a body without a spirit is dead, so also faith without works is dead.

When I say salvation can be achieved by faith alone, I mean to tell you it is faith alone, but that faith involves works and all that Christ teaches that will lead you to salvation. It is not just a belief, but belief combined with action that has saving power.

How sad for people to allow themselves to be deceived by a "lower the bar" theology. That is not, as the Lord says in Scripture, running the race to the finish. That is trying to coast for the last half of the race. The real question is: can you eat only once a week and run a marathon? (And we are in a marathon!) The answer is NO. This marathon takes fuel, perseverance, practice, endurance, love, obedience, giving, asking, taking, suffering and more and it is all lumped together in what God calls faith. Start eliminating the parts you do not want to do, and you are eliminated from the marathon and jump aboard the proverbial rocket sled to hell.

Oh, Satan's false faith will seem great, as all amusement rides are. You will feel a thrill that appears to be from the Holy Spirit, but it is the unholy spirit at work in your life. If you become a corner-cutter you not only do not have faith, you do not have the Holy Spirit, Jesus or the Father. What you have is Satan's full-blown package of deception. The deceiver will attempt to convince you that faith is best accomplished by saying Jesus did it all on the cross. You then think you can do nothing to improve on that and so you assume a coasting position.

They're right. You cannot improve on Christ dying on the cross, but you must cooperate in the salvation that the Crucifixion brought. Scripture says to pick up your cross and follow Jesus. A cross entails suffering. You will not find one saint's story that involves a "lower the bar" theology. The only kinds of saint stories you find are stories of suffering, just like the Christ they followed.

Are you looking for the best Christian church to help you in your faith's journey? Remember my suggestion to the gentleman who was searching. Find the most persecuted Church on the face of the earth and you are on the right track. It is the Catholic Church; the universal Church, the Church for everyone who wants the fullness of faith. It is the only Church that goes back to Christ's founding. Join a "Johnny-come-lately church," a church that started fifteen hundred years or more after Christ and you get a "Johnny-come-lately" theology. You will get 95% of the truth, but is that what you want? Is that what saints are made of - 95% of the truth? Give me the name of one non-Catholic saint. Every saint that was ever proclaimed had authentic faith and was Catholic. Does that not tell you something?

The Lord our God warns us that being of the universal faith, tasting the heavenly gifts (Eucharist) and then turning away, renders no forgiveness. Scripture tells us to hold on to the tradition that was handed down to us. Follow some deceitful, false teacher and look at what God has to say about that:

> Heb 6:1-15 *Therefore, let us leave behind the basic teaching about Christ and advance to maturity, without laying the foundation all over again: repentance from dead works and faith in God, instruction about baptisms and laying on of hands, resurrection of the dead and eternal judgment. And we shall do this, if only God permits. For it is impossible in the case of those who have once been enlightened and tasted the heavenly gift and shared in the holy Spirit and tasted the good word of God and the powers of the age to come, and then have fallen away, to bring them to repentance again, since they are recrucifying the Son of God for themselves and holding him up to contempt.*
>
> *Ground that has absorbed the rain falling upon it repeatedly and brings forth crops useful to those for whom it is cultivated receives a blessing from God. But if it produces thorns and thistles, it is rejected; it will soon be cursed and finally burned.*

So we see God giving us a stern warning about falling from the true faith and from participating in dead faith and performing dead works. This is a firm teaching on faith in the Eucharist. Eat this *supersubstantial* Bread (a term from the Latin *Vulgate)* and you shall live forever. And how often does the Lord tell us to eat this Bread? Daily! Unless you eat this Bread, you have no life in you. That is right. Do not feast on Eucharist and you have no life of faith. With that gem of knowledge in our back pockets, let's move on.

> Mt 8:5-13 *When He entered Capernaum, a centurion approached Him and appealed to Him, saying, "Lord, my servant is lying at home paralyzed, suffering dreadfully." He said to him, "I will come and cure him." The centurion said in reply, "Lord, I am not worthy to have you enter under my roof; only say the word and my servant will be healed. For I too am a person subject to*

authority, with soldiers subject to me. And I say to one, 'Go,' and he goes; and to another, 'Come here,' and he comes; and to my slave, 'Do this,' and he does it." When Jesus heard this, He was amazed and said to those following Him, "Amen, I say to you, in no one in Israel have I found such faith. I say to you, many will come from the east and the west, and will recline with Abraham, Isaac, and Jacob at the banquet in the kingdom of heaven, but the children of the kingdom will be driven out into the outer darkness, where there will be wailing and grinding of teeth."

And Jesus said to the centurion, "You may go; as you have believed, let it be done for you." And at that very hour (his) servant was healed.

Isn't it wonderful how God put every scenario of life in His Book and is always ready to help those who believe?

Luke 11:9-13 *"And I tell you, ask and you will receive; seek and you will find; knock and the door will be opened to you. For everyone who asks, receives; and the one who seeks, finds; and to the one who knocks, the door will be opened. What father among you would hand his son a snake when he asks for a fish? Or hand him a scorpion when he asks for an egg? If you then, who are wicked, know how to give good gifts to your children, how much more will the Father in heaven give the holy Spirit to those who ask him?"*

The key is to develop the faith to believe that you will receive what you ask for as long as it is God's Will. Put nothing in your spare gas can and when you run out of gas, you are out of gas. Fill your life with faith and find the gem therein hidden, for the fruit of faith is still more grace. When you are in true need and God dips into His storehouse of grace, your faith manifests results. The Lord is indeed good, and takes care of His own.

If you pray on a regular basis and experience no results for a time, this is not an indication that God does not exist. It does not necessarily indicate that you have no faith. It could be an indication that it is time for remedial training. It could be a time in the desert. Maybe it is for this reason that God has you reading this book. It is the Lord's desire to have those with difficulty finding faith to find some; and those with some to find more. It is His will that this come about. And it is His will that those who believe that they have great faith to understand how little they truly have, so they will work hard at developing more. Even the saints had to work hard at believing. Look at Saint Peter. He denied Christ three times. And then there is Thomas.

> John 20:24-31 *Thomas, called Didymus, one of the Twelve, was not with them when Jesus came. So the other disciples said to him, "We have seen the Lord." But he said to them, "Unless I see the mark of the nails in his hands and put my finger into the nail marks and put my hand into his side, I will not believe." Now a week later his disciples were again inside and Thomas was with them. Jesus came, although the doors were locked, and stood in their midst and said, "Peace be with you." Then he said to Thomas, "Put your finger here and see my hands, and bring your hand and put it into my side, and do not be unbelieving, but believe." Thomas answered and said to him, "My Lord and my God!" Jesus said to him, "Have you come to believe because you have seen me? Blessed are those who have not seen and have believed." Now Jesus did many other signs in the presence of His disciples that are not written in this book. But these are written that you may come to believe that Jesus is the Messiah, the Son of God, and that through this belief you may have life in his name.*

What is it that you need to believe that Jesus Christ is the Son of God? What is it that you need to start to traverse the mountain of salvation? What is it that you need to run the race to the finish? If your answer is nothing, then go back and start this book from the very beginning, for you have not understood. If your answer is everything that God has to offer or simply grace, then God has granted you more grace to move on to the next Chapter.

NOTES

CHAPTER EIGHT

WORKS

This is where we really get into the dividing of the sheep and the goats. Catholics and Protestants alike protest the concept of works more than anything else.

For you who do not know from where the word Protestant comes, just whack off the "ant" part of the word and you are left with "protest." They are simply people, Catholics, who began protesting against the authentic faith and altered five percent of the doctrine to fit their own beliefs. Works (or good deeds) is one of the areas in which many protesters do not want to participate or acknowledge as necessary for salvation. So their dissent blossomed into an altogether different faith-based theology. New denominations such as Lutheran, Episcopal, and Methodist began to appear. The original split, caused by Martin Luther, (who, incidentally, recanted and confessed his sin on his deathbed,) was the origin of the currently thirty-seven thousand different protesting denominations in existence today. If you are a protester, you have thirty-seven thousand different theologies from which to choose. And guess what? Every one will swear on a stack of Bibles that their denomination is the one true church.

Then there are all of those protesters who stay within the Catholic Church, the ones who will not yield to the teaching authority of the Magisterium, but launch their protests from within and spread their poison as they disguise themselves as sheep. Of the two, I prefer dealing with the first type. But the most dangerous of all are the ones who are dressed as religious, but work for Satan. They cause immeasurable harm to the majority of very good priests who stay obedient to God and to the Church herself. In essence, the dedicated, holy individuals who hang in there and promote God's plan as dictated (and that includes works), have to carry the cross of their falling fellow religious. That, if done well, comes under the title of works and surely leads to sainthood.

We will not cover all of the protesters' fatal complaints here, but just deal with the theology of works. Most protesters do not know or really understand the differences between the Catholic Church and their own selection of the thirty-seven thousand dissenting faiths, but simply follow their false shepherds. Most, in their hearts, believe they are correct in their decision. For the most part, they are very good people who have been duped. In following false teachers they reject authentic Scripture interpretation. The line from the book of James, "*Do you want proof, you ignoramus, that faith without works is useless?*" should be all they need.

I told you I would use it again. I do not know how God could state something more clearly, but when you want to make your point and some "little thing" like Scripture gets in your way, what do you do? You simply throw entire books, or at least some of the verses that contain the Scripture that prove you wrong, out of the Bible. Isn't that convenient? What would God do with people who would discard entire books from His inspired, sacred Word, which we call the Bible? We cannot judge these poor souls or treat them harshly. We can only love them and pray for their return.

There are those who would prefer that we did not address the differences between our faith and those of other religions and I would be the first to agree that the differences cannot be the focus of our relationship. But if we do not, at least in our own ranks, in our own parish missions, and at our Catholic Masses, teach, speak and discuss the differences between the Catholic faith and that of the protesters, what master are we serving? How would an average Catholic learn a defense for the constant attack on our faith by the protester?

My advice for pastors and other priests is this: stop playing down and watering down the Catholic faith to its detriment. We have become so sensitive to ecumenism that Catholics leave the true Church in droves because of the constant attacks against our faith, only to embrace the false doctrine of the protesters. For God's sake, become sensitive to that for a change. The job of the shepherd is to protect the flock. But look at the flock. Where has it gone? The wolves have devoured seventy-three percent of the sheep and still you say, "Be nice to the wolves. Don't ever say anything that would offend the wolves." (*Tongue in cheek*). Does this then not make you a wolf in sheep's clothing? Is this not antichrist?

At times I am called aside by a pastor after a parish mission and instructed not to mention certain subjects again or to bring them up in the future. Your statements on a subject like the Protestant faith are offensive, they will say. It no longer matters to some what it says in Scripture. We have to be politically correct these days. Everybody is going to heaven! I really should bring a wheelbarrow with me sometimes because I could use the fertilizer on my garden. But then again, I do not think these blasphemous encouragements would do anything but kill my plants, as they do the faith of Catholics.

Good works begin at home. If you cannot claim the good work of prospering the Catholic faith, how then could you embrace all of the other works to which God calls us and have them count for something?

> Titus 1:7-16 *For a bishop as God's steward must be blameless, not arrogant, not irritable, not a drunkard, not aggressive, not greedy for sordid gain, but hospitable, a lover of goodness, temperate, just, holy, and self-controlled, holding fast to the true message as taught so that he will be able both to exhort with sound doctrine and to refute opponents. For there are also many rebels, idle talkers and deceivers, especially the Jewish Christians. It is imperative to silence them, as they are upsetting whole families by teaching for sordid gain what they should not. One of them, a prophet of their own, once said, "Cretans have always been liars, vicious beasts, and lazy gluttons." That testimony is true. Therefore, admonish them sharply, so that they may be sound in the faith, instead of paying attention to Jewish myths and regulations of people who have repudiated the truth. To the clean all things are clean, but to those who are defiled and unbelieving nothing is clean; in fact, both their minds and their consciences are tainted. They claim to know God, but by their deeds they deny Him. They*

are vile and disobedient and unqualified for any good deed.

Replace Jewish Christians with Protestants in this Scripture and you have the same scenario. The Jewish Christians mentioned above were the protesters of that day. We had them then, we have them now and we will always have them until Christ returns and personally explains the truth to everyone. It is hard to find a Catholic with the guts or knowledge to handle the job, so we will have to wait for Christ's return. With only a few speakers of the truth left, we will have to wait and wait. How long, oh Lord, how long?

Protestants are not the only ones willing to balk at works. Many Catholics now embrace the false doctrine of works as unnecessary. Let me tell you, they have fallen prey to the enemy. The Scriptures we have discussed cannot be clearer - without works, your chances of making it through the narrow gate of heaven are zero.

To not admonish sinners is failure in itself and could cause the loss of your sainthood, so do not ever be afraid to defend the Catholic doctrine on works or anything contained within our entire Catholic faith. If you fit among the non-defenders of the faith, you automatically become a destroyer of it. Therefore, you may not be heaven-bound.

Catholics reject works for completely different reasons than those of the protesters. The Protestant does it because of false teachers for the most part, but believes in his heart that he is correct. This does not absolve them from their failure, but is most certainly more honorable than the Catholic reason. The reason some Catholics reject works is because they are disobedient and lazy. (I will make a lot of friends with that statement.) The cold, hard facts are not so hard or cold. In fact, the way of Christ is easy. We, as Catholics, simply refuse to do what the Lord asks. Worse yet, many just ignore the Lord and pretend that they never knew about the teachings on works. Believe me when I tell you, God knows every thought that you ever had, bar none, and will play them back for you at judgment day.

With tongue in cheek again, I have to ask this question: is it better to work less, in case this God stuff is not true, than to have wasted all that effort for nothing? That is the mindset of a vast majority of the semi-faithful, the mindset of those for whom getting to heaven is low on their priority list.

I tell you again, it is always better to err on the side of caution in case this God stuff is true, than to make one fatal mistake in your quest for salvation. This is the mindset of the saint bound.

> James 1:19-27 *Know this, my dear brothers: everyone should be quick to hear, slow to speak, slow to wrath, for the wrath of a man does not accomplish the righteousness of God. Therefore, put away all filth and evil excess and humbly welcome the word that has been planted in you and is able to save your souls. Be doers of the word and not hearers only, deluding yourselves. For if anyone is a hearer of the word and not a doer, he is like a man who looks at his own face in a mirror. He sees himself, then goes off and promptly forgets what he looked like. But the one who peers into the perfect law of freedom and perseveres, and is not a hearer who forgets but a doer who acts, such a one shall be blessed in what he does. If anyone thinks he is religious and does not bridle his tongue but deceives his heart, his religion is vain. Religion that is pure and undefiled before God and the Father is this: to care for orphans and widows in their affliction and to keep oneself unstained by the world.*

Not only does the Lord instruct us to be involved in the works for the orphans and widows, but He also demands the same for prisoners and the poor. If we claim to have faith without taking care of these, we have deluded ourselves. Average Catholics hear these marching orders through the Scriptures read and discussed at Mass (if they go to Mass), but then they refuse to get involved, to put the Word into practice. If God asked specifically for these aforementioned projects to be accomplished in each of our lives and we refuse, where would God allow a person like that to go? Hell? What do you think?

This seems like a great place to put in a plug for my orphanages. If you want to be a saint and you have not yet sponsored an orphan or helped build an orphanage, contact me and I will help you get this accomplished. Remember Jerry Lewis and his kids with muscular dystrophy? Well, I have lots of kids myself whose main problems are food, shelter and education. I beg you to help my orphan kids. Helping with orphans is in the realm of works, big time. (See the material for sponsorship at the end of the book.)

> James 1:27 *Religion that is pure and undefiled before God and the Father is this: to visit orphans and widows in their affliction, and to keep oneself unstained from the world.*

> James 2:1-13 *My brethren, show no partiality as you hold the faith of our Lord Jesus Christ, the Lord of glory.*

> *For if a man with gold rings and in fine clothing comes into your assembly, and a poor man in shabby clothing also comes in, and you pay attention to the one who wears the fine clothing and say, "Have a seat here, please," while you say to the poor man, "Stand there," or, "Sit at my feet," have you not made distinctions among yourselves, and become judges with evil thoughts?*

> *Listen, my beloved brethren. Has not God chosen those who are poor in the world to be rich in faith and heirs of the kingdom which he has promised to those who love him? But you have dishonored the poor man. Is it not the rich who oppress you, is it not they who drag you into court?*

> *Is it not they who blaspheme that honorable name which was invoked over you? If you really fulfil the royal law, according to the scripture, "You shall love your neighbor as yourself," you do well. But if you show partiality, you commit sin, and are convicted by the law as transgressors.*

> *For whoever keeps the whole law but fails in one point has become guilty of all of it. For he who said, "Do*

not commit adultery," said also, "Do not kill." If you do not commit adultery but do kill, you have become a transgressor of the law.

So speak and so act as those who are to be judged under the law of liberty.

For judgment is without mercy to one who has shown no mercy; yet mercy triumphs over judgment.

How can we sleep at night with full stomachs, all warm and cozy, knowing that while we slumber, others are starving to death and face eternal sleep because we did not intervene? I know a wealthy man who, when I tried to introduce his children to the Godly art of giving to the poorest of the poor in Africa, protested and refused to allow his children to be involved. Why? There are many children in this country who need help, he said. Whether the children in this country received any help from him, I don't know. I feared, at that time, that there was so little faith in him that there will be no grace at death's door to assume him. I truly feared for the man and his family, so I prayed. I have not yet witnessed anything that could be called a conversion, but I do see God at work in him. He is wealthy enough to travel the world and has now been to Africa. There he witnessed, firsthand, the plight of the poorest of the poor and now he thinks differently. God's grace is at work in him. Maybe some day he will help me build an orphanage.

What would it hurt to teach a child to give to others freely and not selectively? To be too selective in your giving could cause the loss of your reward. I do not mean that you have to give to everyone who asks. There are countless places to which it is wise to give and probably more to which it is unwise. I would never give to the United Way and I ask everyone not to give to them. They support immorality and ungodly behavior, as do the Masons who, likewise, cloak their evil in some good works. What I mean is, if someone has his hand out whom you know feeds starving people and you say, "No, I gave at the office," or "I only support Americans," as the man above said, then I believe that is wrong. There is prejudice in that.

Luke 11:5-8 *And he said to them, "Suppose one of you has a friend to whom he goes at midnight and says, 'Friend, lend me three loaves of bread, for a friend of mine has arrived at my house from a journey and I have nothing to offer him,' and he says in reply from within, 'Do not bother me; the door has already been locked and my children and I are already in bed. I cannot get up to give you anything.' I tell you, if he does not get up to give him the loaves because of their friendship, he will get up to give him whatever he needs because of his persistence.*

The above example would be a good work. The man I mentioned above could not even give out of friendship and that demonstrates separation from God. When we are called upon to respond on behalf of the needy, we must suppose that God sent the messenger and that we should, indeed, respond. It does not always have to be a great sum. It may even be as small as the three loaves of bread or, in the case I am presenting, a dollar bill. But you should respond nonetheless. I'm sure God does not take lack of works lightly.

In all instances you do not have to be directly involved in the work yourself. If you simply, at times, give a donation to a charity, that is doing good works also. We all get many pleas from religious organizations and many of us find them bothersome. I propose this: do not throw them in the trash, but send something to each, even if it is a small donation. If an organization sends out a mailing, it costs them something to do that. To respond by throwing the request in the trash hurts that organization. Sending a few bucks hurts no one, not even you. And if everyone who gets that mailing sends something monthly, then the organization has a monthly income on which they can rely. If you send say, three dollars to ten organizations, that is only thirty dollars a month and you share in all the grace that is being generated through the works of those organizations. All religious organizations pray for their benefactors. So then you have the prayer support of those ten, also. To turn your back on people doing good works hurts you and them. Do you understand this? Sharing your wealth has you involved in the works of the Lord.

This does not preclude you from being actively involved in the works of the Lord. Do not be a check writer only. You will miss out on much grace that way. The Lord tells us to visit the prisoner, the widow, take care of the orphan and feed the poor. Consider the first two as active involvement and the second two although they can be active, as check writing endeavors. You can (and should be) involved in prison ministry in some way. There is a great joy to be had in going to a jail or just writing letters and sharing the Lord with someone who made a mistake. The Lord may treat you with greater mercy if you do.

As for the widows - all you have to do is try this once and you will be hooked. Go to a nursing home or old folks home and ask if there is someone who does not get many visitors. They will come up with a list. Go and visit one of these creatures of God. Take her by the hand and tell her who you are and just talk a while. The Lord will give you the words. After a time, when you decide you must move on, try to get your hand back. The woman will not want to let go. You are the first person to allow Christ to be seen in her life in a long time. There may be some tears and you will then know the joy the Lord wanted you to know through visiting widows.

It becomes obvious after you are involved in works for a while that before your involvement, you had been missing out on the best part of life. Helping others is what life is all about.

We could go on with a more in-depth discussion on faith and works, but why muddy the waters? The book of James settles the argument once and for all. If you want to throw that book out with the others, think about this explanation of the number of God's inspired books. There are seventy-three books in the Catholic Bible. This number consists of seven (7), heaven's number as stated in that Bible, and three (3), God's number. Protesters removed seven (7) books from the inspired universal (universal meaning Catholic) Bible, just so they could attempt to prove their case. Satan left his mark behind. There remained only sixty-six (66) books in the protesters' version of the Bible. And whose number has all the sixes in it?

If you were to attempt to live a life void of good works, you would only prove one thing: your lack of faith. You would demonstrate a selfish lifestyle - one that would not imitate the life of Christ. If you do not imitate the life of Christ, you will not become a saint.

So is it faith and works, or by faith alone, that one is saved?

If you are still obstinate and you want to call your life without works a faith-filled one, go back to Chapter One and start over. If your answer is that you must have faith accompanied by works, and you are now willing to accept the responsibility of being Catholic, to work hard at taking care of God's children and stop turning your back on obedience, continue on to Chapter Nine.

NOTES

Chapter Nine

Tests

I have heard it said that God seldom tests His people. I personally think that all of life is a test, a sort of proving ground for souls. I do not think it erroneous to believe that God sends us tests with whatever frequency He desires, because He is God and we are not. Our Father does not send us tests for their own sake, or to be mean or cruel, but for His Godly reasons and nothing else.

Heavenly tests take many and varied forms. We can see the first test ever in the Garden of Eden, when God ordered Adam and Eve not to eat from the Tree of Life. We all know the end of that story and live today with all of its ramifications. That particular time Satan did not ask God's permission to tempt the two residents, so he also suffered dire consequences. I do not know if Satan has to always ask before he tempts us, but I do know that he asked in the Biblical story of Job. When Job passed all of the tests, God multiplied his wealth and he was much better off after the test than he was before. Could it not then be deduced that tests are for our spiritual betterment?

I see in my own life many of what I would classify as tests being implemented for my edification. I also see the profound good that comes from them.

As a child I had a recurring dream that frightened me immensely. To me, it was more like a nightmare. In this nightmare, I somehow had a lot of money. This was before I was old enough to understand money in a worldly sense. I knew that if you had it, you could buy candy, but that was all I knew. What frightened me was that this huge amount of money was being taken away from me a little at a time and there was nothing I could do about it. The frustration it caused me was life long. I never forgot that nightmare.

After my conversion, I started Gospa Missions, which became a 501(c) 3 private foundation. I began raising funds to do apostolic works of mercy. It was during this time that, on at least five occasions, seemingly good Catholics defrauded my apostolate of sizeable amounts of money. It was very frustrating and caused me to become angry.

After a time it was as if a light went on and I said to the Lord, "I get it now! You are going to have people take money from me until I get over being angry. Okay, I am over it." I was wrong. I am not over it yet, but I know it is an ongoing test. With the grace of God leading me away from this sin of anger, I, one day, will beat it.

Other tests come in the form of pain and trouble. Many will say that these items are just a part of life, but I believe they are more than that. They could be part of original sin and sent from Satan, but no matter where they come from, there are two ways to deal with them. Triumph over the problems and they can afford us much good. Succumb to Satan's call and turn against God because of problems, and we will suffer loss. If trouble comes from Satan in order to cause our downfall and we, through God's help, defeat Satan in his efforts to cause us loss, then we bring glory to God.

Only God knows why he allows malignant tumors to come this world. I believe with all of my heart that we can turn cancer into a gift from God. Please allow me my perception.

> 1 Sam 5:6-12 *The hand of the Lord was heavy upon the people of Ashdod, and he terrified and afflicted them with tumors, both Ashdod and its territory.*
>
> *And when the men of Ashdod saw how things were, they said, "The ark of the God of Israel must not remain with us; for his hand is heavy upon us and upon Dagon our god."*
>
> *So they sent and gathered together all the lords of the Philistines, and said, "What shall we do with the ark of the God of Israel?" They answered, "Let the ark of the God of Israel be brought around to Gath." So they brought the ark of the God of Israel there.*

But after they had brought it around, the hand of the Lord was against the city, causing a very great panic, and he afflicted the men of the city, both young and old, so that tumors broke out upon them.

So they sent the ark of God to Ekron. But when the ark of God came to Ekron, the people of Ekron cried out, "They have brought around to us the ark of the God of Israel to slay us and our people."

They sent therefore and gathered together all the lords of the Philistines, and said, "Send away the ark of the God of Israel, and let it return to its own place, that it may not slay us and our people." For there was a deathly panic throughout the whole city. The hand of God was very heavy there; the men who did not die were stricken with tumors, and the cry of the city went up to heaven.

Deu 28:27 *The Lord will strike you with Egyptian boils and with tumors, eczema and the itch.*

Who will strike you? The Lord! God sent all kinds of plagues to Egypt's Pharaoh so he would let God's people go. The particular items sent, locusts, a bloody river and the sort did not seem like gifts to the Pharaoh, but they certainly were for the Jews. We cannot always credit Satan for disruptions in our lives, but most certainly should glorify God for everything that comes our way, good or seemingly bad.

If I ever get cancer, I pray the first thing that comes out of my mouth when the doctor tells me I have it is, "Thank you, God." Why? God says to thank Him in *all* things. What does a person generally do when he is diagnosed with cancer? He prays - sometimes for the first time in a very long time. What is it that causes one to pray? The Holy Spirit. What generally happens to the family and friends of the person who has cancer? They find themselves praying and again, sometimes for the first time. What is it that causes one to pray? The Holy Spirit! So I can only figure that if cancer came into my life it would come for a very good reason. If it was allowed to come into my life by God and it caused me to pray more, then it is good.

Please do not try to rob God of all His tools that He uses to bring about salvation for His people. I thank God for the many tears I have cried over my conversion. I have been led to believe it is called the gift of tears.

> 1 Samuel 2:6-10 The *Lord puts to death and gives life; he casts down to the nether world; he raises up again. The Lord makes poor and makes rich, he humbles, he also exalts. He raises the needy from the dust; from the ash heap he lifts up the poor, To seat them with nobles and make a glorious throne their heritage. He gives to the vower his vow, and blesses the sleep of the just. "For the pillars of the earth are the Lord's, and he has set the world upon them. He will guard the footsteps of his faithful ones, but the wicked shall perish in the darkness. For not by strength does man prevail; the Lord's foes shall be shattered. The Most High in heaven thunders; The Lord judges the ends of the earth, now may he give strength to his king, and exalt the horn of his anointed!"*

Our Lord, out of love, intervenes in His people's lives on a regular basis and many times the result is a profound conversion. The Lord gives and the Lord takes away. If you have not received a test from the Lord, you can bet that it is on the way. Pick up that cross and carry it.

> Gen 22:1 *Some time after these events, God put Abraham to the test.*

> Deu 8:2 *Remember how for forty years now the Lord, your God, has directed all your journeying in the desert, so as to test you by affliction and find out whether or not it was your intention to keep his commandments.*

> Mt 26:41 *Watch and pray that you may not undergo the test. The spirit is willing, but the flesh is weak.*

James 1:1-10 *James, a servant of God and of the Lord Jesus Christ, to the twelve tribes in the Dispersion: Greeting. Count it all joy, my brethren, when you meet various trials, for you know that the testing of your faith produces steadfastness. And let steadfastness have its full effect, that you may be perfect and complete, lacking in nothing. If any of you lacks wisdom, let him ask God, who gives to all men generously and without reproaching, and it will be given him. But let him ask in faith, with no doubting, for he who doubts is like a wave of the sea that is driven and tossed by the wind. For that person must not suppose that a double-minded man, unstable in all his ways, will receive anything from the Lord. Let the lowly brother boast in his exaltation and the rich in his humiliation, because like the flower of the grass he will pass away.*

1 Cor 3:13 *The work of each will come to light, for the Day will disclose it. It will be revealed with fire, and the fire (itself) will test the quality of each one's work.*

Rev 3:10-13 *Because you have kept my message of endurance, I will keep you safe in the time of trial that is going to come to the whole world to test the inhabitants of the earth. I am coming quickly. Hold fast to what you have, so that no one may take your crown. "The victor I will make into a pillar in the temple of my God, and he will never leave it again. On him I will inscribe the name of my God and the name of the city of my God, the new Jerusalem, which comes down out of heaven from my God, as well as my new name. Whoever has ears ought to hear what the Spirit says to the churches."*

So we see that everyone will undergo a test, perhaps multiple tests, but if we hold fast to the Lord's teaching, He will keep us from harm's way and we will wear a crown of victory.

The big danger is the false teachers and the clever way Satan works through them. Employ great caution in deciding to whom you will listen and know that there is no one with all of the answers outside the Lord.

If, at this point in your life, you do not have a cross, do what the Lord says to do. Take what you have and sell it. You will then have a cross.

There are those who asked God for a cross and received a very large one. Remember, Saint Rita asked and received. She requested to be able to suffer part of the passion and received a thorn in her head. If you want to be on God's winning team, ask to share in whatever it is that God desires of this world.

If you are willing to accept all the tests that God has to offer, please continue on to Chapter Ten.

NOTES

CHAPTER TEN

TITHING

This is where a lot of people will want to throw this book away. Remember the asbestos suits? Hang in there.

Let me ask this question point blank: do you give to God His fair share of your time, talent and treasure? If you cannot answer in the affirmative, read this chapter very carefully, because it may just save your soul.

If you are already a tither, please do not jump ahead, figuring that you do not need this section. Allow grace to help you to improve. Perhaps the percentage you are currently giving should only be the beginning. Perhaps God expects more. Move forward from that beginning and see the glory that comes from giving God's way. It is in giving that you receive.

In the Old Testament, God demanded ten percent of your time, talent and treasure from the first fruits, right off the top. If you were not a tither, *you put your salvation at risk.*

Although the New Testament does not specifically mention a ten percent tithe, that does not absolve us from giving. In fact, under the New Covenant, the requirement may be more than ten percent for some people and less for others. Our God, in giving us free will, allows us now to determine, on our own, how much we will give. Sad to say, many do not even think about their salvation when they share their wealth. If you want heaven to be your home, think about what you are giving very carefully.

If you are giving little when you should be giving much, please take some of the monies you are stealing from God and invest in the asbestos suits I have been mentioning, because it is going to be hot down there. (I say that to be humorous, but there is truth in it.)

Know this: you came into this world with nothing. All that you received while you where here came from God and when you die, the record of what you did with God's possessions will testify for or against you on judgment day.

If we only would read the Bible and know what God demands of us, maybe then we would have a holy fear of Him. But today, hardly a person fears the Lord because the world and most everybody in it teaches against God. The false teachers that claim that no one is going to hell are going to hell themselves and would like to take you with them.

> Mt 25:14-46 *"It will be as when a man who was going on a journey called in his servants and entrusted his possessions to them. To one he gave five talents; to another, two; to a third, one—to each according to his ability.*
>
> *Then he went away. Immediately the one who received five talents went and traded with them, and made another five. Likewise, the one who received two made another two. But the man who received one went off and dug a hole in the ground and buried his master's money.*
>
> *After a long time the master of those servants came back and settled accounts with them. The one who had received five talents came forward bringing the additional five. He said, 'Master, you gave me five talents. See, I have made five more.' His master said to him, 'Well done, my good and faithful servant. Since you were faithful in small matters, I will give you great responsibilities. Come, share your master's joy.'*
>
> *(Then) the one who had received two talents also came forward and said, 'Master, you gave me two talents. See, I have made two more.' His master said to him, 'Well done, my good and faithful servant. Since you were faithful in small matters, I will give you great responsibilities. Come, share your master's joy.'*
>
> *Then the one who had received the one talent came forward and said, 'Master, I knew you were a demanding*

person, harvesting where you did not plant and gathering where you did not scatter; so out of fear I went off and buried your talent in the ground. Here it is back.' His master said to him in reply, 'You wicked, lazy servant! So you knew that I harvest where I did not plant and gather where I did not scatter? Should you not then have put my money in the bank so that I could have got it back with interest on my return?

Now then! Take the talent from him and give it to the one with ten. For to everyone who has, more will be given and he will grow rich; but from the one who has not, even what he has will be taken away. And throw this useless servant into the darkness outside, where there will be wailing and grinding of teeth.'

"When the Son of Man comes in his glory, and all the angels with him, he will sit upon his glorious throne, and all the nations will be assembled before him. And he will separate them one from another, as a shepherd separates the sheep from the goats.

He will place the sheep on his right and the goats on his left. Then the king will say to those on his right, 'Come, you who are blessed by my Father. Inherit the kingdom prepared for you from the foundation of the world. For I was hungry and you gave me food, I was thirsty and you gave me drink, a stranger and you welcomed me, naked and you clothed me, ill and you cared for me, in prison and you visited me.'

Then the righteous will answer him and say, 'Lord, when did we see you hungry and feed you, or thirsty and give you drink? When did we see you a stranger and welcome you, or naked and clothe you? When did we see you ill or in prison, and visit you?' And the king will say to them in reply, 'Amen, I say to you, whatever you did for one of these least brothers of mine, you did for me.'

Then he will say to those on his left, 'Depart from me, you accursed, into the eternal fire prepared for the devil and his angels. For I was hungry and you gave me no food, I was thirsty and you gave me no drink, a stranger and you gave me no welcome, naked and you gave me no clothing, ill and in prison, and you did not care for me.'

Then they will answer and say, 'Lord, when did we see you hungry or thirsty or a stranger or naked or ill or in prison, and not minister to your needs?' He will answer them, 'Amen, I say to you, what you did not do for one of these least ones, you did not do for me.' And these will go off to eternal punishment, but the righteous to eternal life."

We hear these Scriptures and many like them all the time at Mass and more often if we go to daily Mass. Are we to think God had them placed in the Bible for no reason or because He wanted to hear Himself talk? Why are we such fools as not to take the words of salvation and put them into practice?

Let's focus on that word 'stealing.' How could someone steal from God and make it into heaven with that sin unforgiven? You can't! How often have you gone to confession and admitted that you stole a portion of your income from God? That is what the average Catholic does, steals from God, but no one ever thinks of it that way.

Mal 3:8-21 *Dare a man rob God? Yet you are robbing me! And you say, "How do we rob you?" In tithes and in offerings! You are indeed accursed, for you, the whole nation, rob me. Bring the whole tithe into the storehouse, That there may be food in my house, and try me in this, says the Lord of hosts: Shall I not open for you the floodgates of heaven, to pour down blessing upon you without measure?*

For your sake I will forbid the locust to destroy your crops; and the vine in the field will not be barren, says the Lord of hosts. Then all nations will call you blessed, for you will be a delightful land, says the Lord of hosts.

You have defied me in word, says the Lord, yet you ask, "What have we spoken against you?"

You have said, "It is vain to serve God, and what do we profit by keeping his command, and going about in penitential dress in awe of the Lord of hosts? Rather must we call the proud blessed; for indeed evildoers prosper, and even tempt God with impunity." Then they who fear the Lord spoke with one another, and the Lord listened attentively; and a record book was written before him of those who fear the Lord and trust in his name. And they shall be mine, says the Lord of hosts, my own special possession; on the day I take action. And I will have compassion on them, as a man has compassion on his son who serves him.

Then you will again see the distinction between the just and the wicked; between him who serves God, and him who does not serve him. For lo, the day is coming, blazing like an oven, when all the proud and all evildoers will be stubble, And the day that is coming will set them on fire, leaving them neither root nor branch, says the Lord of hosts. But for you who fear my name, there will arise the sun of justice with its healing rays; And you will gambol like calves out of the stall and tread down the wicked; They will become ashes under the soles of your feet, on the day I take action, says the Lord of hosts.

Many Catholics prefer to shower their children and grandchildren with gifts than to ever share the proper amount with God's poor or even the Church, for that matter. But when you do it God's way, a whole new world opens up. You can live heaven right here on earth. When you do it your way, a disaster is lurking.

Deu 7:13-15 *He will love and bless and multiply you; he will bless the fruit of your womb and the produce of your soil, your grain and wine and oil, the issue of your herds and the young of your flocks, in the land which he swore to your fathers he would give you. You will be blessed above all peoples; no man or woman among you shall be childless nor shall your livestock be barren. The Lord will remove all sickness from you; he will not afflict you with any of the malignant diseases that you know from Egypt, but will leave them with all your enemies.*

And you thought cancer, misfortune and the like just happened. Fail to meet the proper sharing demands of the Lord and you will find more problems in your life than you know what to do with. Take heed and know the Scriptures, for your sainthood depends on it. Your sins will not only bring to you punishment and affliction, but to your children, grandchildren and beyond. It is not that God is mean. To the contrary, He is doing all He can to get us into heaven. It is we who are mean to ourselves by not listening to God.

Exodus 20:6, 20 *For I, the Lord, your God, am a jealous God, inflicting punishment for their fathers' wickedness on the children of those who hate me, down to the third and fourth generation; but bestowing mercy down to the thousandth generation, on the children of those who love me and keep my commandments.*

When the people witnessed the thunder and lightning, the trumpet blast and the mountain smoking, they all feared and trembled. So they took up a position much farther away and said to Moses, "You speak to us, and we will listen; but let not God speak to us, or we shall die." Moses answered the people, "Do not be afraid, for God has come to you only to test you and put his fear upon you, lest you should sin."

One of the really big tests in all of our lives is death - the death of others and our own. We all have to understand that the normal path to heaven is through the portal of death. Don't be beating up on God because someone in your family dies. When we give our first and fair portion to God we will live longer happier lives, but hardly a person gets out alive. All will not be perfect as we wait for that portal to open and God does send those tests. If we are taking care of God's business, we have nothing to worry about.

Why is it we are reluctant to attempt passing God's tests? Even the best of Christ's followers are full of reasons why they can't. Why do we say, "I can't," when God and we both know we *can*? We find it easier to lie to God than perform for Him. Yet in everyday life, we perform. We can't tithe, but we can swim the English Channel. We can't tithe, but we land on the moon. We can't tithe, but we work overtime to make more money to get more things for ourselves and our families. We perform all kinds of feats, day in and day out, for man and country, but generally not for God.

We tell our children they can do anything they want when it comes to sports, and they do. Scholastically, we tell them the same thing – that there are no limits to what they can accomplish. Look at what professional football players endure to win a Super Bowl. As simple humans, we are astounding in what we can achieve, but yet, we try to tell God that we cannot give Him what He demands. The fact is not that we can't do it - we will not do it.

It has a lot more to do with, "I won't," than, "I can't." Why? Because we would rather succumb to Satan's will rather than God's will. It is a fact. We can deny it all we want, but the facts bear out our miserable true selves every time. When we perform, we want to see instant results or some immediate return on our investments. Our problem with what God asks is that His results, His big pay off, is too far away for us to appreciate its true value. In the realm of God, we simply become quitters. Quitters stand a good chance of being on the wrong side of the divide.

Yes, I know most everyone has told you that you are going to heaven. Perhaps your parish priest has even said in his homilies that you and everyone else are going to heaven. I have actually been in churches where the priest stated that every one in his church was going to heaven; that there is not only no hell, but no purgatory. So why try at all? All we have to do is sit back and wait to die and we drift blissfully off to heaven. Why not be a pedophile, gay, adulterer, thief or a backslider?

What fool would buy into that kind of theology? Well, it seems that almost all Catholics and Christians alike think that they can steal from God and still slide right on into heaven! That is dangerous thinking. This is probably why Scripture says that the gate to heaven is very narrow and few find it.

> Heb 11:17 *By faith Abraham, when put to the test, offered up Isaac, and he who had received the promises was ready to offer his only son.*

If Abraham was willing to offer his son's life to please God, actually plunge a knife into his own son, then we know that Abraham loved and trusted God. Do you love and trust God? Would you be willing to give your son's life over to God? The answer for most people is no! We are not even willing to give God a reasonable percentage of our time, talent and treasure, so how and where would we come up with faith to return a son?

> Numbers 18:30-32 *"Tell them also: Once you have made your contribution from the best part, the rest of the tithes will be credited to you Levites as if it were produce of the threshing floor or of the winepress. Your families, as well as you, may eat them anywhere, since they are your recompense for service at the meeting tent. You will incur no guilt so long as you make a contribution of the best part. Do not profane the sacred gifts of the Israelites and so bring death on yourselves."*

He is talking about eternal death here and explains that even when you are the recipient of gifts and handouts, you still owe God a certain percent.

> Deu 14:28-29 *But do not neglect the Levite who belongs to your community, for he has no share in the heritage with you. "At the end of every third year you shall bring out all the tithes of your produce for that year and deposit them in community stores, that the Levite who has no share in the heritage with you, and also the alien, the orphan and the widow who belong to your community, may come and eat their fill; so that the Lord, your God, may bless you in all that you undertake.*

Is this making sense to you yet? You may say this is all Old Testament and that is true, but giving is mentioned in the New Testament in a big way also. Now the choice is yours.

Cor 9:-15 Now it is superfluous for me to write to you about the offering for the saints, for I know your readiness, of which I boast about you to the people of Macedonia, saying that Acha'ia has been ready since last year; and your zeal has stirred up most of them.

But I am sending the brethren so that our boasting about you may not prove vain in this case, so that you may be ready, as I said you would be; lest if some Macedonians come with me and find that you are not ready, we be humiliated -- to say nothing of you -- for being so confident.

So I thought it necessary to urge the brethren to go on to you before me, and arrange in advance for this gift you have promised, so that it may be ready not as an exaction but as a willing gift.

The point is this: he who sows sparingly will also reap sparingly, and he who sows bountifully will also reap bountifully. Each one must do as he has made up his mind, not reluctantly or under compulsion, for God loves a cheerful giver.

And God is able to provide you with every blessing in abundance, so that you may always have enough of everything and may provide in abundance for every good work.

As it is written, "He scatters abroad, he gives to the poor; his righteousness endures for ever." He who supplies seed to the sower and bread for food will supply and multiply your resources and increase the harvest of your righteousness.

You will be enriched in every way for great generosity, which through us will produce thanksgiving to God;

for the rendering of this service not only supplies the wants of the saints but also overflows in many thanksgivings to God.

Under the test of this service, you will glorify God by your obedience in acknowledging the gospel of Christ, and by the generosity of your contribution for them and for all others; while they long for you and pray for you, because of the surpassing grace of God in you.

Thanks be to God for his inexpressible gift!

So do not throw away all of the teachings of the Old Testament, but read them and see what was expected then and apply it more readily to today, knowing what we have been given in the person of Jesus.

2 Chr 31:3-15 *From his own wealth the king allotted a portion for holocausts, those of morning and evening and those on sabbaths, new moons and festivals, as prescribed in the law of the Lord. He also commanded the people living in Jerusalem to provide the support of the priests and Levites, that they might devote themselves entirely to the law of the Lord.*

As soon as the order was promulgated, the Israelites brought, in great quantities, the best of their grain, wine, oil and honey, and all the produce of the fields; they gave a generous tithe of everything. Israelites and Judahites living in other cities of Judah also brought in tithes of oxen, sheep, and things that had been consecrated to the Lord, their God; these they brought in and set out in heaps.

It was in the third month that they began to establish these heaps, and they completed them in the seventh month. When Hezekiah and the princes had come and seen the heaps, they blessed the Lord and his people Israel. Then Hezekiah questioned the priests and the Levites concerning the heaps and the priest Azariah, head of the house of Zadoc, answered him, "Since they began to bring the offerings to the house of the Lord, we have eaten to the full and have had much left over, for the Lord has blessed his people. This great supply is what was left over."

Hezekiah then gave orders that chambers be constructed in the house of the Lord. When this had been done, the offerings, tithes and consecrated things were deposited there in safekeeping. The overseer of these things was Conaniah the Levite, and his brother Shimei was second in charge. Jehiel, Azaziah, Nahath, Asahel, Jerimoth, Jozabad, Eliel, Ismachiah, Mahath and Benaiah were supervisors subject to Conaniah and his brother Shimei by appointment of King Hezekiah and of Azariah, the prefect of the house of God. Kore, the son of Imnah, a Levite and the keeper of the eastern gate, was in charge of the free-will gifts made to God; he distributed the offerings made to the Lord and the most holy of the consecrated things. Under him in the priestly cities were Eden, Miniamin, Jeshua, Shemaiah, Amariah and Shecaniah, who faithfully made the distribution to their brethren, great and small alike, according to their classes.

Tobit 1:6-22 *I, for my part, would often make the pilgrimage alone to Jerusalem for the festivals, as is prescribed for all Israel by perpetual decree. Bringing with me the first fruits of the field and the firstlings of the flock, together with a tenth of my income and the first shearings of the sheep, I would hasten to Jerusalem and present them to the priests, Aaron's sons, at the altar.*

To the Levites who were doing service in Jerusalem I would give the tithe of grain, wine, olive oil, pomegranates, figs, and other fruits. And except for sabbatical years, I used to give a second tithe in money, which each year I would go and disburse in Jerusalem. The third tithe I gave to orphans and widows, and to converts who were living with the Israelites. Every third year I would bring them this offering, and we ate it in keeping with the decree of the Mosaic law and the commands of

Deborah, the mother of my father Tobiel; for when my father died, he left me an orphan.

When I reached manhood, I married Anna, a woman of our own lineage. By her I had a son whom I named Tobiah. Now, after I had been deported to Nineveh, all my brothers and relatives ate the food of heathens, but I refrained from eating that kind of food. Because of this wholehearted service of God, the Most High granted me favor and status with Shalmaneser, so that I became purchasing agent for all his needs. Every now and then until his death I would go to Media to buy goods for him. I also deposited several pouches containing a great sum of money with my kinsman Gabael, son of Gabri, who lived at Rages, in Media.

But when Shalmaneser died and his son Sennacherib succeeded him as king, the roads to Media became unsafe, so I could no longer go there. During Shalmaneser's reign I performed many charitable works for my kinsmen and my people. I would give my bread to the hungry and my clothing to the naked.

If I saw one of my people who had died and been thrown outside the walls of Nineveh, I would bury him. I also buried anyone whom Sennacherib slew when he returned as a fugitive from Judea during the days of judgment decreed against him by the heavenly King because of the blasphemies he had uttered. In his rage he killed many Israelites, but I used to take their bodies by stealth and bury them; so when Sennacherib looked for them, he could not find them.

But a certain citizen of Nineveh informed the king that it was I who buried the dead. When I found out that the king knew all about me and wanted to put me to death, I went into hiding; then in my fear I took to flight.

Afterward, all my property was confiscated; I was left with nothing. All that I had was taken to the king's palace, except for my wife Anna and my son Tobiah. But less than forty days later the king was assassinated by two of his sons, who then escaped into the mountains of Ararat. His son Esarhaddon, who succeeded him as king, placed Ahiqar, my brother Anael's son, in charge of all the accounts of his kingdom, so that he took control over the entire administration.

Then Ahiqar interceded on my behalf, and I was able to return to Nineveh. For under Sennacherib, king of Assyria, Ahiqar had been chief cupbearer, keeper of the seal, administrator, and treasurer; and Esarhaddon re-appointed him. He was a close relative-in fact, my nephew.

It is in giving that you receive and that is the name of that tune. Giving is not a popular subject in the realm of Catholic people, but I pray that this will touch your heart to the point that you will reconsider giving, and giving God's way.

David Parkes, a famous Catholic sinner, I mean *singer*, and I, sang one of Frank Sinatra's songs at a conference where my presentation on tithing was made. The song, "My Way." David sang it well; I, on the other hand, not so well.

David introduced us this way: "We are going to sing a duet. Thomas is going to take the girl's part, and I ..." Well, the nerve of the man! Me doing the girl's part! Parkes has quite a sense of humor. David continued after I gave him a good trashing, "Some years back, I released an album called *Songs of Love and Despera...er, Inspiration.* On that album...it's an album of love songs...I did the "Wind Beneath My Wings" and a few other beautiful love songs, but I put another song on it, as well. It is a song I sang for fourteen years with the band, six nights a week, and you know what used to annoy me was the amount of royalties that I paid to Frank Sinatra. And the other really annoying part was that for fourteen years, six nights a week, I used to mention his name and he never once mentioned mine.

"This song was originally written by Paul Anka and it's probably the most conceited song ever written. But I, through the inspiration of the Holy Spirit, changed just one word. And by virtue of changing that one word, it has probably made it the most complete song ever written. Thomas was very taken when he heard me sing it and when it came out on the album and he has written about it in his second book...isn't that right Thomas? *Miracles and How to Work Them.* We are going to try to sing it together. Now as I said, I saw a few of you falling asleep earlier on, but unfortunately, more of you are falling asleep now than you were earlier. We're not going to tell you what the one word is that was changed, what we want to see, Thomas, is if they are paying attention. Cue the orchestra."

And now the end is near,
and so I face the final curtain.
My friends, I'll say it clear;
I'll state my case, of which I'm certain.
I've lived a life that's full;
I've traveled each and every highway.
And more, much more than this,
I did it *God's* way.

Regrets, I've had a few,
but then again, too few to mention.
I did what I had to do
and saw it though, without exemption.
I planned each chartered course,
each careful step, along the byway,
and more, much more than this,
I did it *God's* way.

Yes, there were times, I'm sure you knew,
when I bit off more than I could chew.
But through it all when there was doubt,
I ate it up and spit it out.
And through it all, I stood tall,
and did it *God's* way.

I've loved, I've laughed and cried;
I had my fill, my share of losing.
And now as those tears subside,
I find it all so amusing.

To think I did all that, and may I say, not in a shy way.
Oh, no, oh, no, not me, I did it *God's* way.

For what is a man? What has he got?
If not himself, then he has naught.
To say the things he truly feels,
and not the words of one who kneels.
The record shows, I took the blows
and did it God's way. Yes, it was *God's* way.

Well, let's thank David for allowing God to change one word in that song and making it the perfect song. And I want to thank David Parkes for setting up this whole scenario of *In Giving You Receive.* When you give, you certainly do it God's way.

The idea of God giving to us seems to be a lost art, and it's not God's fault; it seems to be we who are at fault, because we work too hard at stopping God from giving us His gifts.

Through my whole working life, I did quite well. Although I lied to get out of high school, the creativity I used to get out of high school seemed to allow me do well in the world. And in my success, there was one thing lacking - my willingness to share it. I figured that I worked so hard and if I got myself a Mercedes-Benz - well, doggone it, I deserved it! And if I drove my Lincoln Continental around town - well, I deserved it. I worked hard. I had a four-wheel-drive vehicle to go out into the woods, to play around, to hunt, to take to those remote places where the fishing was the best, and hey, what the heck, I worked hard for it. It was mine; I had a right. I had even worked overtime, and with the paychecks that they would give me for working overtime, and along with the money my wife, Mary, had earned on a national television game show, we bought a boat big enough to spend weekends on, and we realized we were living that American dream. Life was good to us.

But there was always something missing, and I couldn't figure it out. Why was owning a Mercedes-Benz so much fun for such a short period of time? As for the boat, it seemed great. I never felt the way many boaters felt. They say there is an old adage about boating - that the two happiest days in a boat owner's life are the day he buys the boat and the day he sells the boat – that wasn't true in my life. How I loved that boat! I was so proud of it. I would polish it and wax it. I had worked hard for that boat and it was justifiably mine. But soon it became a hollow joy. Something was missing, and I didn't know what it was. I didn't realize what it was until God came into my life!

He came and changed my life. Even my wife, Mary, says that through watching what God was doing for me, her life was changing, although quite a bit more slowly. I am the first to admit that I got in the way of her conversion. I tried to shove God down her throat, and that did not work, so I finally did it God's way. What a difference. *It is in giving that you receive.* What was I giving? I was giving up doing it my way.

One day, I was sitting on our boat, convinced by God that I had to start getting rid of stuff in my life. I said, "Okay, Lord, You've got me convinced. I could be doing better things in this world then sitting on a boat at a yacht club, so I'm willing to sell this boat and use the proceeds to start doing Your work. But how are You going to convince *her*?" And I looked across the boat to my wife. At that moment, Mary looked up and said "Honey, did you ever think of selling this boat?"

Praise the Lord! He just makes it so easy, sometimes. All you have to do is to be willing to surrender your problems to the Lord and all of a sudden, He just starts taking care of business. So we ended up selling the boat and launching a new apostolate. I gave more and more of my life to the Lord, and people shared in that. And I started to find the happiness that I was looking for, because when I shared with others, joy came to me in a way I never perceived it could. It was marvelous.

What I didn't know was that it was just the beginning. At that particular time, I didn't know that I was going to walk out of my career in broadcast journalism. But God, very slowly, very patiently, worked in both our lives.

So with the boat gone, we gradually left our former way of life behind. Many of our friends left us. And looking back, it was easy. God makes it easy. Soon we were on the road for Jesus

Christ and we started giving our lives as a married couple in the Catholic Church, giving our lives in time, talent and treasure. I really believe the Catholic Church needs some Catholic families giving their lives so that the rest of the world might see Jesus Christ in the family. People working and giving their lives to God is God's plan for us.

So now we were working hard, but together. Everything we have belongs to God and we try to share abundantly. Through Gospa Missions, our foundation, we've built an orphanage in Africa. We'll be starting another one soon.

We also helped rebuild churches in Bosnia and Croatia, which were destroyed during the war there. We attended the rededication of the newly rebuilt St. Anne Church in Dubrovnik, Croatia, in 1999. The damage to that church had been so great that the bishop of the diocese of Dubrovnik, Zelimir Puljic, had already made the decision to bulldoze it. But we said, "Wait, maybe we can raise some funds to help. And so we did. With Gospa Missions' donations and with the help of others, the church was rebuilt. What a celebration! It was fantastic. The people cried, I cried, my wife cried, just to see the joy in the hearts of people who got their church back. The Serbians had blown it up and God returned it to them, better than before.

At the dedication, they invited me forward to say a few words.

I asked the people of the parish, "Is your church better now or the way it was before?" They said, "Oh, it's much better now. It's more beautiful. It is the same church but it's more beautiful." I said, "Whom do we have to thank for that?" And they said, "God, of course." I said, "Of course, God, but who else?"

You could see the puzzlement on their faces, trying to figure this out. Then they shouted, "You!" And I said, "No, not me. It's the Serbians. We have to thank the Serbians."

There was a dead silence in the congregation as they heard me speak the word that had caused them so much pain. The Serbians! As what I said sank in, they were all mumbling and grumbling. The moment before, they'd had joy in their hearts;

they had their church back. Here in front of them was one of the people in the world, a very distant neighbor, who had helped give it back to them, and they were excited to have me there. But all of a sudden there was silence.

I could just hear them protesting. "Have you gone mad, Mr. Rutkoski? The Serbians are the ones who blew it up. They're our archenemies. We hate them."

"With an attitude like that," I said, "the Serbians will get into heaven before you do. We pray that God will forgive us our trespasses as we forgive those who trespass against us. So unless you forgive the Serbians, you, yourself, cannot get into heaven. Don't let them be the stumbling block for you."

The message didn't sit well with these Croatians who were hurt and bitter, but surely it was a seed planted. There was joy in my heart that day, in the heart of my wife and all of Gospa Missions, and I pray to the Lord that there is joy in every one of you who helped us rebuild that church, because we, at Gospa Missions, do not have high paying jobs. So we cannot rebuild churches. It was they who donated to Gospa Missions who actually rebuilt that church. *It's in giving that you receive,* and the Lord pays back a hundredfold. So if you were part of that project, please share in our joy. Along with your giving to Gospa Missions for causes like this, please tithe part of your time in prayer so the Croatians will forgive the Serbians.

Some believe the Lord promised us a hundred percent return on what we give to Him. What He actually promised was a hundredfold return. There is a big difference between a hundredfold and a hundred percent. Let's say we invest one thousand dollars in a mutual fund. A hundred percent return would be two thousand dollars. A hundredfold return would be one hundred thousand dollars. Big difference, isn't there?

So why do we have such a hard time sharing what we have with the Lord? Do you ever notice in Scripture that the people God respected the most were the people who gave from their want? They were giving until it hurt. I didn't understand that process for most of my life. Before my conversion, I gave almost nothing to God's causes. Afterward, I was giving up my life, giving up my job, but it didn't seem like I was taking hard cold cash and handing it over to somebody. It was just a little bit at a time. The total amount I gave grew, but if I had to walk into the bank and draw out all of my funds and give it to the poor and ponder where my next meal would come from, I wonder how I would have felt then?

The Lord is smarter than that. He started to work on me, to show me that if you give to the Lord, the Lord does give back a hundredfold. I can remember, early on in my conversion, someone, during a phone conversation, asked me if I had a devotion to the Infant Jesus of Prague. I said, "No, I know of the Infant Jesus of Prague, but I don't know anything of the devotion. I just see that little statue in a dress and often wondered about that."

This person then said, "What I am going to do is send you a little infant Jesus of Prague and a devotional book." I was appreciative.

That same day I had ordered something for myself; it was the Catholic Bible on a CD-ROM that I could put in my computer and do my Bible studies. About a week later, two packages arrived in the mail at the same time. The one package I opened had the little statue of the Infant Jesus of Prague. I put him right up on the monitor of my computer workstation. I got the little devotional book out, and sat it on my desk. I opened up the other package, which was that Bible computer program.

I started to install the program, and as it was installing, I took that devotional book and I started to read it. I read in the booklet how people would ask the Infant of Prague for financial help in things that were really necessary. Often the money would come to them; often it came to the penny. I was impressed, but the computer program was all loaded in and I was in a hurry to try it out, so I put the devotional book aside and I fired up that Bible program on the computer.

I'm not someone who is well-trained in Scripture, but I remembered a few famous phrases, so I went to the part of the program where you type in some words, and the program will perform a search of the entire Bible and find those words, as many times as they occur. So I typed 'Upon this rock.' When I typed it, the program said "No occurrence." I thought to myself, "Well, I must have spelled it wrong or something. "Upon this rock...how do you spell 'upon'...? I think I know how to spell 'rock.' It looks right. I typed again, 'Upon this rock.'

"No occurrence" came up again! Maybe I'm spelling 'this' wrong. You know I lied to get out of high school. I know I have a terrible problem with spelling, but nothing would come out of my search, no matter what I did. I got a bit frustrated, but in my frustration I heard in my head to type in ...I think it was Luke 2 (I was working with the King James version at that time. Forgive me, it was the only one I had.) So I typed Luke 2 and up came a phrase on the computer screen. It was a Scripture talking about how the Magi came to honor the Infant Jesus, and I looked up at that little statue of the Infant Jesus on my computer. I thought, "I wonder how many times the word 'infant' appears in the Bible?" I typed in 'Infant' and it appears one time – I had stumbled upon the only place in the whole Bible that the word 'infant' appeared. I was impressed by what I heard in my head.

I was just putting this computer office together, and I was getting some new equipment to aid me more in my evangelization. I had just gotten a new fax machine, unpacked it and was busy installing it. I'd never had a fax machine in my life. I'd just had a brand new telephone line put in for this fax. I connected the phone line to the fax and plugged the power cord into the wall. The next process was in turning the switch on to the fax machine. As this was accomplished, immediately a piece of paper started coming out of the fax. My first thought was that they must put in a test page so that as soon as you start it up, this test page comes out so you can see that it is working.

The page came out of the fax machine and I tore it off. The fax was not a test page at all. It read: "Two containers of food are stranded in Louisiana at the harbor, waiting for someone to donate $2,500 per container. If you can help, please send a check."

I thought to myself, "How can this be? This company doesn't put that kind of test page in the machine. How could somebody who couldn't possibly know my fax number, send me a fax? How could it be that it came just the second I plugged in the machine? What difference does it make, there are people starving to death in Bosnia, I've got to help."

Retrieving Gospa Missions' checkbook, I looked at the balance. Gospa Missions, at that particular time had about twenty-seven hundred and some odd dollars in the checking account. I called the telephone number that was on that fax and I asked, "Do you folks have stranded food sitting on a dock in Louisiana?" They said yes, and I replied, "I don't know how I got your fax, but I got it, and really believe it's a miracle. I want to help. I am going to pay for one of those containers to be sent to Bosnia." They responded, "Praise the Lord, that's very kind of you."

I told them, "You've got to understand that I would pay for both containers if I had the money, but I don't have many benefactors who support my mission." They assured me that they were grateful for my paying for one container.

It was my plan to write out a check in the morning and send it off. I couldn't sleep that night; I was thinking, "What if no one sends the funds to cover the other container? These people are starving to death and here's the food sitting on a dock waiting for a benefactor. It will probably rot there if someone doesn't pay to ship it over."

I called the man back in the morning and I said, "I am sending you a check for five thousand dollars. I want you to know that I do not have five thousand dollars, but I am convinced, with all my heart, that God will take care of this."

"Thank you for your faith," he said and we ended the conversation. The check was made out for five thousand dollars. I don't know if the little statue of Jesus on the computer winked at me or not, but something was going on.

I put that check into the mail, returned to the house and the phone rang. It was a man with whom I was casually acquainted.

"Mr. Rutkoski, I just got a Christmas bonus from my boss and I would like to share it with your apostolate." "Thank you very much, I replied. "At this particular moment of my life, I can use a little sharing."

I wasn't going to tell him that I had just bounced a big check, but I said, "How much are you sending?" It was the exact amount to make good on that mailed check for five thousand dollars. The Infant Jesus of Prague came through just like that little devotional book said He would. *It is in giving that you receive.*

I was willing to give more than I had and the Lord took care of the problem. There is so much joy in receiving from the Lord that way. This kind of interaction with God encourages your conversion. It makes you have greater hope, faith and obviously, more charity. Even if it is from the Old Testament, I feel sorry for people who do not tithe at least ten percent to our Lord. They may not only be stealing from Him, but they could be robbing themselves of the treasure not made of gold. The grace lost in not giving generously from the heart could also be the cause of spiritual failure.

God is the only one we can trust. He takes care of business, so why do you and I have the reputation of being the worst Christian givers on earth? If God will do all these things in our lives, why do we have such a reputation? It's not as though we haven't earned it. Why isn't giving and its benefits so much better known within the Catholic Church?

> Jeremiah 13:1-15 *The Lord said to me: Go buy yourself a linen loincloth; wear it on your loins, but do not put it in water. I bought the loincloth, as the Lord commanded, and put it on. A second time the word of the Lord came to me thus: Take the loincloth which you bought and are wearing, and go now to the Parath; there hide it in a cleft of the rock. Obedient to the Lord's command, I went to the Parath and buried the loincloth. After a long interval, he said to me: Go now to the Parath and fetch the loincloth, which I told you to hide there. Again I went to the Parath, sought out and*

took the loincloth from the place where I had hid it. But it was rotted, good for nothing!

Then the message came to me from the Lord: Thus says the Lord: So also I will allow the pride of Judah to rot, the great pride of Jerusalem. This wicked people who refuse to obey my words, who walk in the stubbornness of their hearts, and follow strange gods to serve and adore them, shall be like this loincloth which is good for nothing. For, as close as the loincloth clings to a man's loins, so had I made the whole house of Israel and the whole house of Judah cling to me, says the Lord; to be my people, my renown, my raise, my beauty. But they did not listen.

Now speak to them this word: Thus says the Lord, the God of Israel: Every wine flask is meant to be filled with wine. If they reply, "Do we not know that every wine flask is meant to be filled with wine?" say to them: Thus says the Lord: Beware! I am filling with drunkenness all the inhabitants of this land, the kings who succeed to David's throne, the priests and prophets, and all the citizens of Jerusalem. I will dash them against each other, fathers and sons together, says the Lord; I will show no compassion, I will not spare or pity, but will destroy them.

We keep selling ourselves on the great mercy of God and how He is going to forgive even the iniquities we do not ask to have forgiven. We are sadly mistaken. God set aside His chosen Jews and struck them, so why would He be so merciful to us Gentiles? We conveniently forget God's justice. The Lord our God treats all with equity and so He will not spare us. If we do not change and return to the Lord as a holy people, we will see God's wrath. Let there be no mistake about it, we will suffer for our lack of giving. Yet there will be people who read this and believe I am wrong, and I am not.

To those who turn back to God with all of their heart, there is where we find the mercy of our Father in heaven. In returning to Him as prodigal sons and daughters, we receive grace.

God was not finished teaching me about giving and receiving. There came a time that I needed a new car for Gospa Missions and I said to the Lord, "I need a new car." The Isuzu Trooper I was driving had many miles on it and it was time to replace it or risk investing a lot of money to keep it roadworthy. I said to the Lord, "When You send me to speak some place and I am driving, You expect me to be there on time. It would just be better if we get a new car that we could trust. Besides, this one is six years old." An afterthought was, "If you are going to get me a new car, Lord, why don't You make it a Ford Expedition… maybe green?"

If you are going to ask, you might as well ask for what you really need. If you don't ask for what you need, He might send you a tiny Volkswagen Bug when you need a S.U.V. What am I going to do with a Volkswagen? That's great transportation, but I have to haul all of our religious goods around to raise funds to build orphanages. Sometimes I have to get there in deep snow. So I was asking for a sports utility vehicle with four-wheel drive.

I was driving down the road that following week, on my way to evening Mass, and in front of me were six cars and a tractor-trailer. I was a bit upset because I was late. This tractor-trailer has his left turn signal on to turn onto PA Route 528. A vehicle that size is not allowed on Route 528 because it has a ten-ton weight limit. But sure enough, that driver turned left, and I followed behind him and the other six cars. At about ten miles an hour he labored up the first hill…ten miles an hour over the backside of the hill. Then it was ten miles an hour up the next hill…I was getting more upset…all of a sudden, I couldn't believe what was happening.

Right before my eyes, I saw the truck now coming down the hill backwards, and he crushed the six cars in front of me, one at a time. I'm thinking to myself, "My God, I am not going under that truck." My wife was sitting beside me, but we were not talking about it; this was happening so fast we didn't have time to talk about it. To escape being crushed by this tractor-trailer, I made a hard right. I did not care what was to the right; I was not going under the truck. Splooosh, right into a pond, and the Isuzu sank halfway up its doors. It was December in Pennsylvania and the water was very cold…I was freezing stuff off while sitting there. Surely the thought went through my mind, "Way to go, God. I asked you for a new car; now look what You did." Judges of God is what we are. God is in the midst if working a miracle in my life and I'm complaining to Him.

The next day the insurance company came. "Mr. Rutkoski, we are going to total your Isuzu." I was puzzled. "Why," I said, "it's only wet?" The adjustor replied, "Once they're wet up to that level, we want no part of them." I said, "It wasn't even the whole way in the pond, only the front end." He basically repeated, "Once they are in the water we don't want to support them."

I was quite frustrated "How much are you going to give me?" You know what dealing with insurance companies is like. You never really know what kind of a deal you're going to get. The agent said, "We are going to give you $16,500.00."

"You are going to give me what? Why would you give me $16,500.00 for an Isuzu that's six years old and has all those miles on it?" The guy looked at me and asked, "Are you arguing with me?" I came to my senses quickly. "No, no – write the check."

Then I asked, "What are you going to do with the Isuzu?" The reply was, " We will sell it to a junk yard."

"Could I buy it?" I asked. "Yes, if you want." He did a little math and said, "You can buy it for $4,000.00. In fact, this is what I'll do right now. I'll write you a check for $12,500.00 and you keep the Isuzu." "You've got a deal." I answered. My best guess was that the Isuzu was worth probably $10,000.00 the way it sat there.

I had taken the Isuzu home, dried it all out and cleaned it up. When I turned the key after I finished, it fired right up and ran like a top. A buddy of mine actually offered me $10,000.00 for the Isuzu after I had cleaned it up. Now remember, I lied to get out of high school, so my math isn't that great. I need your help here….I have a check for $12,500.00 in my hand, a guy offers me $10,000.00 for the car…am I correct in my figures? Was

I getting what amounted to $22,500.00 for an Isuzu for which I paid less than $20,000.00 brand new six years prior, right out of the show room? My goodness, God was tithing to me! This is wonderful! Why was I beating God up in the middle of this great miracle?

That is how our God works when you are in need and you are in His favor. I was giving my life to God and He was proving to me that it is *in giving you receive*. I don't know how you get your cars, but you might consider other alternatives. If it is not obvious to us that we have too much unshared wealth in the United States, it is to God. The Lord gave us this great wealth so we might share it with others, but most do not and there is a price to be paid for that failure. Some pay the price now and some will pay the price of this failure later, but most assuredly it will be paid. Do not ever delude yourself to think you do not have to share equitably your wealth with the poor.

I was speaking in Titusville, Pennsylvania, years ago. As I came into the church, I asked the pastor where I could set up my religious goods to sell. He told me I could set them up right there in the church. I looked at him and said, "In the church? No, I can't set them up in the church." He responded, "Of course you can. Just set them up here in the corner or someplace." I said "No, no, don't you remember the Scripture where the Lord came into the temple, and He saw people selling doves, and lambs there. He flipped over tables and He started reading the riot act to these guys. I'm not going to have God come into this church and start flipping over my tables. I would prefer to give this stuff away first." He said, "That's fine. Give it away."

That night I gave away about eight hundred dollars worth of religious goods and books. Well, Gospa Missions operates on a small budget. Eight hundred dollars is a large amount of money to us. But it wasn't worth having God showing up and flipping over the tables. I didn't need that kind of lesson, so I just gave it away. About three weeks after the talk, we got a letter and a check in the mail from a woman who hadn't even attended. She stated in her letter that her mother and her sisters came to hear me talk and they had told her all about it. All of them had been very touched by the presentation. It had really changed their lives - given them a new perspective. They also were impressed at the end when I gave everything away. They said they couldn't understand how I could afford to do that. The family had said to the writer of the letter, "He said in the presentation that he didn't have a job; he had no income. How could he give all these items away?"

This correspondent was working in Tennessee at the time. When she relocated there to assume her new position, her employer had given her a certain amount of money to cover moving expenses. She said it hadn't cost her that much to move. However she managed to do it, she ended up with a check in her hands for around eight hundred dollars. She thought, "I might just use this to get some new tires for my car, and just as quickly changed her mind. She heard in her head, "Give it to a mission."

"Okay, I'll give it to a mission," she replied. All of a sudden, two and two equaled four in her life, because her parents told her about a mission that gave all their religious items away. Gospa Missions was the one to whom she decided to send that check. It covered precisely all the things we gave away that night. You can't beat God. He takes care of business every single time. Only fools do not get to see God in action.

Not only did that gift pay for all the religious goods we gave away, the donor was so impressed that she wanted to go on pilgrimage with us. In July of 1999, she went on pilgrimage with Gospa Missions – which included the rededication of St. Anne Church in Dubrovnik, Croatia.

She really enjoyed herself on that trip. As I mentioned, I like a good time. I like to pray hard and I like to play hard. So on this pilgrimage, we prayed hard. We said fifteen decades of the Rosary each day, we went to Mass every day, we fasted a couple of days, but while we were in Dubrovnik for the rededication of St. Anne Church, we rented a three-masted schooner. It was filled with everything we needed for a day of partying on the Adriatic: fresh mackerel, smelt, vegetables, beer and wine. Most everyone took along bathing suits, and there we were in the middle of the Adriatic diving off the boat and we were having just a great time.

It took great convincing to get the captain of that ship to let us dive off of that boat. We really wanted to take advantage of this great adventure. We were like kids again, and we were having a blast. When we finished swimming in the sea, and it was time to get back on the boat, we were exhausted from all the water activity. Turns out that the only way to return to the ship was to climb up a rope! The twenty-foot distance was easy enough for the young folks to climb, but then there was me, this old man. I fought with everything I had to get back up this rope, as did the other elderly people who had jumped into the water with us. Finally, we got everybody back in the boat. We were rejoicing while we opened up a beer. I thanked the Captain for allowing us the experience. Then asked him, "Why don't you have a ladder? Wouldn't it make it easier for people who dive off of this boat to use a ladder to get back aboard?" He revealed, "I used to have a ladder, and people did dive off of the boat all the time. But then sharks were discovered in the water, so I put a stop to the diving.

"SHARKS! You mean there are sharks in this water? If I had known that I would have had no problem getting up that rope."

Our young donor had such a good time on that trip, and we had some conversations about this and one day she said to me, "You know, I really feel like giving my life to God, just as you did." I said, "Why don't you come to Gospa Missions and give your life there." I say that to almost everybody I meet and I say that to you as reader of this book also (especially if you know how to develop a web site. We really need somebody who knows the Internet.) Every once in the while, somebody takes me seriously, and this young woman did. And she walked out of her career, a career that paid her well. When she announced that she was leaving, her company offered her a promotion and wanted to send her to sunny California. She turned them down and told her employer that she was going to give her life to God. Backing up her words with action, she came to Gospa Missions a few months later and became our general manager.

She made a very big difference in Gospa Missions. In fact, she invited another woman, Betty Diegelman, to give her life to

God and Gospa Missions as our bookkeeper. And did we need a bookkeeper. But do you see what happened from one act of giving? The impact of each and every act of giving brings with it a tidal wave of grace. I was not willing to insult the Lord by selling stuff in a church and so I gave everything away. So we see that God replaced all the money, and sent us a very talented general manager and bookkeeper and the Mission continued to grow. *It is in giving that you receive.*

When you give from your want, it works. Do you understand that? To give from your surplus is not something that impresses God all that much, but when you feel what you give, you become God's friend. The trouble with Catholics is that they do not trust God enough; they don't have the faith of that mustard seed God mentions. If you do not try to share an equitable portion of your time, talent and treasure, you will not see much of your God in action. Action, that is, in a positive way. If you do not do it His way, you may also see Him in action, but it is not the kind of action you really want to see.

For this next scenario to have the proper impact, you have to understand that I was speaking to a Catholic audience when I told the following story:

I was speaking in Puerto Rico and it was related to me that there was a local Protestant minister who had a neat style of operating. With everybody in his congregation sitting down, he would say to them, "You see that gold you all have on? To whom does that belong: those rings, the earrings the bracelets, the watches, the chains – to whom does all that gold belong?"

"What do you think they said? Remember, these are Protestants in his audience, not Catholics. They shouted out, 'God!' So I figure we will try that today. 'To whom does all your stuff belong?" The response was half-hearted, to say the least. So I responded, 'Hey, the other folks were really excited. They yelled it out from their hearts.' Now I love the Protestants dearly, and I see that sometimes they out perform us Catholics, but I also know we can do better. They out-sing us, they out-give us, they out-evangelize us, and they are taking people out of the Catholic Church. But I know that if we were encouraged, we could do better. So let's just try to do a little better right now.' And I tried again in a little louder voice, "Do you see that gold you have on: the rings, the watches, and the bracelets? TO WHOM DOES THAT GOLD BELONG?' The response came back a little more exuberant than the previous one – 'God!'

"That's pretty good. You really did much better. The Protestants really screamed it out, but you were almost there. There's hope for you," I promised.

'Guess what that minister said then? Quite excitedly he said, 'You're right – it all belongs to God. You've learned your lesson well. Guess what? He's calling it in today. Pass it up here.' And they started taking it off: their watches, their necklaces, their bracelets and they are putting it in the collection plate. Pretty impressive, is it not? Could you imagine watching the excitement of people giving to God in a big way? So I kind of figured we'd try that today. Why don't we just pass the hat right now and you all can put in your jewelry, and everything gold? Wouldn't that be great?' I heard a deafening silence and then a few chuckles. I responded with, "There are two chances of that, right?

I played around with that from talk to talk and I tried to convince Catholics to do that, in a joking way. Sometimes I would say, "I am probably embarrassing you, watching as I am, so I will turn around." I turn around and there would be Jesus up there on the wall, at the front of the church and I'd say, "Are they doing it, Lord?" No, they weren't.

One day at a presentation of mine, about eight times into telling the story and playing around with my Catholic friends, after the free will offering, there was a little gold ring in the basket. A tear trickled down my cheek, and I thought, "Look at that – there was a Protestant in the audience."

I joked around with this for several months until I found myself speaking in Washington State. I ended the talks that same way. I didn't know this happened until the following year when I returned to Washington, but one lady in the audience took my appeal to heart. That next year the woman approached me and said, "Mr. Rutkoski, last year you were here and you were joking about the Protestant minister in Puerto Rico who had his flock pass up all their gold. When I heard that I said to God, 'Lord, we are not wealthy people. We are farmers and we just barely make it from year to year. I don't have any gold to give this man except my wedding band. You certainly wouldn't want me to give him my wedding band?'

She said, "I have not been able to get the wedding band off my hand in six years – I've tried soap, I've tried oil, I've tried everything and I cannot get it off. 'I'll tell you what, Lord. You make that ring come off, and I'll give it to the man.' She revealed that, at that moment, she reached down and pulled on the ring and it slid right off her finger. The woman put her wedding band in the collection plate.

She then informed me that a cherry blight had come to the cherry farmers of Washington State that year. Most everybody lost their crop - but not them. Their farm had harvested a bumper crop of the most select cherries they'd ever grown. They sold them to the Japanese for a premium price. She claims they had never done so well.

"It was the ring," she stated. Of course it was. It was the widow's mite. She had given from their want, something as cherished as a wedding band.

Now many people are willing to give us their wedding rings and it's because their marriages are falling apart. If the marriage is working, the rings are something very prized in a family. Maybe you want to hand yours down to your children; it is not easy to part with, but this woman found out that *it is in giving that you receive.*

I see it played out over and over and over again. There are churches, Catholic Churches (can you believe it?), that have started stewardship programs in their parishes. These programs essentially re-introduce to parishioners the time-honored tradition of tithing. Can you guess what is happening in those parishes? They no longer have to do parish festivals. They no longer have to run bingo games, sell raffle tickets or hold bake sales.

They no longer have to strain to create challenging ways to coax a little giving out of their members. Instead of putting their efforts toward raising funds, they turned their fund raising efforts to spiritual matters. The parishes begin to grow. The faith of the members of the church became stronger. People would pray for the sick and the sick would get well. *It's in giving that you receive.*

The parishes are now starting to get vocations. All God has to see you doing is taking care of His business. And when you do it God's way, a whole world opens up, like a flower on Easter morning. The lily blooms, becomes something very beautiful, and all of a sudden you can see God at work in your life.

I come to encourage you. The readers of this book are from all walks of life. God expects a portion from each and every one of us. At this point in history, that portion is far below what God seems to expect. Start giving more today and then you can go on from there and increase your giving as you see grace come. But if we all start giving more, we will see growth in our Church once again. And our Church can use some growth. So what do you think? Can we wake up and start doing what God asked for a long time ago? Can we start putting in our fair share in the basket every week?

If you start giving more, you are probably going to have to help your pastor get dressed, because you are going to shock the pants right off him. Catholics who now actually are giving the proper amount - who are these people? They must be converts from the Protestant churches. If this is true, we could use a lot more of them. There are things we can learn from Protestants and much they can learn from Catholics.

Someone asked me this question after one of my tithing presentations: "Should I give a percentage of my net or of my gross?" Think about it. "God pays back a hundredfold," I told him. "Do you want a hundredfold return on the net or the gross?" We need to get smart in our investing in God.

If you try this out for six months, you will find out how much God meant tithing as a gift for you. I don't know if this happened in your state, but there was one man out there paying for billboards to be put all over the United States. They are black signs with white letters and they proclaim a variety of thoughts from God in a humorous way. I am sure one of them says, "You know that tithing thing? I meant that. Signed God." Another sign read, "What part of 'thou shalt not…' don't you understand? Signed God." There were millions of dollars worth of these billboards. It was one man investing to point out to us that God meant that. And tithing or giving – God meant that. So I encourage you to find out what my wife and I have found out: it is in giving that you receive. You will find the joy of the Lord in giving, your conversion will move forward and we will all benefit in the Catholic Church from your newfound hope. God will bless every one of us when each one of us steps forward to do a little more.

Ladies and gentlemen, may I present, for your edification, the slam-dunk of giving. Many people could possibly lose their salvation over this and if they don't lose their salvation, spend a lot of time in purgatory for it. There is a document that we sign before we die, our last will and testament and because of this document many will suffer. Let me give you a piece of Scripture here so you will know from where I am coming.

> Luke 19:12-27 *So he said, "A nobleman went off to a distant country to obtain the kingship for himself and then to return. He called ten of his servants and gave them ten gold coins and told them, 'Engage in trade with these until I return.' His fellow citizens, however, despised him and sent a delegation after him to announce, 'We do not want this man to be our king.' But when he returned after obtaining the kingship, he had the servants called, to whom he had given the money, to learn what they had gained by trading. The first came forward and said, 'Sir, your gold coin has earned ten additional ones.' He replied, 'Well-done, good servant! You have been faithful in this very small matter; take charge of ten cities.' Then the second came and reported, 'Your gold coin, sir, has earned five more.' And to this servant too he said, 'You, take charge of five cities.' Then the other servant came and said, 'Sir, here is your gold coin; I kept it stored away in a handkerchief, for I was afraid*

of you, because you are a demanding person; you take up what you did not lay down and you harvest what you did not plant.'

He said to him, 'with your own words I shall condemn you, you wicked servant. You knew I was a demanding person, taking up what I did not lay down and harvesting what I did not plant; why did you not put my money in a bank? Then on my return I would have collected it with interest.' And to those standing by he said, 'Take the gold coin from him and give it to the servant who has ten.' But they said to him, 'Sir, he has ten gold coins.'

'I tell you, to everyone who has, more will be given, but from the one who has little, even what little he has will be taken away.

Now as for those enemies of mine who did not want me as their king, bring them here and slay them before me.'"

The reason God placed this parable in Scripture is for all to understand that the Lord has invested much in each one of us and He expects a return. You came into this world with nothing. When you leave this world, you will leave with nothing. All that you possessed while you were here belonged to God; it was only on loan to you. Now you have a decision to make prior to your death. Are you going to return to God what is rightfully His, with interest, or are you going to squander what is God's on your children? If you have children in great need, God will not be outraged if you help them. If you take what is God's and give it to children who already have so much, and who will only buy more possessions with it, more than likely you will offend God. And it will cost you much.

An intelligent, Godly individual, will see that all that he has gathered here on earth will be his legacy after his death and go on supplying the grace for his sainthood long after his bodily demise.

I beg of you to start investing in your heavenly retirement today. Far too many people save for their very short earthly retirement and invest almost nothing in a retirement that will last forever.

To the contrary, instead of investing in sainthood, many people give to dogs and let God's creatures with eternal souls die a horrible death of starvation. One only has to do a little research to find out the billions of dollars that Americans spend on pets rather than feeding starving human beings. God provides for all animals in the wild and expects us to provide for each other. A great portion of our possible sainthood is based on how well we take care of each other.

> Luke 10:25-37 *There was a scholar of the law who stood up to test him and said, "Teacher, what must I do to inherit eternal life?" Jesus said to him, "What is written in the law? How do you read it?" He said in reply, "You shall love the Lord, your God, with all your heart, with all your being, with all your strength, and with all your mind, and your neighbor as yourself." He replied to him, "You have answered correctly; do this and you will live." But because he wished to justify himself, he said to Jesus, "And who is my neighbor?" Jesus replied, "A man fell victim to robbers as he went down from Jerusalem to Jericho. They stripped and beat him and went off leaving him half-dead.*
>
> *A priest happened to be going down that road, but when he saw him, he passed by on the opposite side. Likewise a Levite came to the place, and when he saw him, he passed by on the opposite side. But a Samaritan traveler who came upon him was moved with compassion at the sight. He approached the victim, poured oil and wine over his wounds and bandaged them. Then he lifted him up on his own animal, took him to an inn and cared for him. The next day he took out two silver coins and gave them to the innkeeper with the instruction, 'Take care of him. If you spend more than what I have given you, I shall repay you on my way back.' Which*

of these three, in your opinion, was neighbor to the robbers' victim?" He answered, "The one who treated him with mercy." Jesus said to him, "Go and do likewise."

All of your giving does not have to go to the Catholic Church, but I would advise you to give at least five percent of your income to the Church, thus multiplying your average church donation by five times. The other portion you should distribute to people who are doing God's work as lay people. I do not consider the United Way a Godly act of giving; in fact I believe that it helps Satan more. If you give to Planned Parenthood or the NOW organization, these are big problems and they will cost you dearly. If you give to the American Cancer Society or any other health-related foundation or non-Godly entity, I believe you are wasting God's precious money. You can donate for a possible cure down the road or you can feed a starving human today. Which is better?

The first is a possible help in the future and the second is guaranteed help and is a directive by God Himself. So why choose research over certain death for starving people?

He who has ears, let him hear. If you have a problem with giving to God what is rightfully His, I do not know if going back to the beginning of this book is going to help you. I personally believe that your sainthood is becoming doubtful. Get down on your knees and beg God for a renewal of conscience. If you are willing to start giving your fair share and take care of God's business, continue on to Chapter Eleven. You are becoming a possible candidate for sainthood.

NOTES

Chapter Eleven

Love

Love is probably the most misinterpreted, most misused word in existence. You can use Webster's explanation to try to define love, but it will not. When the world's interpretation is applied, it cannot get you into heaven. It will not make you a saint.

There is nothing more beautiful than two people in love. A husband and a wife, absolute best friends, supporting and building each other up, leading each other to sainthood - that is love. When we procreate and bring children into the world and raise those children to honor, respect and fear God - that is love.

To strive to please God our Father in all we do - that is love. To try to bring as many souls to the Lord as we can before our inevitable death - that is love.

To feed the poor, visit the widows and prisoners and take care of an orphan - that is love.

To place others' needs before our own and living a life that one would lay down so another's life may be spared - that is love.

Here is when authentic love takes a turn from God and gets you involved in division. When you live for yourself, you divide yourself from God. When you gather and store for yourself, you turn from God. Here is a prime example of self-love. "If you loved me you would __________" (fill in the blank). That's division.

Two people say they are "in love." One coerces the other to break God's laws to prove what? Love? Not hardly. A man and a woman, not married to each other in the eyes of God, cannot engage in any kind of sexual relationship and expect to go to heaven. The sin would be a death sentence unless they repent, go to confession and give up their sins against God's law on the use of sexuality and begin to live according to God's word and the teaching of the Church.

If you are a person who longs for a hot, sweaty and impassioned premarital moment, then you are not a person on the correct path to authentic love. Love is not found in words or the back seat of a Chevy. Love is silent action manifested in wonderful deeds. Love is a young man never attempting to topple virginity until he is married.

It was Jewish law to stone a man and a woman for the offense of having sex before marriage and for adultery. If the same were true today, we would not have many men and women alive, would we? A real man or a real woman is one who respects not only each other, but God's laws and enjoys being obedient to those laws.

Two males or two females are sexually attracted to each other and they act out their fantasies and they want to call that love. You cannot do that, leave it unforgiven, and be a saint. You cross that chasm and end up on the wrong side.

Being a practicing homosexual is not love; it is sin. I don't care if it is your son, daughter, mother, father or your pastor, it is mortal sin to be actively involved in a gay lifestyle and if you do not help them to get out of the sin, it could cost you *your* salvation. Am I my brother's keeper? YES! Anyone who tries to sell you on the goodness of gay relations has handed their soul over to Satan. They have crossed the great divide and entered into darkness. Do not confuse homosexuality tendencies with sin. If one is inclined to become involved in homosexuality and fights off the inclination, that person is on the correct path.

> Romans 1: 18–32 *The wrath of God is indeed being revealed from heaven against every impiety and wickedness of those who suppress the truth by their wickedness. For what can be known about God is evident to them, because God made it evident to them. Ever since the creation of the world, his invisible attributes of eternal power and divinity have been able to be understood and perceived in what he has made. As a result, they have no excuse; for although they knew God they did not accord him glory as God or give him thanks. Instead, they became vain in their reasoning, and their*

senseless minds were darkened. While claiming to be wise, they became fools and exchanged the glory of the immortal God for the likeness of an image of mortal man or of birds or of four-legged animals or of snakes. Therefore, God handed them over to impurity through the lusts of their hearts for the mutual degradation of their bodies. They exchanged the truth of God for a lie and revered and worshiped the creature rather than the creator, who is blessed forever. Amen.

Therefore, God handed them over to degrading passions. Their females exchanged natural relations for unnatural, and the males likewise gave up natural relations with females and burned with lust for one another. Males did shameful things with males and thus received in their own persons the due penalty for their perversity. And since they did not see fit to acknowledge God, God handed them over to their undiscerning mind to do what is improper.

They are filled with every form of wickedness, evil, greed, and malice; full of envy, murder, rivalry, treachery, and spite. They are gossips and scandalmongers and they hate God. They are insolent, haughty, boastful, ingenious in their wickedness, and rebellious toward their parents. They are senseless, faithless, heartless, ruthless. Although they know the just decree of God that all who practice such things deserve death, they not only do them, but give approval to those who practice them.

If we just look at the "degrading passions" part, it is enough to make you ill. This is the part the promoters of active homosexuality do not want you to know about. And before you find out the truth, they want laws passed to have their lifestyle legally protected. For the past several years, national television shows display gays as kind, loving, normal people. They want to adopt children. Do gay couples want to adopt children because they are compassionate towards the plight of these children? Or are they are impassioned in a predatory way and see the children as fair game for a perverse lifestyle?

You can ask a gay person what it is that he does in the relationship that replaces marital intercourse. It is doubtful that you will get honest answers from someone who has surrendered to the evil one, so just use your imagination to figure out what they are really doing in the name of love. If you need or want an explanation, call me. My number is in the back of the book and I will explain it to you.

Now ask yourself if this is what you want your children learning in school? God destroyed Sodom and Gomorrah for the very reasons listed above and our society wants to label this disgusting perversion as a third lifestyle. If you do not protect your children, the evil one will snatch them up into his web of filth and do it right in your local school, before your very eyes. We have become far too tolerant to the wicked ways of others. If you want to go to heaven, it is time you stood up to defend love.

Evil men, clothed in religious garb, who could be homosexuals themselves, produced a document for our Church called *Always Our Children,* to teach us tolerance and support for gays. There can be no tolerance for the practice of homosexuality, but there can be support for all homosexuals, practicing or not. They are, indeed, our children who need a very big dose of authentic love, correction and forgiveness. Thanks be to God for the orthodox bishops who stood up and said that this document did not reflect the true teachings of the Catholic Church. The document did accomplish one thing: it exposed those on the committee who propagated this lie for what they really are - antichrists. There is no love involved in trying to lead the flock down a path to hell.

How is it that so many of our actions are justified in our minds and make us do battle with God? We tell God, "You are wrong and we are right." What is it? What is it that makes what used to be right, now wrong and what was wrong, now right? It is the evil one. It is the demon or demons in us, directing our thoughts. Do you have demons in you? If you support contraception, abortion, homosexuality, rebellion and the breaking of the Ten Commandments, you have demons. If the sin is mortal and goes uncorrected, you go to hell. You can refute the teachings of the Lord all you want, but one fact remains: God is God and we are not. You cannot alter God's laws to fit your demon's directions and expect to be called a friend of God (a.k.a. saint.) We choose every day whose side we are on. One day you can be a sheep and the next day cross the great divide and become a goat.

You can argue with the Church all you want about its rules, but the fact remains: God gave Peter the right to make rules on earth that would be bound in heaven and when you break those rules in the form of mortal sins and you do not get them repaired, you cross over.

It started with Peter, and those who knew the true love of God and stayed with that Church. Others, in redefining God's laws without any authority and without love, steered multitudes away from the authentic teaching to that of the demon within.

Keep in mind that love is patient and forbearing. Love is something that knows obedience. Demons taught by Satan only know disobedience. So a good rule of thumb to use in discerning who is leading you is obedience. Bishops disobedient to the Magisterium do not know love and will not be saints. Priests disobedient to bishops do not know love and will not be saints. Children after the age of reason who dishonor their parents do not know love and will not be saints. Anyone disobedient to moral civil law that is in tune with God's law, does not know love and will not be a saint.

Let me clarify this. Obviously I am talking about unconfessed sin. How can the world's people who do not confess their mortal sins become saints? This is a touchy subject for many people, but we have to consider that the Catholic Church taught for all of its history that there is no salvation outside of the Church. In recent times we see a modified perspective of this teaching, but I know the Church has never rescinded this dogmatic teaching, nor could it. Can God have one rule for Catholics. one for Jews and still yet another rule for others? Can He? I would not think so. That would not be love. But it is taught today that there are a few loopholes allowing salvation outside the Catholic Church proper, but the applications of those are very limited and difficult to fulfill.

There are those who have abandoned love and taken on the harlot relationship prescribed by Satan himself. The path chosen today by many is not the path to righteousness, but the path to hell. But today we are advised to not mention hell. It is not politically correct. If you talk about hell, you are not a loving person. This discouragement in itself is the talk of the demons. True love is warning someone in danger and telling him or her what that danger is. The reason I am mentioning hell in this book so much is because I love you and because the evil one has been working so very hard to eliminate the word from our vocabulary altogether.

It sounds almost impossible to become a saint, but the truth is, it just takes a small attitude adjustment. Decide today whose side you are on. You need to decide for God. You need to fall in love with God. We cannot really love anyone else until we love God more than all else.

Love, the kind that makes saints, is quite different from what is called love in our conversations, read about in books or see on television. When we love God's way, it is always accompanied by gifts. When used properly love becomes a direct path to sainthood.

> 1 Corinthians 12:1–15:58 *Now in regard to spiritual gifts, brothers, I do not want you to be unaware. You know how, when you were pagans, you were constantly attracted and led away to mute idols. Therefore, I tell you that nobody speaking by the spirit of God says, "Jesus be accursed." And no one can say, "Jesus is Lord," except by the Holy Spirit. There are different kinds of spiritual gifts but the same Spirit; there are different forms of service but the same Lord; there are different workings but the same God who produces all of them in everyone.*
>
> *To each individual the manifestation of the Spirit is given for some benefit. To one is given through the Spirit the expression of wisdom; to another the expression of knowledge according to the same Spirit; to another faith by the same Spirit; to another gifts of healing by the one Spirit; to another mighty deeds; to another prophecy; to another discernment of spirits; to another varieties of*

tongues; to another interpretation of tongues. But one and the same Spirit produces all of these, distributing them individually to each person as he wishes.

As a body is one though it has many parts, and all the parts of the body, though many, are one body, so also Christ. For in one Spirit we were all baptized into one body, whether Jews or Greeks, slaves or free persons, and we were all given to drink of one Spirit.

Now the body is not a single part, but many. If a foot should say, "Because I am not a hand I do not belong to the body," it does not for this reason belong any less to the body. Or if an ear should say, "Because I am not an eye I do not belong to the body," it does not for this reason belong any less to the body.

If the whole body were an eye, where would the hearing be? If the whole body were hearing, where would the sense of smell be? But as it is, God placed the parts, each one of them, in the body as he intended. If they were all one part, where would the body be? But as it is, there are many parts, yet one body. The eye cannot say to the hand, "I do not need you," nor again the head to the feet, "I do not need you." Indeed, the parts of the body that seem to be weaker are all the more necessary, and those parts of the body that we consider less honorable we surround with greater honor, and our less presentable parts are treated with greater propriety, whereas our more presentable parts do not need this. But God has so constructed the body as to give greater honor to a part that is without it, so that there may be no division in the body, but that the parts may have the same concern for one another.

If (one) part suffers, all the parts suffer with it; if one part is honored, all the parts share its joy. Now you are Christ's body, and individually parts of it. Some people God has designated in the church to be, first, apostles; second, prophets; third, teachers; then, mighty deeds; then, gifts of healing, assistance, administration, and varieties of tongues. Are all apostles? Are all prophets? Are all teachers? Do all work mighty deeds? Do all have gifts of healing? Do all speak in tongues? Do all interpret? Strive eagerly for the greatest spiritual gifts. But I shall show you a still more excellent way.

If I speak in human and angelic tongues but do not have love, I am a resounding gong or a clashing cymbal. And if I have the gift of prophecy and comprehend all mysteries and all knowledge; if I have all faith so as to move mountains but do not have love, I am nothing. If I give away everything I own, and if I hand my body over so that I may boast but do not have love, I gain nothing.

Love is patient. Love is kind. It is not jealous, (love) is not pompous, it is not inflated, it is not rude, it does not seek its own interests, it is not quick-tempered, it does not brood over injury, it does not rejoice over wrongdoing but rejoices with the truth. It bears all things, believes all things, hopes all things, endures all things. Love never fails.

If there are prophecies, they will be brought to nothing; if tongues, they will cease; if knowledge, it will be brought to nothing. For we know partially and we prophesy partially, but when the perfect comes, the partial will pass away. When I was a child, I used to talk as a child, think as a child, reason as a child; when I became a man, I put aside childish things.

At present we see indistinctly, as in a mirror, but then face to face. At present I know partially; then I shall know fully, as I am fully known. So faith, hope, love remain, these three; but the greatest of these is love.

Pursue love, but strive eagerly for the spiritual gifts, above all that you may prophesy. For one who speaks in a tongue does not speak to human beings but to God, for no one listens; he utters mysteries in spirit. On the other hand, one who prophesies does speak to human beings, for their building up, encouragement, and solace. Whoever speaks in a tongue builds himself up, but whoever prophesies builds up the church. Now I should like all of you to speak in tongues, but even more to prophesy. One who prophesies is greater than one who speaks in tongues, unless he interprets, so that the church may be built up.

This I declare, brothers: flesh and blood cannot inherit the kingdom of God, nor does corruption inherit incorruption. Behold, I tell you a mystery. We shall not all fall asleep, but we will all be changed, in an instant, in the blink of an eye, at the last trumpet. For the trumpet will sound, the dead will be raised incorruptible, and we shall be changed. For that which is corruptible must clothe itself with incorruptibility, and that which is mortal must clothe itself with immortality. And when this, which is corruptible, clothes itself with incorruptibility and this which is mortal, clothes itself with immortality, then the word that is written shall come about: "Death is swallowed up in victory.

Where, O death, is your victory? Where, O death, is your sting?" The sting of death is sin, and the power of sin is the law. But thanks be to God who gives us the victory through our Lord Jesus Christ. Therefore, my beloved brothers, be firm, steadfast, always fully devoted to the work of the Lord, knowing that in the Lord your labor is not in vain.

As you strive to become Godly you become sanctified. As you strive and seek perfect love, you are seeking sanctification. The honor of sainthood is reserved for those who seek with all their being the loving, living God.

I pray that you will alter your course today, no matter how holy you think you are, so that any imperfection may be ferreted out and the grace of God will fill your entire self so completely that love becomes your trademark. I pray that you will not only know love, but you will be love. Love and sainthood are synonymous.

If you understand all of this, continue on to Chapter Twelve.

NOTES

CHAPTER TWELVE

HUMILITY

Humility is a supernatural virtue whereby one is enabled to make a true and just estimate of herself and she can know in her heart that she came from dust and to dust she will return. Knowing the true value of dust, one then recognizes that all good comes from God. A humble person does not seek honors and esteem, but forwards that to God if it comes in her direction. A humble person is not necessarily meek, so she could stand up in a bold way to defend the Church.

If I were to guide anyone in the direction of humility, I could not, in all honesty, make many suggestions, for I am having great difficulty in that area myself. The best I can do is point you in the direction that I turn to for my own help. I would have to guide you to a book by Thomas a Kempis, *My Imitation of Christ.* The specific book I use here is from the Confraternity of the Precious Blood. Countless scholars and theologians have used this astounding work for hundreds of years to further their journey towards humility and thus on to sainthood. Any time I feel a little puffed up with myself, I get out my audio tape copy of Thomas's work and soon find that I am not what I think I am.

How anyone could read *My Imitation of Christ* and not be humbled by it is beyond my comprehension. Humility is the window to the soul. If someone is truly humble, there is an authenticity to her faith that is obvious. If you want to exit this world with grace, make this book a mandatory read. I have placed here a few short chapters from it for your advancement.

Having an Humble Opinion of Oneself

> All men naturally desire to know, but what does knowledge avail without the fear of God? Indeed a humble farmer that serves God is better than a proud philosopher, who, neglecting himself, considers the course of the heavens.

He who knows himself well is mean in his own eyes and is not delighted with being praised by men. If I should know all things that are in the world and should not be in charity what would it avail me in the sight of God, who will judge me by my deeds?

Leave off that excessive desire of knowing: because there is found therein much distraction and deceit. They who are learned are desirous to appear, and to be called wise. There are many things, the knowledge of which is of little or no profit to the soul. And he is very unwise who attends to other things than what may serve to his salvation. Many words do not satisfy the soul; but a good life gives ease to the mind; and a pure conscience affords a great confidence in God.

The more and better you know the heavier your judgment will be unless your life be also more holy. Be not, therefore, puffed up with any art or science; but rather fear because of the knowledge edge, which is given you. If it seems to you that you know many things and understand them well enough, know at the same time that there are many more things of which you are ignorant. Be not high-minded, but rather acknowledge your ignorance. Why would you prefer yourself to any one, since there are many more learned and skillful in the law than yourself? If you would know and learn anything to the purpose, love to be unknown and esteemed as nothing.

This is the highest science and most profitable lesson, truly to know and despise ourselves. To have no opinion of ourselves and to think always well and commendably of others, is great wisdom and high perfection. If you should see another openly sin or commit some heinous crime, yet you ought not to esteem yourself better: because you know not how long you may remain in a good state. We are all frail, but see you think no one more frail than yourself.

Avoiding Vain Hope and Pride

He is vain who puts his trust in men or in creatures. Be not ashamed to serve others and to appear poor in this world for the love of Jesus Christ. Confide not in yourself, but place your hope in God. Do what is in your power and God will be with your good will. Trust not in your own knowledge, nor in the cunning of any man living, but rather in the grace of God, who helps the humble and humbles those who presume on themselves.

Glory not in riches, if you have them, nor in friends, because they are powerful, but in God, who gives all things, and desires to give Himself above all things. Boast not of the stature, nor beauty of your body, which is spoiled and disfigured by a little sickness. Do not take pride in your ability or talent, lest you displease God, to who belongs every natural good quality and talent, which you have.

Esteem not yourself better than others, lest, perhaps, you be accounted worse in the sight of God, who knows what is in man. Be not proud of thy own works: for the judgments of God are different from the judgments of men; and often times that displeases Him which pleases men. If you have anything of good, believe better things of others that you may preserve humility. It will do you no harm to esteem yourself the worst of all; but it will hurt you very much to prefer yourself before any one. Continual peace is with the humble; but in the heart of the proud is frequent envy and indignation.

Avoiding Rash Judgment

Turn your eyes back upon yourself and see that you judge not the doings of others. In judging others, a man labors in vain, often errs, and easily sings; but in judging and looking into himself he always labors with fruit. We frequently judge of a thing according as we have it at heart: for we easily lose true judgment through a private affection. If God were always the only object of our desire we would not so easily be disturbed at the resistance of our opinions.

But often something lies hid within, or occurs without, which draws us along with it. Many secretly seek themselves in what they do, and are not sensible of it. They seem also to continue in good peace when things are done according to their will and judgment; but if it falls contrary to their desires they are soon moved and become sad. Difference of thoughts and opinions is too frequently the source of dissensions amongst friends and neighbors, amongst religious and devout persons.

An old custom is with difficulty relinquished; and no man is led willingly farther than he himself sees or likes. If you rely more upon your own reason or industry than upon the virtue that subjects to Jesus Christ you will seldom and hardly be an enlightened man: for God will have us to be perfectly subject to Himself and to transcend all reason by inflamed love.

Works Done Out of Charity

Evil ought not to be done, either for anything in the world or for the love of any man; but for the profit of one that stands in need a good work is sometimes freely to be omitted or rather to be changed for a better. For by so doing a good work is not lost but is changed into a better. Without charity the outward work profits nothing; but whatever is done out of charity, be it ever so little and contemptible, all becomes fruitful. For God regards more with how much affection and love a person performs a work than how much he does.

He does much who loves much. He does much that does well what he does. He does well who regards rather the common good than his own will. That seems often to be charity, which is rather natural affection; because our own natural inclination, self-will, hope of reward, desire of our own interest, will seldom be wanting.

He that has true and perfect charity seeks himself in no one thing, but desire only the glory of God in all things. He envies no man, because he loves no private joy, nor does he desire to rejoice in himself; but above all things he wishes to be made happy in God.

He attributes nothing good to any man, but refers it totally to God, from whom all things proceed as from their fountain, in the enjoyment of whom all the saints repose as in their last end. Ah! If man had but one spark of perfect charity he would doubtless perceive that all earthly things are full of vanity.

The Consideration of One's Self

We cannot trust too much in ourselves, because we often want grace and understanding. There is but little light in us and this we quickly lose through negligence. Many times also we perceive not that we are so blind interiorly. We often do ill and do worse in excusing it. We are sometimes moved with passion and we mistake it for zeal. We blame little things in others and pass over great things in ourselves. We are quick enough at perceiving and weighing what we suffer from others, but we mind not what others suffer from us. He that would well and duly weigh his own deeds would have no room to judge harshly of others.

You will make great progress if you keep yourself free from all worldly care. But if you set a value upon anything worldly you will fail exceedingly. Let nothing be great in your eyes, nothing high, nothing pleasant, nothing agreeable to thee, except it be purely God or of God. Look upon all the comfort which you meet with from any creature as vain. A soul that loves God despises all things that are less than God. None but God, eternal and incomprehensible, who fills all things, can afford true comfort to the soul and true joy to the heart.

The Small Number of the Lovers of the Cross of Jesus

Jesus has now many lovers of His heavenly kingdom, but few that are willing to bear His cross. He has many that are desirous of comfort, but few of tribulation. He finds many companions of His table, but few of His abstinence. All desire to rejoice with Him, few are willing to suffer with Him. Many follow Jesus to the breaking of bread, but few to the drinking of the chalice of His passion. Many reverence His miracles, but few follow the humiliation of His cross. Many love Jesus as long as they meet with no adversity. Many praise Him and bless Him as long as they receive consolation from Him. But if Jesus hides Himself, and leaves them for a little while, they either fall into complaints or excessive dejection.

But they that love Jesus for Jesus' sake and not for any comfort of their own bless Him no less in tribulation and anguish of heart than in the greatest consolation. And if He should never give them His comfort, yet would they always praise Him and always give Him thanks.

Oh, how much is the pure love of Jesus able to do when it is not mixed with any self-interest or self love. Are not all those to be called hirelings who are always seeking consolation? Are they not proved to be rather lovers of themselves than of Christ who are always thinking of their own profit and gain? Where shall we find a man that is willing to serve God gratis?

Seldom do we find any one so spiritual as to be stripped of all things. For who shall be able to find the man that is truly poor in spirit and stripped of all affection to all created things? His price is from afar and from the uttermost coasts. If a man gives his whole substance it is still nothing. And if he does great penance it is yet little. And if he attain to all knowledge he is far off still. And if he has great virtue and exceeding fervent devotion there is still much wanting to him, namely, one thing which is chiefly necessary for him. And what is that? That, having left all things else, he leaves also himself and wholly goes out of himself and retain nothing of self love. And when he shall have done all things, which he knows should be done, let him think that he has done nothing.

Let him not make great account of that which may appear much to be esteemed, but let him in truth acknowledge himself to be an unprofitable servant, as Truth itself has said: "When you shall have done all the things that are commanded you, say: We are unprofitable servants. Yet no one is indeed richer than such a man, none more powerful, none more free, who knows how to leave himself and all things, and place himself in the very lowest place.

The Proof of a True Lover

We are not as yet courageous and wise lovers. Because we fall off from what we have begun upon meeting with a little adversity, and too greedily seek after consolation. A valiant lover stands his ground in temptations, and yields not to the crafty persuasions of the enemy. As we are pleased with God in prosperity so let us not displease God when He send adversity.

A prudent lover considers not so much the gift of the lover as the love of the giver. He looks more at the good will than the value and prizes his Beloved above all His gifts. A generous lover rests not in the gift, but in God above every gift. All is not lost if sometimes you have not that sense of devotion towards God or His saints which you think you should have. That good and delightful affection, which you sometimes perceive, is the effect of present grace and a certain foretaste of thy heavenly country, but you must not rely too much upon it, because it goes and comes. But to fight against the evil notions of the mind, which arise and to despise the suggestions of the devil, is a sign of virtue and of great merit.

Let not, therefore, strange fancies trouble you, of what kind so ever they be that are suggested to you. Keep your resolution firm and your intention upright towards God. Neither is it an illusion that sometimes you are absorbed into an ecstasy and presently return to the accustomed weakness of your heart. For these you rather suffer against your will than acquire, and as long as you are displeased with them and resist them, it is merit and not loss.

Know that the old enemy strives by all means to hinder your desire after good and to divert you from every devout exercise, namely from the veneration of the saints, from the pious mediation of Christ's passion, from keeping a guard upon your own heart and from a firm purpose of advancing in virtue. He suggests to you many evil thoughts that he may weary you, and frighten you, that he may withdraw you from prayer and the reading of devout books. He is displeased with humble confession and if he could he would cause you to omit communion. Give no credit to him; value him not, although he often lays his deceitful snares in your way. Charge him with it when he suggest wicked and unclean things, and say to him: Be gone, unclean spirit; be ashamed, miserable wretch; you are very filthy indeed to suggest such things as these to me. Depart from me, you wicked imposter, you shall have no share in me, but my Jesus will be with me as a valiant warrior and you shall be confounded. I would rather die and undergo any torment whatsoever than yield to your suggestions. Be silent, I will hear no more of you, although you so often strive to be troublesome to me. "The Lord is my light and my salvation whom shall I fear? The Lord is the protector of my life, of whom shall I be afraid? "If armies in camp should stand together against me, my heart shall not fear. The Lord is my helper and my Redeemer."

Fight like a good soldier, and if sometimes you fall though frailty, rise up again with greater strength than before, confiding in God's more abundant grace, but take great care that you yield not to any vain gratification and pride. Through this many are led into error and sometimes fall into incurable blindness. Let this fall of the proud, who foolishly rely on their own strength, serve you for a warning and keep you always humble.

Grace and Humility

It is more profitable and more safe for you to hide the grace of devotion and not to exalt yourself, not to speak much of it, not to consider it much, but rather to despise yourself the more and to be afraid of it, as given to one unworthy. You must not depend too much on this affection, which may be quickly changed into the contrary. When you have grace, think to yourself how miserable and poor you are when you are without it. Nor does the progress of a spiritual life consist so much in having the grace of consolation as in bearing the want of it with humility, resignation, and patience, so as not to grow remiss in your exercise of prayer at that time, nor to suffer yourself to omit any of thy accustomed good works. But that you willingly do what lies in you, according to the best of your ability and understanding, and take care not wholly to neglect yourself through the dryness or anxiety of mind, which you feel.

For there are many who when things do not succeed well for them, presently grow impatient or lazy. Now the way of man is not always in his own power, but it belongs to God to give and to comfort when He will, and as much as He will and to whom He will, and as it shall please Him and no more. Some wanting discretion, have ruined themselves by reason of the grace of devotion; they could not weigh well the measure of their own weakness, but followed rather the inclinations of the heart than the dictates of reason. And because they presumptuously undertook greater things than were pleasing to God, therefore they quickly lost His grace. They became needy and were left in a wretched condition, who had built themselves a nest in heaven to the end, that being thus humbled and impoverished they might learn not to trust to their own wings, but to hide themselves under God's. Those who are yet, but novices and inexperienced in the way of the Lord, if they will not govern themselves by the counsel of discreet persons, will be easily deceived and overthrown.

And if they will rather follow their own judgment than believe others who have more experience, their future is full of danger if they continue to refuse to be drawn from their own conceit. They that are wise in their own eyes seldom humbly suffer themselves to be ruled by others. It is better to have little knowledge with humility and a weak understanding, than greater treasures of learning with self-conceit. It is better for you to have less than much, which may puff you up with pride. He is not so discreet as he ought to be who gives himself up wholly to joy, forgetting his former poverty and the chaste fear of God, which dreads the loss of that grace which is offered. Neither is he so virtuously wise who, in the time of adversity or any tribulation whatsoever, carries himself in a desponding way and conceives and reposes less confidence in the Lord than he ought.

He who is too secure in time of peace will often be found too much dejected and fearful in time of war. If you could but always continue humble and little in your own eyes and keep your spirit in due order and subjection, you would not fall so easily into danger and offence. It is a good counsel that when you have conceived the spirit of fervor you should meditate how it will be with you when that light shall leave you. And, when it shall happen, remember that the light may return again, which, for your instruction and God's glory, has withdrawn from you for a time.

Such a trial is oftentimes more profitable than if you were always to have prosperity according to your will. For a man's merits are not to be estimated by his having many visions or consolation, nor by his knowledge of the Scriptures, nor by his being placed in a more elevated station. But by his being grounded in true humility and replenished with divine charity; by his seeking always purely and entirely the honor and sincerely despising himself and being better pleased to be despised and humbled by others than to be the object of their esteem.

— *My Imitation of Christ*

The best way to develop humility is through spiritual direction. If you try to direct yourself, you will only deceive yourself. Be very careful in choosing a spiritual director because obedience is the key to humility. If you choose a spiritual director who is not well-rooted in his faith and humble himself, you will be worse off than when you started.

You will find humility to be the most elusive saint-like trait to acquire and it will take much effort on your part. It will not be your friend if you do not put your mind to the task and work tirelessly to accomplish it. The old saying, bite your tongue, just may be the best advice of all. It is much better to be kind and passive in situations where our nature instinctively demands a fiery response.

It is much better to take the back seat in life and be called to the front, than to suffer embarrassments of stepping forward yourself. As I said at the beginning of the chapter, I am having a hard time in this area and I need to be diligently on guard twenty-four hours a day. Please pray for my success as I will yours.

It should be obvious that you're not going to develop great humility by simply reading this chapter, so you can advance to Chapter Thirteen by making a commitment to work hard at humility and take advantage of a spiritual director. If you're willing to do that, continue on.

NOTES

Chapter Thirteen

Prayer

I would not want to mislead you by having you think this chapter is a panacea for having a great prayer life. I will only touch on the basic subject of prayer and give a few insights as to what has worked for me. There are many books that deal with prayer and I cannot recommend one to you because I have not read any of them. I do know from my own research that you have to be careful to whom you listen. There are books that attempt to teach people to pray a certain way and it is dangerous territory. Eastern mysticism and prayers often have New Age ties. Reiki, a system for channeling energy into healing power, tai chi and the like, which are often passed off as valid Catholic spiritual endeavors, are to be avoided. We do have retreat houses offering classes on these, as faith builders, and it is a dangerous step away from authentic Catholic teaching.

I do not know how each of you prays. I only know that I have prayed in a form surely not pleasing to God. I know that, at times, I have read my prayers, said my prayers, but not prayed my prayers. I know at times I have drifted off somewhere while saying my Rosary and found when I returned to reality, I was at the end of five decades. I never realized that I'd said all five. That prayer was probably not a prayer at all, unless I became contemplative. When I first started praying the Rosary I went a bit fast so I could get it done. Prayer is not about speed; it is about talking to God.

Before I go further, I want to let you know that, for me, there is a difference between prayers and praying. Prayers are structured, something you read or recite. Praying is talking to God, just as you would talk to your best friend. Both have their place.

I have noticed and corrected some of my speedy prayer problems. I guess when I realized that I was saying prayers to, or talking to God, at a speed that I would not use when I was talking to a friend, I changed my prayer style. If any of us continues with fast-paced prayer, we must realize that God could only infer that we do not want to spend much time with Him. If I don't want to spend time with God now, what would make me think that God would want me in heaven with Him after I die? What would make me think that I was saint material?

I can remember a conversation I had with one of my former pastors, Father Ken Oldenski. I was explaining to him that I was having a hard time saying all fifteen decades of the Rosary, as the Blessed Mother asked. We never got on the subject of the fifteen decades. What Father Ken brought to my attention was the word 'saying.' He explained that we do not 'say' the Rosary, we 'pray' the Rosary. That sound teaching has stuck with me until this very day. Father Ken brought to my attention something that I believe many people have a problem with, 'saying' the Rosary instead of 'praying' it.

Could you imagine if God equipped us with a prayer meter and it only logged legitimate prayer time? The meter would not compile any time that was not 'from the heart' prayer. I cannot help but wonder if we would advance the meter past zero very often. I know for certain that the Kentucky Derby Rosary I used to say would not make the meter move. The Kentucky Derby Rosary is one said so fast that you sound like a racetrack announcer, rather than a person having a conversation with the Blessed Virgin Mary and God. The Rosary prayed, scratch that, *said* very fast would not count as prayer. So why waste God's time and ours, saying prayers that count for nothing? On the other hand, what if the so-called prayers we say are offensive to God. Rather than being answered or helping to pay off our purgatory debt, they actually increased the time due? That in itself is a reason to analyze and ponder our prayer methodology.

Prayer is meant to enhance our relationship with the Lord, but if we analyze our prayer pattern, we would find much of it is "I want, I need, could You fix this or that. Lord, my wife doesn't pray so well. Will You fix her?" Seven days a week, three hundred and sixty-five days a year, God is bombarded with our requests. Could you imagine what kind of computer it would take to handle all of that inbound information? I surely would not want to work in the heavenly fulfillment department if all of those prayers had to be answered. I sure am glad I am not God. Bet you are, too!

Are all prayers answered? My answer may shock you, but I believe they are. I really do think all prayers are answered, but many times the answer is NO! And God's time in answering our prayers may not fit our agenda. Absolutely, God hears all prayers. There was never a prayer said that God did not hear. But if God answered all the prayers the way we want them to be answered, what a mess this world would be. I guess it is already a mess because of our unwillingness to implement what the Church asks of us. If all prayers were answered in the way we want, the lotto wouldn't even be worth winning - too many people with whom to have to split it.

There is an aspect in our communication with God that we forget far too often. "Here I am, Lord, I come to do Your will." At what point do we plug in doing for God to balance all of the requests we have?

There is an art in having prayers answered and it lies in the combined effort of this book. Plug into your life what you find here and you will find what I found. You get from your prayers what you put into them. I'm going back to the concept of 'for every action there is an equal and opposite reaction' again. I see now and quite vividly, that when I prayed little and backed up those prayers with little action, I had little hope of God actually answering my prayers in the affirmative. But here I testify to the truth: God answers many prayers for those who know Him. My second book, *Miracles and How to Work Them,* demonstrates that well. In there you will find many prayers answered.

We need to learn how to pray effectively so all of the problems mentioned in this book can not only be addressed, but addressed sucessfuly.

How do we learn to pray so that God may be interested in answering our prayers? I find most all of my answers in the Bible. The primary source of perfect prayer, outside of Mass, is demonstrated with the prayers of Jesus. The areas of bold type are great hints as to the posture to have in prayer and perfect approach. Try these and you will see improvement in your prayer life.

Prayers of Jesus

Mt 6:5-9 *"When you pray, do not be like the hypocrites, who love to stand and pray in the synagogues and on street corners so that others may see them. Amen, I say to you, they have received their reward. But when you pray, go to your inner room, close the door, and pray to your Father in secret. And your Father who sees in secret will repay you. In praying, do not babble like the pagans, who think that they will be heard because of their many words. Do not be like them. Your Father knows what you need before you ask him. This is how you are to pray:*

Our Father in heaven, hallowed be your name, your kingdom come, your will be done, on earth as in heaven. Give us today our daily bread; and forgive us our debts, as we forgive our debtors; and do not subject us to the final test, but deliver us from the evil one.

Mt 11:25 *At that time Jesus said in reply, "I give praise to you, Father, Lord of heaven and earth, for although you have hidden these things from the wise and the learned you have revealed them to the childlike.*

John 11:41-44 *So they took away the stone. And Jesus raised his eyes and said, "Father, I thank you for hearing me. I know that you always hear me; but because of the crowd here I have said this, that they may believe that you sent me." And when he had said this, he cried out in a loud voice, "Lazarus, come out!" The dead man came out, tied hand and foot with burial bands, and his face was wrapped in a cloth. So Jesus said to them, "Untie him and let him go."*

John 17:1-26 *When Jesus had said this, he raised his eyes to heaven and said, "Father, the hour has come. Give glory to your son, so that your son may glorify you, just as you gave him authority over all people, so that he may give eternal life to all you gave him.*

Now this is eternal life, that they should know you, the only true God, and the one whom you sent, Jesus Christ. I glorified you on earth by accomplishing the work that you gave me to do. Now glorify me, Father, with you, with the glory that I had with you before the world began. "I revealed your name to those whom you gave me out of the world. They belonged to you, and you gave them to me, and they have kept your word. Now they know that everything you gave me is from you, because the words you gave to me I have given to them, and they accepted them and truly understood that I came from you, and they have believed that you sent me. I pray for them. I do not pray for the world but for the ones you have given me, because they are yours and everything of mine is yours and everything of yours is mine, and I have been glorified in them. And now I will no longer be in the world, but they are in the world, while I am coming to you.

Holy Father, keep them in your name that you have given me, so that they may be one just as we are. When I was with them I protected them in your name that you gave me, and I guarded them, and none of them was lost except the son of destruction, in order that the Scripture might be fulfilled. But now I am coming to you. I speak this in the world so that they may share my joy completely. I gave them your word, and the world hated them, because they do not belong to the world any more than I belong to the world. I do not ask that you take them out of the world but that you keep them from the evil one.

They do not belong to the world any more than I belong to the world. Consecrate them in the truth. Your word is truth. As you sent me into the world, so I sent them into the world.

And I consecrate myself for them, so that they also may be consecrated in truth.

"I pray not only for them, but also for those who will believe in me through their word, so that they may all be one, as you, Father, are in me and I in you, that they also may be in us, that the world may believe that you sent me. And I have given them the glory you gave me, so that they may be one, as we are one, I in them and you in me, that they may be brought to perfection as one, that the world may know that you sent me, and that you loved them even as you loved me. Father, they are your gift to me. I wish that where I am they also may be with me, that they may see my glory that you gave me, because you loved me before the foundation of the world. Righteous Father, the world also does not know you, but I know you, and they know that you sent me. I made known to them your name and I will make it known, that the love with which you loved me may be in them and I in them."

Luke 22:41-48 *After withdrawing about a stone's throw from them and kneeling, he prayed, saying, "Father, if you are willing, take this cup away from me; still, not my will but yours be done." (And to strengthen him an angel from heaven appeared to him. He was in such agony and he prayed so fervently that his sweat became like drops of blood falling on the ground.)*

When he rose from prayer and returned to his disciples, he found them sleeping from grief. He said to them, "Why are you sleeping? Get up and pray that you may not undergo the test." While he was still speaking, a crowd approached and in front was one of the Twelve, a man named Judas. He went up to Jesus to kiss him. Jesus said to him, "Judas, are you betraying the Son of Man with a kiss?"

Luke 23:33-35 *When they came to the place called the Skull, they crucified him and the criminals there, one on his right, the other on his left. (Then Jesus said,*

"Father, forgive them, they know not what they do.") They divided his garments by casting lots. The people stood by and watched; the rulers, meanwhile, sneered at him and said, "He saved others, let him save himself if he is the chosen one, the Messiah of God."

Luke 23:46 *Jesus cried out in a loud voice, "Father, into your hands I commend my spirit;" and when he had said this he breathed his last.*

For whom do we pray? The first person to pray for is yourself. Scripture tells us to get the plank out of our own eye first. If you are married with children, the second group of people on your list should be your spouse and your children. Your children are the next generation to lead the world to God. Mess up there and you have messed up big time. Of course, you have to pray for your spouse to keep the marriage going, but the evil one is especially interested in your children.

Every aspect of a child's life has Satan waiting to spring his trap. Schools are one such trap trying to spiritually kill your children. Sad to say, even many Catholic schools are involved. If you have the Internet, please go to www.national-coalition.org (National Coalition of Clergy and Laity.) There you will find enough information to frighten you senseless regarding the promotion of blatant sex education in place of the teaching of true Catholic faith and morals.

One such sex education program, which is very widespread and apparently authorized by many U.S. bishops, is titled "Growing in Love." This Kindergarten – Grade 8 curriculum contains offensively explicit language and situations in a way that can damage the faith of children and erode their moral sense, say Rev. Ignacio Barreiro STD, JD, and Kristin Sparks of Human Life International.

Mother's Watch is an organization of mothers against sex education in schools. An article in the Summer/Fall 2001 issue of their magazine states that, " 'Growing in Love's' repetitive emphasis on genitalia, feel-good sexual acts and explicit details of such acts could only have been developed by homosexual/lesbian pedophiles who care nothing about the purity of children and the sanctity of the Church."

The article goes on to reveal that "'Growing in Love' teaches perverse sexual acts of oral and anal sex as foreplay. Masturbation is also repeatedly discussed and masturbation with a partner is mentioned beginning in grade three and often thereafter." After reading a course description and excerpts from the publication, I can tell you that it gets worse – much worse.

Because of this and the other current crises which are enveloping the Church today, Mary K. Smith, president of NCCL, calls for three steps to help set the Church in the U.S. on course:

1. Vatican appointment of a special papal legate to chair the USCCB

2. Vatican appointment of a special apostolic visitor to each diocese to oversee reform of the clergy (and laity.)

3. Application of the Church's traditional prohibition of classroom sex education in Catholic schools and restoration of catechesis in Catholic faith and morals.

I applaud Mrs. Smith's suggestions. The Vatican has to get involved before we lose still more generations of Catholics to the liberal trap.

The amount of threat that comes from your children's playmates through peer pressure is astounding also. Television and all media have a plan of action against your kids. And then there is the home computer. The Internet can be a tremendous asset to them, but there are such ample amounts of evil to be discovered, to the point of killing them morally ten times over. Computer games such as "Dungeons and Dragons" are designed to involve and familiarize your children with the occult, to say nothing of the assault by those constantly pushing pornography. Often you do not even have to be searching it out – it just invades your screen.

I purchased a new sound card for my computer and it came with a free game. As the program fired up, words flashed on the screen such as *kill, suicide, sex* and the like. Be careful what you allow your children to see.

It takes much prayer to keep Satan at bay. The best prescription for a prayer life that I know of, is this; Daily Mass, fifteen decades of the Rosary each day, fasting on bread and water on Wednesdays and Fridays, confession each month and conversion of the heart every day.

There are those who give me a hard time because I sell this spirituality package firmly. I am the first to admit there are other ways to holiness, but this is the only way that I know that works for me and the results have been astonishing. I have been encouraged by some to back off a bit and to them I say, "Get thee behind me, Satan." We have big problems in the Church today and big problems take big time prayer and fasting.

There are always folks who want the bar a bit lower so they will not feel guilty when they do little. I know someone with a Catholic apostolate who explains why he cannot make it to daily Mass. He states that he is too busy in the studio trying to record Christian music so he can support his family. When you trade the most powerful prayer in existence for anything else, even your family, you withdraw support from them. There is no greater support you can give anyone than Mass. There are those who move from town to town for various reasons and those reasons are generally not Godly. Who is it that moves so he may make it to Mass every day? Someone who has a desire of achieving sainthood.

> Luke 12:16-42 *Then he told them a parable. "There was a rich man whose land produced a bountiful harvest. He asked himself, 'What shall I do, for I do not have space to store my harvest?' And he said, 'this is what I shall do: I shall tear down my barns and build larger ones. There I shall store all my grain and other goods and I shall say to myself, "Now as for you, you have so many good things stored up for many years, rest, eat, drink, be merry!"'*

But God said to him, "You fool, this night your life will be demanded of you; and the things you have prepared, to whom will they belong? Thus will it be for the one who stores up treasure for himself but is not rich in what matters to God." He said to (his) disciples, "Therefore I tell you, do not worry about your life and what you will eat, or about your body and what you will wear. For life is more than food and the body more than clothing. Notice the ravens: they do not sow or reap; they have neither storehouse nor barn, yet God feeds them. How much more important are you than birds!

Can any of you by worrying add a moment to your lifespan? If even the smallest things are beyond your control, why are you anxious about the rest? Notice how the flowers grow. They do not toil or spin. But I tell you, not even Solomon in all his splendor was dressed like one of them. If God so clothes the grass in the field that grows today and is thrown into the oven tomorrow, will he not much more provide for you, O you of little faith? As for you, do not seek what you are to eat and what you are to drink, and do not worry anymore. All the nations of the world seek for these things, and your Father knows that you need them. Instead, seek his kingdom, and these other things will be given you besides.

Do not be afraid any longer, little flock, for your Father is pleased to give you the kingdom. Sell your belongings and give alms. Provide money bags for yourselves that do not wear out, an inexhaustible treasure in heaven that no thief can reach nor moth destroy. For where your treasure is, there also will your heart be. "Gird your loins and light your lamps and be like servants who await their master's return from a wedding, ready to open immediately when he comes and knocks. Blessed are those servants whom the master finds vigilant on his arrival. Amen, I say to you, he will gird himself, have them recline at table, and proceed to wait on them. And should he come in the second or third watch and find them prepared in this way, blessed are those servants.

> *Be sure of this: if the master of the house had known the hour when the thief was coming, he would not have let his house be broken into. You also must be prepared, for at an hour you do not expect, the Son of Man will come." Then Peter said, "Lord, is this parable meant for us or for everyone?" And the Lord replied, "Who, then, is the faithful and prudent steward whom the master will put in charge of his servants to distribute (the) food allowance at the proper time?"*

Who is it who would trade prayer and God's way for earthly security? Only a fool. Make everything you do a prayer. Make your sleep a prayer by commending to God your spirit before you drift off. Make your work a prayer by inviting God to guide you through every step. Make your play a prayer by thanking God constantly for the opportunity to do so. Pray before all meals and even to the point of giving thanks for a glass of water. He who does not pray and give thanks before he places anything in his mouth reaps judgment.

When you pray and it feels good, that is God's gift to you. When you pray and you are experiencing great distraction, as most people do, and you persevere in your prayer, that is your gift to God. Pray without ceasing.

Outside of Mass, the Rosary is the weapon of choice. I know I covered the Rosary in the prior chapter, but here, under the heading of prayer, I would like to give you the insights of Pope Pius V from his Apostolic Constitution on Praying the Rosary, dated September 17, 1569, *Consueverunt Romani:*

> The Roman pontiffs, and the other holy fathers, our predecessors, when they were pressed in upon by temporal or spiritual wars, or trouble by other trials, in order that they might more easily escape from the these, and having achieved tranquility, might quietly and fervently be free to devote themselves to God, were wont to implore the divine assistance, through supplications or litanies to call forth the support of the saints, and with David to lift up their eyes unto the mountains, trusting with firm hope that thence would they receive aid.

1. Prompted by their example, and as is piously believed, by the Holy Ghost, the inspired blessed founder of the Order of Friars Preachers, (whose institute and rule we ourselves expressly professed when we were in minor orders), in circumstances similar to those in which we now find ourselves, when parts of France and of Italy were unhappily troubled by the heresy of the Albegenses, which blinded so many of the worldly that they were raging in most savagely against the priests of the Lord and the clergy, raised his eyes up unto heaven, onto that mountain of the glorious Virgin Mary, loving Mother of God. For she by her seed has crushed the head of the twisted serpent, and has alone destroyed at all heresies, and by the blessed fruit of her womb has saved a world condemned by of the fall of our first parent. From her, without human hand, was that stone cut, which, struck by wood, poured forth the abundantly flowing waters of graces. And so Domenic looked to that simple way of praying and beseeching God, accessible to all and wholly pious, which is called the Rosary, or Psalter of the Blessed Virgin Mary, in which the same most Blessed Virgin is venerated by the angelic greeting repeated one hundred and fifty times, that is, according to the number of the Davidic Psalter, and by the Lord's Prayer with each decade. Interposed with the these prayers are certain meditations showing forth the entire life of Our Lord Jesus Christ, thus completing the method of prayer devised by the Fathers of the Holy Roman Church. This same method Saint Dominic propagated, and it was spread by the Friars of Blessed Domenic, namely, of the aforementioned Order, and accepted by not a few of the people. Christ's faithful, inflamed by these prayers, began immediately to be changed into new men. The darkness of the heresy began to be dispelled and the light of the Catholic faith to be revealed. Sodalities for this form of prayer began to be instituted in many places by the Friars of the same Order, legitimately deputed to this work by their superiors, and confreres began to be enrolled together.

2. Following the example of our predecessors, seeing that the Church militant, which God has placed in our hands,

> in these our times is tossed this way and that by so many heresies, and is grievously troubled, troubled and afflicted by so many wars, and by the depraved morals of men, we also raise our eyes, weeping but full of hope, unto that same mountain, whence every aid comes forth, and we encourage and admonish each member of Christ's faithful to do likewise in the Lord.
>
> — Rome, September 17, 1569

We see by this document that we are not the first to be so troubled, but who could be having more trouble than we?

One great way you can help stop division in community prayer, where two or more are gathered, is for all to know the correct way to pray, that is, everyone saying the same words. If Jesus is present, and He is, why pray in a way that is confusing?

One church I attend has a handsome number at daily Mass. And not only do they attend daily Mass, they start a half hour early. The extra time is so they can pray Divine Mercy and five decades of the Rosary. This is all very honorable, but I try not to show up until after the Divine Mercy prayer. Why? Because instead of saying, "For the sake of His sorrowful passion, have mercy on us and on the whole world" - they say - "For the sake of Jesus' (*pronounced Jesuses*) sorrowful passion, have mercy on us and on the whole world. The word Jesus' (*pronounced Jesuses*) is very difficult to say and is incorrect. Thanks be to God, with a loving encouragement, the problem was fixed. If you get in a habit of saying prayers in the wrong way and you go somewhere else and are invited to lead Divine Mercy or any prayer, then you bring that confusion to all of those people. It becomes difficult to focus on your intentions when the words are very foreign.

There is tremendous confusion over the Hail Mary prayer. Some say, "The Lord is with *thee"* and some say, "The Lord is with *you*." Some say, "Blessed *art thou"* and some say "Blessed *are you*." To my knowledge, the official Roman Catholic form is with the *thees* and *thous* intact. We rob the poetry from the prayer when we modernize it. It would be like taking all of the thees and thous out of Shakespeare.

The Saint Michael Prayer is said so many different ways; people are always stumbling over it.

I was speaking at a conference one time and gave a demonstration on how confusing our prayers were when words were changed. After my presentation, a priest from that diocese got up and stated that the prayers were officially changed in that diocese and everyone should unite in the new way. The problem with that is when we change prayers from diocese to diocese, we fall into Satan's trap of confusion.

Part of Satan's game plan is to bring confusion to prayer and he uses just one person to start. Pride comes upon a person and he believes he can make the prayer a little more holy by changing a word or two. The next thing you know, the new version is spreading like fire and the result is prayer confusion. Stay with the proper wording in prayers and we will all benefit from them.

I hope you will decide to pray more, and more correctly. The best place to pray is in front of Jesus in adoration and if that is not available, then in front of the Tabernacle.

The world is very transient these days and many times we are in a diocese other than our own and we stumble over the prayers. That is why Christ gave us the Universal Church, so all would be uniform. The Church was that way, in celebrating the Latin Mass, but somebody wanted to change it and now we have a war over which Mass is correct.

I know one man who will not go to daily Mass because daily Masses are not in Latin. He misses out on the Bread on Life and the greatest prayer of all, and why? Because of the confusion caused by change.

I personally like the Mass in English so I can pray along, but I see his point. He believes that most of the reverence has disappeared from the Mass and he is quite correct. The movie industry used to have Catholic Masses in their productions because they were awesome in their ritual and so inspiring. There are not many Catholic Masses in productions today, for many reasons to be sure. But one reason would certainly be its lack of grandeur. Although the Mass itself is far from ordinary, its contemporary manifestations are for the most part, sadly lacking in the ceremony, elegance and inspiration it once had. A second reason that Mass upsets many people is because of the immodesty in dress. We have lost our sense of morality in attending Mass. We will talk more about that in Chapter Fifteen.

You do not have to be very observant to notice that the reverence in church is diminishing rapidly and the change has hurt us badly. Joseph Cardinal Ratzinger has called for a revised Mass to be initiated that would reinstate the feeling of reverence. I applaud that idea, but as slowly as the Church moves, it could take fifty years.

All we can do is try to stick to as much uniformity as possible and try to survive these changing times. Every week it seems as though there is another change to which we are expected to become acclimated. It is difficult.

To sum up, I can only echo the words of the Blessed Mother when she said, "Pray, pray, pray! Why? Imagine life as a large set of scales. Now place all that you do for God on one side. Place tithing, works, prayer suffering, love, Mass, confession and time spent with the Lord on His side of the scale. Now place all that you do for the world on the other side. Place television, sports, vacations, movies, video games, internet, socializing, and so much more on the other side. Which way is your scale going to tip? If it is tipping moderately toward God, pray. If it is only tipping a little toward God, pray, pray. If your scale is skewed toward life, pray, pray, pray. You can only imagine why she says what she does. And remember; the family that prays together, stays together.

You are doing great so far. You are absorbing God's grace and the hope for the Church is, indeed, in you. We have surely lost many readers at this point and only those sincerely interested in healing division and procuring sainthood are still with us. Praise the Lord! Give thanks to God in all things and proceed to Chapter Fourteen.

NOTES

Chapter Fourteen

Evangelization

Evangelization is something sorely needed in the Catholic Church today. Many people are just showing up at Mass on Sunday and it is not enough. Not only do we have to learn how to evangelize, but also we need to be evangelizing ourselves.

There are so many good priests working so hard to try to improve the spirituality of the flock, but the resistance they meet is so disheartening. Lay people are just too busy to be concerned much about their spiritual journey. This stems from the mindset of the Church over the last forty years. As I stated earlier, we have been trying to shy away from the subject of punishment, judgment and hell. In doing so, we have convinced practically everyone that they're already going to heaven. If that is the case, everyone is already a saint, so why even try at all? Therein lies the reason and the need for evangelization.

I encountered a priest who was so concerned about the salvation of those entrusted to him that merely inviting me to give a four-day parish mission at his church was not enough. He wanted me to come two days early, to be present at all the Masses prior to the mission and to extend a personal invitation for each person to attend the nightly sessions. I was impressed with his efforts. Not only did he want me to extend the invitation to each person personally, but he had also been announcing the event for weeks in advance, he had placed the announcement in the bulletin several times and put it in the local Catholic and secular papers. What more could have been done to invite people to a parish mission? What more could have been done to have them present for something they need very badly? I guess I could spend a month or more in advance of the parish mission, knocking on doors of the parishioners, as the Jehovah's Witnesses do, but the time that would take would cut down the number of presentations I could give by about ninety-five percent.

In assuming that the pastor had done more than enough to get the attention of most of his flock, I was satisfied that the church would be full. That only goes to show how much I have to learn about Catholic spirituality. The church was far from packed. My wife Mary and I have joked about something that really isn't all that funny. We'll comment about the large crowds at the bars or the bingo halls in the vicinity of the churches at which we speak, and say that is where all the parishioners are.

Even as uneducated as I am, I know that people are more interested in entertainment than in salvation, so if you're going to be at all Masses to issue a personal invitation, you had better be somewhat entertaining or your pitch will not work at all. In my invitations I deliver a serious message and offer plenty of reasons for people to come, but I also have them laughing out loud. While they're laughing, I tell them not to be so frightened about a parish mission being boring, that we're going to have a great time. Then I leave them with a stock line after I invite everyone to attend. I say, "I have arranged for the Jehovah's Witnesses to show up at your door at precisely 7:00 p.m. each night (exactly the time the mission begins), so you have a choice. You can sit at home and wait for them or you can come to the church and deal with me. May God bless you in your decision."

That leaves them laughing hard and shaking my hand on the way out or slapping me on the back like we were lifelong friends.

I have been a Catholic evangelist long enough not to be disappointed at the size of a crowd. I would travel halfway around the world for one person. It could justify my existence. So the night of this grandiose effort, when not all that many people showed up I was not disappointed. But I did do one thing. I asked how many people were enticed into coming by my personal invitation at all the Masses that weekend. *One* young woman raised her hand as she said, "And I can't stay all that long. I have someplace to go." Everyone laughed, as did I. The remarkable thing was that she found the evening so exciting, she forgot about her previous appointment and ended up staying the entire evening. The woman returned the other nights of the parish mission as well, and she surely received a boost in the right direction.

So many times after one of these parish missions, people express to me how they wish their whole family had attended. They found out that parish missions were are not as boring as they'd first thought.

For as much as the Holy Father has called for a new evangelization, little has been done. It needs to start at the pulpit. People are always thanking me for reading them the riot act at my presentations. They enjoy hearing the truth, even when it is as hard-hitting as when I deliver it. It is refreshing and it is evangelizing. Many religious are afraid of the one or two people who raise "hell" when they do not like the truth they heard in a homily. As a result, so often we hear some watered-down version of the truth.

If we want to be evangelists, priest and layperson alike, we need to speak the truth. The truth will set us free. Don't worry about the collections, Father. God will take care of that when the truth is delivered. Maybe that is why the donations are down. People are paying for what they get. Give little truth and you get little in return.

One good thing to remember is that evangelization begins at home. Then the whole family can live a Christ-centered life and others will notice. Then evangelization is happening without your even saying a word.

NOTES

Chapter Fifteen

Mass

If you want to be a saint you must understand the Mass and participate in it frequently. In the test in Chapter Two, question one, you learn that you can go to Mass more than just on Sunday. Most Catholics believe that Sunday attendance is all they need to be holy. Yet participating in Sunday Mass is actually the least you can do and still stay Catholic. If you miss Mass on a Sunday through your own fault for something less than a serious reason, it is a grave sin and you should not receive Holy Communion again until you have confessed it.

I met a priest, originally from Ireland, while on a speaking tour in Alaska and ended up evangelizing at his parish. He thought it was great that lay people were getting involved in the Church to the extent that I was. But after the presentation he tried to convince me that God was everywhere and you did not have to attend Mass at all to achieve salvation. My wife, Mary, and I did our best to set him straight, but I believe we failed.

Mary and I were together again on a speaking tour in Mexico. We were invited by some friends to participate in a Bible study at a private residence in Guadalajara. There were several couples, a Catholic priest and a Catholic nun present. In the course of the evening, the subject turned to Mass and again Mary and I were subject to a professed religious trying to convince us that missing Mass on Sunday was not a problem. It was the American nun who explained the same scenario that the priest in Alaska was selling.

I appealed to the Mexican priest who was present to set her straight, but I ended up being chastised for my lack of charity. Imagine being charged with the lack of charity for defending the authentic teaching of the Catholic Church. It is happening more and more as dissenters make their move to overthrow the Church as we know it and implement their own rules. They are sly ones. These change-mongers do it inch-by-inch, revising what they want, and then claiming it to be American Catholic tradition.

The Mass is under attack by Satan. He is using dissenting religious to bring about a false shortage of priests. It is an orchestrated campaign by fallen religious to destroy the male priesthood and thus try to force their liberal agenda, which includes women priests. The Holy Father has stated over and over that the Catholic Church does not have the authority to institute a woman's ordained priesthood. It does not matter to the protesting faction that is attempting to overthrow the Church. They do not care how many people miss Mass, because their game plan is the destruction of the Mass as we know it today. These dissenters do not care how much the Church suffers.

It is my observation, after having attended Mass at over a thousand different Catholic churches, that we now use approximately seventy-five percent altar girls and only twenty-five percent altar boys. How could such a dramatic change come about in such a short time? It has to be orchestrated. I believe it to be an attack on the male priesthood.

Not only is there an attack on the male priesthood through attempts to eliminate altar boys, but also there has been a coup working for years to overthrow the seminaries and it was quite successful. You would have to read the book, *Goodbye, Good Men* by Michael S. Rose, to understand fully what I am talking about. In a nutshell, in as many seminaries of which Satan could take control, his dissenters systematically implemented a plan to reject good, young men with loyalty to the teachings of the Church and opted to fill the seminaries with like-minded, liberal thinking men, a large number of whom are practicing homosexuals. The plan again was to bring scandal to the Church and force the issue of women priests.

The Mass is the prized gem that Christ left behind to sustain us until His return. Satan believes if he can destroy the Mass, he wins. That fool did not read the end of the book. God stated specifically in Scripture that the gates of hell would not prevail against the one, holy, catholic and apostolic Church.

But all of this should give you tremendous insight to how important the Mass is in your life. If Satan is trying to destroy it with all his might, it must mean that it is very good for us.

But lay people take the Mass in a very casual way. Attendance on any given Sunday in the last forty years has plummeted to an all-time low of twenty-seven percent. Use of the sacrament of Confession, the ultimate preparation for Mass, has also plummeted to an all-time low with some exceptions. Active participation and even polite interest in the Mass, such as with paying attention to what's actually happening and even singing, seems to be sagging.

A great indignation that one could cast upon the Lord during Mass is to walk out early, yet many people walk out during the time from Communion to the final blessing or while a final song of praise is being lifted to the Lord. Next time you are at Mass, check out how many are left in the pews when the final hymn is over. We are a busy people, God. We have places to go.

I saw a sign one time at the back of a church that put a big smile on my face. The sign simply read, "Judas left early, too." If we truly want to be saints and remain on the right side of the divide, we must regain our respect for Mass. We must regain the reverence we once had at Mass. We must set aside the dissenters' program of "community" at Mass and focus not on each other, but God. All of the talking before Mass, the holding of hands at some churches during Mass and the sign of peace is all an attempt to be community-minded. We have one hundred and sixty seven hours a week to be community-minded and generally one hour is reserved for God. Why in the world can we not stay focused on God for that one hour rather than be led to have still more community. Sometimes I get so upset at the constant elevation of community and the downplay of the Lord at Mass that at the sign of peace I turn to my wife and say, "And may great division come to your family also." I do that in remembrance of the Lord saying, "I come not to bring peace, but division." (She knows I am joking.)

It doesn't take a very bright observer to notice that, as the dissenters stripped churches, removed the kneelers and demanded that people stand during the Consecration of the Mass, reverence plummeted. As tabernacles were moved from sight, reverence plummeted. As the words of many of the Scriptural texts were altered and the words of the hymns changed to align with the feminist agenda, reverence plummeted. No, you don't have to be too bright to see that our Church is in a lot of trouble.

These are the days that will make great saints. If simple people like you and I, realizing the seriousness of the attack our Church is under, and respond with our lives, perhaps we would more easily join the ranks of the greats in sainthood. The right response, I believe, will entail showing up at Mass more often. The reason the Eucharist is called "daily bread" in the Our Father prayer, is because God, Our Father, wants us to be fueled on the Eucharist daily. Each day we are permitted to attend as many Masses as we desire, but we can only receive the Eucharist two times in the course of a day. For the second reception, Mass must be attended fully, from start to finish. I am often challenged on my teaching of daily Mass and daily bread being one in the same. Many listeners also dispute the number of times we're allowed to receive the Eucharist each day. Allow me to present the proof from *The Code of Canon Law (rev. 1985).*

> Canon 917 – A person who has received the Most Holy Eucharist may receive it again on the same day only during the celebration of the Eucharist in which the person participates, with due regard for the prescription of can. 921, 2.
>
> The purpose of this canon is twofold: on the one hand, to promote active participation in the Eucharist including the full sacramental sharing in the Lord's Body and Blood; on the other hand, to prevent the abuse of receiving multiple Communions out of superstitions, ignorance, or misguided devotion.
>
> The 1917 Code (CIC 857) forbade the reception of Communion more than once a day except in danger of death or in need of impeding irreverence. The law was mitigated repeatedly after Vatican II to allow more frequent opportunities to receive twice on the same day. This canon greatly simplifies the post-conciliar legislation by permitting the reception of Communion twice in a day for any reason, provided the second reception occurs in the context of the Eucharist at which

> one is actually participating. Such participation implies minimally one's physical presence at the Eucharist. It excludes a second Communion outside of Mass except as Viaticum, and it also excludes a second Communion during a Mass at which one is not participating, such as when one enters in the course of the Mass only to receive Communion.

I would like to suggest another book for you to read - *The Lamb's Supper* by Scott Hahn. It would be senseless for me to try to attempt to explain to you how profound the Mass is when Scott's book does it so well. Scott was a Protestant theologian who discovered the one true Church and came aboard. He is now a professor of theology at Franciscan University in Steubenville. For most of his years as a Protestant, he studied the Bible. The book of Revelation was the one that he always failed to understand, as have all Protestants for over four hundred years. He found the truth and the excitement of Revelation being played out as he sat through his first Catholic Mass. This new understanding helped to cause his profound conversion.

As hard as Satan tries to destroy the Mass, God is right there supplying the grace for us to understand how astounding it is. There is great hope to be found in all of the people, lay and ordained alike, living an authentic Catholic faith.

"The Mass is the most perfect form of prayer!" (*Pope Paul VI*)

For each Mass we hear with devotion, Our Lord sends a saint to comfort us at death. (*Revelation of Christ to St. Gertrude the Great*).

Saint Pio, the stigmatic priest, said the world could exist more easily without the sun than without the Mass.

The Cure d'Ars, St. Jean Vianney said that if we knew the value of the Mass we would die of joy.

A great doctor of the Church, St. Anselm, declares that a single Mass offered for oneself during life may be worth more than a thousand celebrated for the same intention after death.

St. Leonard of Port Maurice supports this statement by saying that one Mass before death may be more profitable than many after it.

"The Holy Mass would be of greater profit if people had it offered in their lifetime, rather than having it celebrated for the relief of their souls after death." *(Pope Benedict XV).*

Once, St. Teresa was overwhelmed with God's goodness and asked Our Lord, "How can I thank you?" Our Lord replied, "Attend one Mass."

You can see by those who ran the race before us that there is great hope; so don't lose heart. There are problems ahead to be discussed in Chapter Sixteen, but we need to know what we are up against to prepare the best defense.

I hope you are understanding this Great Divide. It obviously exists in the Church today and your persistent striving for sainthood is the best posture for you to hold. It will help you be a survivor of the confusion and chaos we sometimes have to get through.

If you want to be active and part of the solution rather than passive and part of the problem, move on.

NOTES

CHAPTER SIXTEEN

THE CHURCH

This is a distressing chapter and may be quite shocking to some Pollyanna Catholics, but it must be said. Archbishop John P. Foley, the president of the Pontifical Council for Social Communications, gave the following advice when he opened the World Congress of Catholic Journalists on September 17, 2001:

> I would ask, first, that you have an unwavering dedication to truth—not to ideology, not to personal prejudice, not to political correctness or social conformity, but the truth. You will be called upon every day to report facts and the old adage of journalism is "Get it first, but first get it right."

The archbishop appealed to us journalists to be men and women of hope. My response to that is applause. But hope cannot be always clothed in touchy-feely stories that do not deal with the facts.

Many times when journalists write the truth, they are chastised. The hope I am looking for is in you and in the many good priests and bishops of the world who live and teach the truth. If we lived and taught the truth united and consistent, there would be nothing for journalists against our faith at which they could point a finger. Sadly, there is much occurring today to merit pointed fingers in the Church. As time passes, the truth is getting harder to find. And so the stones are thrown. But remember that telling the truth is not throwing stones. I can only hope that we one day stand united to defeat the evil that is festering in our Church today. When you and I live the truth - that is hope.

She, the bride of Christ, is delicate and beautiful. She is not to be trampled upon and disgraced with constant bickering. There will always be those who will desire to impart their will upon this bride and resist being obedient to the Magisterium. Ravenous wolves in sheep's clothing have come and are still coming. Pope

Paul VI said, "The darkness of Satan has entered and spread throughout the Catholic Church, even to its summit. Apostasy, the loss of faith, is spreading throughout the world and into the highest levels within the Church" (October 13, 1977). In other words, smoke has entered the sanctuary. Satan has put in place his own, and their purpose? To dismantle all the good that your God has poured upon this world. The evil one has enslaved them in his service and all the wrong that they do, they justify so easily. They sugar coat their venomous words and lead many astray. They are the dividers. But who is it that gets the label 'divider' today? It, many times, is the one who is most obedient to the truth.

Pope Paul VI knew full well about what he was talking when he said, "Do not participate in the auto-demolition of the Church, that is the destruction from within."

There is a book titled, *AA-1025: The Memoirs of an Anti-Apostle.* It makes "food-for-thought" reading if you're interested in the subject of destruction of the Church from within - and you should be.

It must be God's will for this subject to be discussed here because this very day, myriad material kept coming into my possession, showing the evil path that many church leaders choose. Yesterday brought me this distressing news headline: "U.S. bishops appoint Clintonite pro-aborts to twelve member abuse board."

How could the American Catholic bishops, in any good conscience, appoint Leon Panetta, a professed pro-abortion leader, to a lay, Catholic, moral evaluation board? The very reason this board is being created is to deal with the tremendous sexual scandal in the priesthood today. How could someone involved in an equally evil sexual scandal - the killing of innocent babies in the mother's womb - be elected by bishops to guide them and us in moral decisions?

In an effort to save at least some, God calls upon you to stand for what is true. He calls upon you to embrace a life of sanctification. If it is not you who will lay down your life for the bride of Christ, then who? God has, in every generation, called upon a select few to come forward. Can you comprehend your invitation? You are called to the light side of the *Great Divide.*

Can you stand with the Thereses, the Faustinas and a Joan of Arc? You can, if you choose to, be a Francis or a Thomas. If you desire it, your Father in heaven will send the grace.

God created the Church for you and He wants you to be a saint within it. Will you say yes? Please keep in mind that all who say no will go to hell. Now that you've decided to be a saint, arm yourself with all the weapons that God provides to those who choose to defend His Church - prayer and fasting.

We have talked about the sin of active homosexuality, but where does the Church stand on this subject? The Holy Father and the Vatican are quite clear on it.

Here is a recent headline that appeared in the *Seattle Post-Intelligencer*: "Fight gay rights laws, Vatican tells U.S. bishops."

The article stated that the Vatican Congregation, which had issued guidelines in 1986 on pastoral care of homosexuals, said its recommendations were prompted by a flurry of proposed laws in the United States. In several cities and states, debates have been continuing on how far to extend homosexual rights. Ballot measures are pending in several states.

> "U.S. bishops generally have been less stringent than the Vatican in opposing homosexuality (emphasis added). In a 1990 document on sexuality, (*Human Sexuality: a Catholic Perspective for Education and Lifelong Learning* from what was then the National Council of Catholic Bishops), the bishops voted to reduce to a footnote the Vatican's 1986 declaration that homosexuality is an objective disorder and added that it isn't sinful" (emphasis added).

"Isn't sinful" is a lie!

A priest in the diocese of Santa Fe, New Mexico, has told me personally that three-fourths of all priests in his diocese are homosexual. He also told me that he was under such extreme pressure to become one of them, that it was difficult to endure. Now, with the book, *Goodbye, Good Men,* revealing homosexual practices in the seminaries and the recent sex scandal in the Church, this all becomes more believable. You would have to be blind not to see the smoke.

Some bishops have already resigned, e.g., Archbishop Rembert Weakland of Milwaukee, because of their homosexuality. All of this demands this question to be asked: exactly how many priests and bishops are involved in the mortal sin of active homosexuality? Is it because so many are involved in the sin that it goes unchecked? Why else would bishops refrain from teaching against a sin even though it is in direct opposition to Scripture and the Magisterium? The problem is so troublesome that this relevant passage from St. Paul bears repeating:

> Romans 1:26-32 *Therefore, God handed them over to degrading passions. Their females exchanged natural relations for unnatural, and the males likewise gave up natural relations with females and burned with lust for one another. Males did shameful things with males and thus received in their own persons the due penalty for their perversity.*
>
> *And since they did not see fit to acknowledge God, God handed them over to their undiscerning mind to do what is improper. They are filled with every form of wickedness, evil, greed, and malice; full of envy, murder, rivalry, treachery, and spite. They are gossips and scandalmongers and they hate God. They are insolent, haughty, boastful, ingenious in their wickedness, and rebellious toward their parents. They are senseless, faithless, heartless, and ruthless. Although they know the just decree of God that all who practice such things deserve death, they not only do them, but give approval to those who practice them.*

The Old Testament story of Sodom and Gomorrah could not make the sinfulness of it any clearer. It is time to bring everything to the front so that we can get the sin of our Church, behind us and move on to holiness. We have been tolerant far too long. If we want to be saints, we must amass the greatest campaign of prayer and fasting that has ever been launched in the history of the Church. You must start a campaign in your own church to enlist as many people as you can to form an army of prayer and fasting warriors. We must become daily recipients of the Eucharist. We must pick up the Rosary and we must fast diligently. This division can be closed if the truth is lived in all Catholics.

Sin always starts small and escalates. When Satan gets his foot in the door, it is difficult to get him out. He tries to make everything acceptable and he does it over long periods of time. Allow me to share with you a letter written to the highest authorities of the Franciscan University in Steubenville. I received a copy from the author, a young man attending that school:

> I am writing as a concerned male student who, along with many other men on campus, suffers watching our sisters in Christ continue to dress immodestly. Our concern is not only for ourselves but also for the women. As the weather gets warmer, the clothing becomes more revealing. I understand it is not their intention to entice us by wearing seductive clothing, however this is the reality. I do believe most students at F.U.S. desire to grow in their faith. More women would be conscious of how they dressed if they knew how it affected their brothers and how it frustrates their own growth in purity and humility.
>
> The Franciscan University 1999-2001 catalog states that, "Students are expected to dress in a manner that expresses Christian charity and respect for self, fellow students, faculty, staff and academic life." It emphasizes that such clothing must be modest and appropriate for both the classroom and particularly the chapel. Merely enforcing this policy, however, will not transform hearts and minds to understand a deeper truth; how one's outer expression is a reflection of their interior disposition. I pray that our Lady, model of purity, will afford you the opportunity to address these issues so to help us grow in holiness. May

the Holy Spirit enable us to see the wisdom and beauty in guarding our bodies, thus helping us to develop virtue and become more charitable toward one another.

—A Concerned Student

There were similar letters written, but it only goes to show us how Satan starts small. We are out of control in many areas in the Church today. The same complaints can be made about how people dress when they attend Mass. Twenty years ago you wouldn't dare wear short shorts to Mass, but today it's not a problem. I have actually seen a female lector's underwear as she sat in the sanctuary with her skirt ten inches above her knees, waiting for her turn to work for God. Is that working for God or against Him? There is little sense of modesty in Church today and that is because modesty is not mentioned much from the pulpit. And now we see people coming to Mass wearing shorts, halter tops, strapless dresses, blue jeans - anything but appropriate clothing.

I have never been in a Catholic school in recent years where I was not embarrassed to see the kind of skirts the girls are permitted to wear. Skirts well above the knee are not how we should be encouraging young Catholic girls to dress. And the same goes for the home front. What has happened to parents' minds when they send their little girls out half-naked? There is a lack of leadership from the top down. The Church needs to correct itself in this area today, not talk about it for twenty years and then do nothing. I am sure the Vatican mandates modesty, but enforcement, as we have seen in our Church lately, is practically non-existent.

The music in the Church is out of control, as well. Most of the songs are being neutered and are generally sung so slowly that we're losing the joy in the celebration of Mass. It is now evident that music directors for some parishes are writing their own versions of songs to be used in the liturgy. The end result is that few people know the melodies and because they're unfamiliar with how to sing that version, they do not sing at all.

Too many times at Mass there are solos sung, whether by an individual or a choir. Mass is not a place for exhibitions or performances. The sanctuary area is often so strewn with cables, microphones, instruments and music stands because the music has been moved up front. It is a terrible distraction and reduces the reverence that we need so badly. We are told it is to encourage "community participation." But does it? Is that even what we really need? Our focus is supposed to be on the Lord.

If you have a music ministry, make sure you are not involved in the following and your chances of being a saint increase. I came upon this article which expresses my own feelings very well. Thanks to *Mentor Magazine* for permission to reprint it here:

> Why Are They Vandalizing Our Hymns?
>
> Vandalism can be towards words as well as buildings and the worst vandals are those who, without any ecclesiastical authority, are vandalizing our hymns both old and new. The opening verse of "Faith of our Fathers" has not yet been changed to "Values of Everyone's Parents and Guardians" but when it does, remember that this warning was served.
>
> Many great hymns have been desecrated. Father Faber is one of the greatest of all English poets, let alone hymn writers. One of the greatest of his hymns is "O, Come and Mourn with Me a While." It contains the wonderful line, 'Have we no tears to shed for him while soldiers scoff and Jews deride?'
>
> First of all, the word 'Jews' was seized upon by the thought-police and was replaced with 'men'. But even that was not good enough. The same censors decided that the word 'men' was sexist in the hymn's context. Thus the new ecclesiastically correct version in *Liturgical Hymns Old & New* is, 'While soldiers scoff and people sneer'. Now, apart from how ludicrous this sounds, it does not rhyme. Faber, a genius with words, has the 'ide' rhyme going through the second line of each of the seven verses of this great hymn. But the vandals do not care about that. They have neither ear nor brain.

So do not think that a name as great as that of Newman can be spared their vandalism. Can you believe that *Liturgical Hymns, Old & New* has the temerity to alter "Firmly, I Believe, and Truly"? In the second verse - famously set to inspired music by Elgar in *The Dream of Gerontius* - Newman actually wrote, 'And I trust and hope most fully/ In that manhood crucified;' but the feminist thought police, who obviously know better than the great cardinal, have changed it to 'In the Savior crucified'. Out goes 'manhood', even though Newman gave it a precise theological meaning, which follows on from, what he set down in the first verse.

The spoilers are not prejudiced against old hymns; they will ruin modern hymns just as freely. Nor do they hesitate to correct the words of Our Blessed Lord Himself. One of the best modern hymns is "I Am the Bread of Life." We all know the first verse: 'He who comes to me shall not hunger/ He who believes in me shall not thirst/ No one can come to me/ unless the Father draw him'. Well we can all hunger and thirst now because this hymn has been politically corrected: 'I am the bread of life/YOU who come to me shall not hunger/and who believe in me shall not thirst/ No one can come to me/Unless the father beckons.' (*A Celebration Hymnal for Everyone.*)

Among many hymns with ruined words are these: "I'll sing a Hymn to Mary" (can't have wicked men blaspheming); "Come, Come, Come to the Manger" (Christ cannot be the savior of mankind); and "To Jesus' Heart All Burning" (the sacred heart is forbidden from burning with love for men.)

Indeed, any hymn is likely to be changed if it upsets the politically correct. These latter-day book-burners censor many hymns simply by omitting entire verses - as they have with, for example, a "Purgatory in Lord for Tomorrow" verse - or, better still, from their point of view, by doing away with entire hymns.

We must not now ask God to Bless the Pope, though that hymn is perhaps the most loved of Catholic hymns among the English and Irish faithful; and we must also tolerate the hymn books to which I have referred not containing a single hymn about the Holy Souls. In the style of Faulty Towers, these hymn-spoilers seem to have as their abiding motto, "Don't mention Purgatory."

How should we fight back against these vandals? First, our bishops should insist, as they used to do and as Canon Law requires them to do, that all hymn books carry an imprimatur. This would give them a chance to review whether changes are heretical, rather than just being idiotic.

Meanwhile, parishes that have been saddled against their wishes with politically correct hymn books should demand their money back from the publishers. This can certainly be done, under the terms contained in the Trades Descriptions Act. If you advertise a book as containing 'hymns of old' and then allow the alteration of words of the old hymns before you put them in that book, you are deceiving the public and that public becomes entitled to have its money back.

Any respectable publisher, if he (or she) feels they must alter the words of hymns, ought to warn people prominently, in advance, of the changes. Additionally, the person responsible for ordering new hymn books should be told to insist that all hymns in deliveries received contain the proper words. They should insist, too, on "God Bless Our Pope" and at least one hymn for the poor forgotten Holy Souls.

Some Catholic schools, like Stoneyhurst and the London Oratory, have their own hymn books. This avoids the situation in which they might feel that they have to insult their pupils' intelligence with feminist versions of hymns, but why in the first place should schools be put into a position where they feel they have to resort to this?

> It is not my intention to publicize one particular book of hymns, but I can helpfully observe that *The Catholic Hymn Book* (Gracewing) has, to my knowledge, the proper version of all hymns and contains both "God Bless our Pope" and Newman's "Help Lord the Souls."
>
> As for the poor Catholic in the pews, pray to Our Blessed Lady we will be able to keep the finest words to honor her and her son.
>
> —*Eric Hester*

As I said earlier, Hester expresses my very sentiments. If we play around with God's word to suit our personal theology, we could be sinning. Don't go there. Leave such things for those whose sights are not on heaven. Do life God's way.

We have become so fragmented by countless different liturgies at Mass that we do not know when to sit, stand or kneel. I have been present at churches where all three were being done at the same time. In some parishes, if you do not follow the way some dissenter, in creating his own liturgy, wants it, you may be ridiculed in front of the entire congregation out loud. It has happened and not just a few times.

In the *Adoremus Bulletin*, I found an article titled "Bishops to 'Adapt' Liturgy Rules." The complete document can be found at www.adoremus.org/0501liturgyrules.html. From this article we get an aerial perspective of the battleground. I think you'll find it quite interesting.

I personally get a kick out of the explanation given by some liturgists when they try to explain why we should stand at the consecration. Allow me to glean and place here, for your edification, an insight from the *New Oxford Review*, February, 1999. Titled "At the Name of Jesus Every Knee Shall Remain Unbent," the complete article can be found at www.catholicliturgy.com/index.cfm.FuseAction/ArticleText/Index/6subIndex/94/Article Index/18.

The norm in the United States is kneeling between the Sanctus and the Lord's Prayer, for the entire Eucharistic Prayer.

The article advises that some liturgists have been arguing that this is incorrect, that Catholics should stand at the Consecration (as D. Phillipart wrote in the *U.S. Catholic* in July, 1993.) Kneeling, he said, "is a penitential posture, and is like mourning on Easter...." Phillipart would restrict kneeling to penitential times, private prayer and extraliturgical devotions. If Christ is present in all the Mass, "why kneel at the consecration?" He asks that without cracking a smile and no tongue in cheek. He really believes his statement.

If he is stating this because Scripture says where two or more are gathered, Christ is present, then he is not differentiating between Christ being present spiritually and being present in Body, Blood, Soul and Divinity. This, in fact, implies that he does not believe in the Real Presence. It also dismisses, out of hand, the Scripture that says, "At the name of Jesus, every knee shall bend." Thank God, that for the most part, bishops agree that kneeling is the correct posture. But still they vacillate and allow that, for the sake of "unity," if you are ordered off your knees by your particularly stubborn bishop, you should stand. I ask this: is it not better to ask those rebellious bishops who refuse to unify with the rest of us and their brother bishops, to get in line, rather than asking entire dioceses to offend Jesus Christ?

The rebellion in the leadership runs from completely stopping perpetual adoration to rejecting the *mandatum* from the Holy See for theologians to teach what the Catholic Church teaches. I would suggest to the bishops to do a study contrasting the Diocese of St. Petersburg, Florida, where perpetual adoration was ordered stopped and the Diocese of San Antonio, Texas, where the bishop ordered it implemented. I understand that there's tremendous spiritual growth in San Antonio and many more vocations.

The last chapter in this book is titled, "And The List Goes On." That is a very appropriate statement here. I could write a book based solely on how distorted and unholy our Mass is becoming, but it has already been written and it's called *Mass Confusion*. It is time that our bishops realized that the books that are being written today: *Mass Confusion*, *Goodbye, Good Men*, *Amchurch Comes Out*, *What Went Wrong With Vatican II?*,

Shaken by Scandals, and many others, are a direct reflection on the lack of leadership our Church is experiencing today. Many times the leadership complains about those who are bold enough to write these books, but the fact is - they need to be written. Eighty years of continual liberal advancement and constant deterioration of the faith in our generation is the proof that these books need to be written and read. The handwriting is not only on the wall.

It is not my point to try to be yet another negative voice in the Catholic Church today. God knows we have enough of that, but at what point do all the problems become addressed? Do we wait until there are no parishioners left? Do we wait for the contributions to drop from the miserable one percent of Catholics' income to zero percent? Well, I don't think you will have to wait long. People are cutting off the funds they used to give to dissenting parishes to make a statement and I agree with them. I do not agree that we should stop giving to God, only to parishes and dioceses that refuse to follow the Magisterium. Send your checks to the Vatican until those straying parishes and dioceses come to their senses. (I will get a lot of fertilizer for that statement.)

We see mismanagement in our corporations and how the government has now passed laws to make the leadership more accountable. The fact is, we have those kinds of laws in the Roman Catholic Church, but few enforce them. The only prison that awaits the offenders is on the other side of the *Great Divide.* That would be a shame.

I personally have been the target of an attempted seduction in a confessional. A priest has demanded that I leave his church (I was there just to attend Mass) and when I refused, he invited me outside to fight him! I have been screamed at and insulted by the very people who are supposed to be the example to the world. We can keep saying, "They're only human," all we want. But every profession or occupation has a code of ethics and conduct that has to be lived so that order is maintained. We, in the Church, somehow, have gotten out of control. I get letters often from people complaining that they write to their bishops about serious problems and either they receive no reply or at times, an insulting one.

I can't even explain to you how bad I feel for the majority of wonderful priests and bishops in this country and around the world. The cross that they have to carry because of our continual tolerance of dissenters in this Church has to be a crushing weight. I know of religious who have become physically sick over the weight of defending the true Church. To constantly be hearing about fellow priests and their failures has to weigh them down immensely. To have such a shadow cast on the noblest of professions is a crying shame.

How can we expect to be saints if we just stand by and watch all of this destruction come to the one, holy, catholic and apostolic Church? We must rise and do battle for the bride of Christ.

If you are willing to fight the good fight, mostly through prayer and fasting, to regain the poor lost souls that were once good lay people, priests and bishops, then be brave enough to tackle Chapter Seventeen.

NOTES

CHAPTER SEVENTEEN

TRACK RECORD

The track record for people of this period in time is not a shining example for one to imitate. We have become greedy, giving less than one percent of our income to God, self-centered, spiritually lazy and we have lost seventy-three percent of the Mass attendance in the Church in a mere forty years. This is not 'get into heaven' material. Coupled with a great lack of leadership, this may be one of the most dangerous times to be alive in all of history; that is if you can get out of the womb.

Beware!

Mt 3:7-12 *When he saw many of the Pharisees and Sadducees coming to his baptism, he said to them, "You brood of vipers! Who warned you to flee from the coming wrath? Produce good fruit as evidence of your repentance. And do not presume to say to yourselves, 'We have Abraham as our father.' For I tell you, God can raise up children to Abraham from these stones.*

Even now the ax lies at the root of the trees. Therefore every tree that does not bear good fruit will be cut down and thrown into the fire. I am baptizing you with water, for repentance, but the one who is coming after me is mightier than I. I am not worthy to carry his sandals. He will baptize you with the Holy Spirit and fire.

His winnowing fan is in his hand. He will clear his threshing floor and gather his wheat into his barn, but the chaff he will burn with unquenchable fire."

Do not go to anyone for advice or guidance that has already proven his untrustworthiness. Beware of the Pharisees and Sadducees of even this day that disregard obedience and faithful teaching. Be at arms length of those that alter the word of your God and make a mockery of His miracles. Do not allow them to touch you least what has infected them may infect you. Demons are a screwed lot and are always looking for someone new to inhabit. Living in a state of grace and relying solely on the Lord your God is your only defense.

Take the words 'Pharisees' and 'Sadducees' and replace them with 'bishop' and 'priest' and you find that the world has not improved at all. In fact, it most likely has gone downhill. We have many good priests and bishops and we should thank God every day for them, but we are also inundated with those who have given their lives over to the evil one. This is very risky for me to talk about because there seems to be such a climate of revenge found in the world these days. But how could I live with myself if I did not warn you about the danger? How would God treat me for being a coward? If John the Baptist, encouraged by God, spoke openly of the brood of vipers then, I guess it is God who wants it to be addressed right about now. As I have said, I am not in a popularity contest. I want you to be a saint and I am willing to risk all to help this be accomplished.

I would like to tell you a story to show you how the teaching above plays itself out today, in exactly the same manner as taught by John. If you want to be a saint, there are things you need to know. Please also be aware that I find no joy in the telling of anyone's failures and most of all because of the long list of my own failures. But there is a big difference between failing before your conversion and failing after being put in charge of God's House. Also know that I have been banned from speaking in one diocese for relating the truth in one of my editorials. That is the kind of revenge of which I spoke earlier.

If you do not invest your time in obtaining knowledge of God and praying for that knowledge, how will you know if what is being taught is or is not of God? The world is a trap for those destined for the pit, but you are not of this world. You have already proven that you desire what is above by reading that which leads to holiness. Continue on in constant pursuit of sainthood and sainthood will be yours. Ask anything of the Father in the name of Jesus Christ and it will be granted, as long as it is the Father's will. Your Father in heaven wants you to be a saint.

In this section I want to present how God constantly works in our lives to help us understand simple truths. Here we deal with a single Mass and one man's complete failure. I will leave the names and places out of the following story so as not to damage anyone's reputation.

Let us just say this happened somewhere in Canada. I had an experience with a priest there and it frightens me to this very day to see how some priests have given their lives over to Satan. They surrender to the point that they lose even the simplest knowledge they received in high school in spite of the fact that most of them have advanced degrees. Believe me, you have to know truth from fiction when you go to Mass these days or you could lose your very soul. Be like lambs, but wise like foxes.

I gave a presentation at a Catholic church one evening and all went well. In the morning, before leaving the area, I came back to the same church for Mass. At the time of the homily, the priest addressed me from the pulpit.

"Thomas, we do things a little different at weekday Mass here," he said. "I invite those in attendance to comment on the readings. As you are a guest, I will have you go first. Please tell us your feelings on today's Scripture."

I sighed a deep sigh, knowing I was in the presence of someone who had little regard for the authentic teaching of the Catholic Church. It breaks my heart to see religious all too willing to separate themselves from the rubrics and liturgy of Roman Catholicism, only be replaced with their own deceived notion of how they want it to be or rather how Satan wants it.

My response was, "Father, lay people are not allowed to do homilies." He was unrelenting and insisted to a point that it was embarrassing. I stood up and said, "I will only give in because the readings are some of my favorites and there is so much confusion over this subject that it needs clarifying." This was obviously God's will and not mine. I could not believe I was giving in. The Scripture was the following (I have obviously included more than the reading covered that day):

Exodus 14:11–*15:13 And they said to Moses, "Is it because there are no graves in Egypt that you have taken us away to die in the wilderness? What have you done to us, in bringing us out of Egypt? Is not this what we said to you in Egypt, 'Let us alone and let us serve the Egyptians'? For it would have been better for us to serve the Egyptians than to die in the wilderness." And Moses said to the people, "Fear not, stand firm, and see the salvation of the Lord, which he will work for you today; for the Egyptians whom you see today, you shall never see again. The Lord will fight for you, and you have only to be still."*

The Lord said to Moses, "Why do you cry to me? Tell the people of Israel to go forward. Lift up your rod, and stretch out your hand over the sea and divide it, that the people of Israel may go on dry ground through the sea. And I will harden the hearts of the Egyptians so that they shall go in after them, and I will get glory over Pharaoh and all his host, his chariots, and his horsemen. And the Egyptians shall know that I am the Lord, when I have gotten glory over Pharaoh, his chariots, and his horsemen."

Then the angel of God who went before the host of Israel moved and went behind them; and the pillar of cloud moved from before them and stood behind them, coming between the host of Egypt and the host of Israel. And there was the cloud and the darkness; and the night passed without one coming near the other all night. Then Moses stretched out his hand over the sea; and the Lord drove the sea back by a strong east wind all night, and made the sea dry land, and the waters were divided. And the people of Israel went into the midst of the sea on dry ground, the waters being a wall to them on their right hand and on their left.

The Egyptians pursued, and went in after them into the midst of the sea, all Pharaoh's horses, his chariots, and his horsemen. And in the morning watch the Lord in the pillar of fire and of cloud looked down upon the host of the Egyptians, and discomfited the host of the Egyptians, clogging their chariot wheels so that they drove heavily; and the Egyptians said, "Let us flee from before Israel; for the Lord fights for them against the Egyptians." Then the Lord said to Moses, "Stretch out your hand over the sea, that the water may come back upon the Egyptians, upon their chariots, and upon their horsemen."

So Moses stretched forth his hand over the sea, and the sea returned to its wonted flow when the morning appeared; and the Egyptians fled into it, and the Lord routed the Egyptians in the midst of the sea. The waters returned and covered the chariots and the horsemen and all the host of Pharaoh that had followed them into the sea; not so much as one of them remained. But the people of Israel walked on dry ground through the sea, the waters being a wall to them on their right hand and on their left. Thus the Lord saved Israel that day from the hand of the Egyptians; and Israel saw the Egyptians dead upon the seashore.

And Israel saw the great work, which the Lord did against the Egyptians, and the people feared the Lord; and they believed in the Lord and in his servant Moses.

Then Moses and the people of Israel sang this song to the Lord, saying, "I will sing to the Lord, for he has triumphed gloriously; the horse and his rider he has thrown into the sea. The Lord is my strength and my song, and he has become my salvation; this is my God, and I will praise him, my father's God, and I will exalt him. The Lord is a man of war; the Lord is his name. "Pharaoh's chariots and his host he cast into the sea; and his picked officers are sunk in the Red Sea. The floods cover them; they went down into the depths like a stone. Thy right hand, O Lord, glorious in power, thy right hand, O Lord, shatters the enemy. In the greatness of thy majesty thou overthrowest thy adversaries; thou sendest forth thy fury, it consumes them like stubble. At the blast of thy nostrils the waters piled up, the floods stood up in a heap; the deeps congealed in the heart of the sea. The enemy said, 'I will pursue, I will overtake, I will divide the spoil, my desire shall have its fill of them. I will draw my sword, my hand shall destroy them.' Thou didst blow with thy wind, the sea covered them; they sank as lead in the mighty waters. "Who is like thee, O Lord, among the gods? Who is like thee, majestic in holiness, terrible in glorious deeds, doing wonders? Thou didst stretch out thy right hand, the earth swallowed them. Thou hast led in thy steadfast love the people whom thou hast redeemed; thou hast guided them by thy strength to thy holy abode.

I said, "Father, in the United States, theology has become so tainted that the Holy Father himself had to intervene and address the theologians. He demanded that they return to teaching what the Catholic Church teaches.

"Pertaining to this story in the Bible, the theologians of my country, at times, explain that the Jews knew where the stones were and crossed over on the stones. The Egyptians, in failing to know where those stones were, drowned in the sea."

Quite a prophetic interpretation of Scripture, is it not?

The priest replied, "Obviously, Mr. Rutkoski, you do not understand tides. Tides are caused by wind. Here in Canada, we have very large tides. In Victoria, we have tides as high as twenty-five feet and that is exactly how the Jews crossed the sea safely. They crossed at low tide. By the time the Egyptians got there it was high tide and they drowned in the deep water."

What I meant when I said above that some have lost even the knowledge they learned in high school is this tide story. I learned in high school that tides were caused by the gravitational pull of the moon, not wind. I also have the basic knowledge that when a body of water is at low tide on one side, it is at high tide on the other and could not aid anyone in crossing.

Why would anyone want to dismantle God's miracles? It is to make God less important and the person doing the dismantling more important. These deconstructionists are on a head trip, with heads full of demon suggestions. The sad thing is that they do not even understand how foolish they sound.

After the Mass, I said my goodbyes to the pastor and was about to depart. A young woman came up to me and asked if I would give her a blessing. I responded by saying, "Why would you ask me to give you a blessing when there's a Catholic priest standing here? She immediately turned to the priest and asked him for a blessing.

The priest reached for the young woman and placed his hand on her head and began to say something I could not understand. The woman immediately started to scream. "Stop, stop," she yelled. "Get your hands off of me."

I could not believe what I was seeing. The woman broke out in hives from head to toe. Enormous hives, about the diameter of a softball. She ran outside screaming, and I chased after her. When I caught up to her, I asked what was wrong. She explained to me that when the priest laid his hand on her head she saw something horrible and ugly. I laid my hand on her head and I said a little prayer and the hives went away.

In trying to glean some understanding of what had just happened, the thought that passed through my mind, based on the false teaching in the Mass, was that he might be possessed. It was the only thing I could think of that might cause such a frightening episode.

I have not experienced only a few of these kinds of things, but so many that it causes me much dismay. I thank God for allowing me to experience these evil episodes. They are what allow me to understand how real Satan is and how vigilant I must be in defending myself. We all have to be on our guard twenty-four hours a day. Most people take their salvation for granted, but in reality, we are so fragile that hell is only one mortal sin away.

If my intention is to be a saint, then I should know what it is that gets me the closest to being in heaven now. I cannot allow myself to focus on all the evil that surrounds us. I must focus on Jesus Christ.

I find it amazing how the Lord drops spiritual bombshells in our lives and then gives us a lifetime to ponder them. It is in pondering everything that God places in each of our lives, our personal, private revelations, that we will start to experience heaven now, or at least part of it. One such instance happened to me probably in 1988 or 1989. The reason I cannot trace the chronological order of so much of what has happened to me is because I failed to journal. I believe if we used the ability that God has given us, we would all be able to see in retrospect how much the Lord is interacting with us. That is one of my big failures.

In the infancy of my conversion, I had an insatiable hunger for the Word. Not that this desire has died out, but back then it was a brand new experience for me. A thought, an inspiration about a Scripture would come to mind. Thanks be to God I had the Bible on computer and so I could sit down and research what it was that passed through my mind. In this case, I was being drawn to understand something profoundly theological. Believe me, I was not equipped for it then and am certainly not equipped for it now. I am not a theological person. It was not meant for me to understand then. God was giving me a lifetime to think about it and I do think about it a great deal.

This inspiration drew me to the Old Testament and the Angel of Death coming to Egypt. If you notice this story is the precursor to the story above about crossing the sea.

> Exodus 12:1-32 *The Lord said to Moses and Aaron in the land of Egypt, "This month shall stand at the head of your calendar; you shall reckon it the first month of the year. Tell the whole community of Israel: On the tenth of this month every one of your families must procure for itself a lamb, one apiece for each household. If a family is too small for a whole lamb, it shall join the nearest household in procuring one and shall share in the lamb in proportion to the number of persons who partake of it.*

The lamb must be a year-old male and without blemish. You may take it from either the sheep or the goats. You shall keep it until the fourteenth day of this month, and then, with the whole assembly of Israel present, it shall be slaughtered during the evening twilight. They shall take some of its blood and apply it to the two doorposts and the lintel of every house in which they partake of the lamb. That same night they shall eat its roasted flesh with unleavened bread and bitter herbs.

It shall not be eaten raw or boiled, but roasted whole, with its head and shanks and inner organs. None of it must be kept beyond the next morning; whatever is left over in the morning shall be burned up. "This is how you are to eat it: with your loins girt, sandals on your feet and your staff in hand, you shall eat like those who are in flight. It is the Passover of the Lord. For on this same night I will go through Egypt, striking down every first—born of the land, both man and beast, and executing judgment on all the gods of Egypt-I, the Lord!

But the blood will mark the houses where you are. Seeing the blood, I will pass over you; thus, when I strike the land of Egypt, no destructive blow will come upon you. "This day shall be a memorial feast for you, which all your generations shall celebrate with pilgrimage to the Lord, as a perpetual institution.

For seven days you must eat unleavened bread. From the very first day you shall have your houses clear of all leaven. Whoever eats leavened bread from the first day to the seventh shall be cut off from Israel. On the first day you shall hold a sacred assembly, and likewise on the seventh. On these days you shall not do any sort of work, except to prepare the food that everyone needs. "Keep, then, this custom of the unleavened bread. Since it was on this very day that I brought your ranks out of the land of Egypt, you must celebrate this day throughout your generations as a perpetual institution.

From the evening of the fourteenth day of the first month until the evening of the twenty-first day of this month you shall eat unleavened bread. For seven days no leaven may be found in your houses. Anyone, be he a resident alien or a native, who eats leavened food shall be cut off from the community of Israel. Nothing leavened may you eat; wherever you dwell you may eat only unleavened bread."

Moses called all the elders of Israel and said to them, "Go and procure lambs for your families, and slaughter them as Passover victims. Then take a bunch of hyssop, and dipping it in the blood that is in the basin, sprinkle the lintel and the two doorposts with this blood. But none of you shall go outdoors until morning. For the Lord will go by, striking down the Egyptians. Seeing the blood on the lintel and the two doorposts, the Lord will pass over that door and not let the destroyer come into your houses to strike you down. "You shall observe this as a perpetual ordinance for yourselves and your descendants. Thus, you must also observe this rite when you have entered the land, which the Lord will give you as he promised.

When your children ask you, 'What does this rite of yours mean?' you shall reply, 'This is the Passover sacrifice of the Lord, who passed over the houses of the Israelites in Egypt; when he struck down the Egyptians, he spared our houses." Then the people bowed down in worship, and the Israelites went and did as the Lord had commanded Moses and Aaron.

At midnight the Lord slew every first-born in the land of Egypt, from the first-born of Pharaoh on the throne to the first-born of the prisoner in the dungeon, as well as all the first-born of the animals. Pharaoh arose in the night, he and all his servants and all the Egyptians; and there was loud wailing throughout Egypt, for there was not a house without its dead.

During the night Pharaoh summoned Moses and Aaron and said, "Leave my people at once, you and the

Israelites with you! Go and worship the Lord as you said. Take your flocks, too, and your herds, as you demanded, and be gone; and you will be doing me a favor."

Normally when I read Scripture it goes flying over my head and this one did. I could not understand anything about the Scripture other than God teaching the Pharaoh a lesson and trying to make him release the Jews.

I was then led to a Scripture in the New Testament, the teaching that came from the Last Supper.

> John 6:35-64 *Jesus said to them, "I am the bread of life; whoever comes to me will never hunger, and whoever believes in me will never thirst. But I told you that although you have seen (me), you do not believe. Everything that the Father gives me will come to me, and I will not reject anyone who comes to me, because I came down from heaven not to do my own will but the will of the one who sent me.*
>
> *And this is the will of the one who sent me, that I should not lose anything of what he gave me, but that I should raise it (on) the last day. For this is the will of my Father, that everyone who sees the Son and believes in him may have eternal life, and I shall raise him (on) the last day."*
>
> *The Jews murmured about him because he said, "I am the bread that came down from heaven," and they said, "Is this not Jesus, the son of Joseph? Do we not know his father and other? Then how can he say, 'I have come down from heaven'?" Jesus answered and said to them, "Stop murmuring among ourselves. No one can come to me unless the Father who sent me draw him, and I will raise him on the last day. It is written in the prophets: 'They shall all be taught by God.' Everyone who listens to my Father and learns from him comes to me. Not that anyone has seen the Father except the one who is from God; he has seen the Father.*

Amen, amen, I say to you, whoever believes has eternal life. I am the bread of life. Your ancestors ate the manna in the desert, but they died; this is the bread that comes down from heaven so that one may eat it and not die.

I am the living bread that came down from heaven; whoever eats this bread will live forever; and the bread that I will give is my flesh for the life of the world."

The Jews quarreled among themselves, saying, "How can this man give us (his) flesh to eat?"

Jesus said to them, "Amen, amen, I say to you, unless you eat the flesh of the Son of Man and drink his blood, you do not have life within you. Whoever eats my flesh and drinks my blood has eternal life, and I will raise him on the last day. For my flesh is true food, and my blood is true drink. Whoever eats my flesh and drinks my blood remains in me and I in him.

Just as the living Father sent me and I have life because of the Father, so also the one who feeds on me will have life because of me. This is the bread that came down from heaven. Unlike your ancestors who ate and still died, whoever eats this bread will live forever."

These things he said while teaching in the synagogue in Capernaum. Then many of his disciples who were listening said, "This saying is hard; who can accept it?" Since Jesus knew that his disciples were murmuring about this, he said to them, "Does this shock you? What if you were to see the Son of Man ascending to where he was before? It is the spirit that gives life, while the flesh is of no avail. The words I have spoken to you are spirit and life. But there are some of you who do not believe." Jesus knew from the beginning the ones who would not believe and the one who would betray him.

When I read this I knew instantly that there was a connection between the use of the body and blood of the lamb in the Old

Testament and the use of the body and blood of the lamb in the New Testament. It became so clear to me that unless you eat the body and drink the blood of Jesus Christ, you really do not have life in you. And ignorance has nothing to do with the death spoken of here, just as ignorance had nothing to do with the death of the animals in the Old Testament. You either do what God says or you die.

I experienced this somewhere round 1988. And now I see in Scott Hahn's book, *The Lamb's Supper*, this very scenario spelled out in a very theological way. This only goes to show me that God is trying very hard to deal with a not-so-scholarly person like myself as well as the very scholarly, like Scott Hahn. He is trying to lead us all to holiness.

Remember, unless your holiness surpasses that of the bishops and priests, the Pharisees and the Sadducees, you will not obtain sainthood. Your track record must be remarkable. You shall not have had a cowardly bone in your body. Stand up and be counted, Christian soldier, and march on to Chapter Eighteen.

NOTES

CHAPTER EIGHTEEN

INDULGENCES

While on a speaking tour in Florida, a new friend of mine, John Youngblood, gave me a little present. It was an old prayer book titled *The Treasury of the Sacred Heart*, dated 1912. When he gave me the gift we were at about 10,000 feet flying from Lakeland to North Palm Beach. As we flew with John and our pilot, Bill Meehan, I opened the prayer book and instantly found this next addition to this book. The first chapter was on indulgences. The first paragraph quoted Matthew 16:19, *"Thou art Peter,"* setting up the fact that the Catholic Church has the God-given right to institute great help in our becoming saints, thus we get the gift of indulgences.

The second paragraph introduced me to Saint Alphonsus. Saint Alphonsus tells us that in order to become a saint, nothing is more needed than to gain all the indulgences we can; and Saint Leonard of Port Maurice says something to the same effect. If you are not a collector of indulgences, you'd better get to it.

> Sin produces two bitter fruits in the soul: the guilt that deprives us of grace, the friendship of God, and the punishment, which is due that sin. We have to be aware of God's justice. This punishment is of two kinds, temporal and eternal. The guilt of sin and the eternal punishment due to it (hell), are remitted, through the merits of Jesus, in the sacrament of penance (confession); but the temporal punishment must be atoned for in this life or in the next (purgatory) unless cancelled by indulgences, or by acts of penance, or by other good works. An indulgence is, therefore, the remission of the temporal punishment due to actual sin already forgiven in the sacrament of penance as to the guilt and the eternal punishment. This remission is made by the application of the merits and satisfactions of Jesus, with those of the Blessed Virgin, and of all the saints, which have all their value from Christ, who is the only mediator of redemption.

There are two sorts of indulgences – plenary and partial. A partial indulgence remits only part of the temporal pain due to sin. By a plenary indulgence we gain the remission of all temporal punishment due to sins forgiven, provided we have the proper disposition and comply with the conditions required. These conditions are: to be in the state of grace and to have the intention of gaining the indulgence. But this intention may be virtual, that is, we may have formed it previously, though from distraction or inadvertence, we do not think of it when we fulfill the conditions of the indulgence, for the intention continues, Unless it be revoked by a contrary act, or cease by too great length of time. It is recommended, therefore, in our morning prayers, to form an intention of gaining all the indulgences that are annexed to the prayers and other pious actions we perform during the course of the day, and to apply them for ourselves or for the dead. Don't do this and the indulgence is lost.

To gain a plenary indulgence, we must confess and communicate (receive the Eucharist). Communion must be received on the day a plenary indulgence is to be obtained, unless it be otherwise prescribed in the grant. This is a very good reason to attend Mass daily. Confession may be made on the day previous, and weekly penitents may gain several indulgences in the same week without confessing previous to each indulgence. We must likewise, in most cases, pray for the pope's intention. For this purpose we may say five Our Fathers and Hail Marys in honor of the five wounds of Our Lord, for the exaltation of the Catholic Church, propagation of the faith, peace among Christian princes, the extirpation of heresy, the conversion of sinners, and for all the intentions of the Holy Church.

To gain the *full* effect of a plenary indulgence, we must be free, not only from mortal sin but even from every attachment to venial faults. Keep in mind that one can have all venial sins removed by blessing oneself with holy water and doing it with the intention of removing those smaller sins. If a person labored with all his power to make satisfaction and complied with all the requisite conditions, and if he were truly penitent, and so well disposed as to gain the full effects of a plenary indulgence, should he die immediately after, his soul would suffer nothing in purgatory, but would go directly to heaven. The same may be said of the faithful departed whenever, in their favor, we fully gain a plenary indulgence which is applicable to them; the soul to whom the indulgence is applied, that moment is liberated from the painful flames and received into glory, provided the divine justice deigns to accept it in her favor. How desirable, therefore, is it to procure the dispositions necessary to gain these celestial treasures! It would be, however, a fatal delusion for anyone to make himself certain of having obtained the remission of all punishment due to mortal sin by gaining an indulgence so as to neglect the practice of penance. This would be an infringement of the divine precept, "bring forth fruits worthy of penance."

As mentioned, I received an old book as a gift, and the rules on indulgences have changed some. There is a new *Handbook of Indulgences* issued by the Holy See on June 29, 1968. There are three general concessions in regard to the gaining of a partial indulgence. The definitions of indulgences have stayed pretty much the same but the extreme importance of this particular subject demands that you read the Vatican's *Handbook of Indulgences*. There's also a small book titled *New Regulations on Indulgences* by Father Winfrid Herbst.

Indulgences have gotten a bad rap because of the terrible practice of selling them in the days of Martin Luther. Greedy religious decided this was a great and easy ways to raise funds and allow the punishment due one's sins to be eliminated for a price. Sounds like things haven't changed all that much in the Church. But one thing has changed - an indulgence is *bona fide* if you follow the Church's prescription and you don't slip somebody a quick twenty bucks. You can spare yourself a lot of suffering in purgatory.

If today you would go to confession, go to Mass, receive the Eucharist and fulfill all the requirements of a plenary indulgence, you'd be a saint. It would be best if you died that second. Is that something you want? If you're not going to attempt taking your own life, but are willing to allow God's divine providence to make that decision and stay in that state of grace until He does, you just may cross the *Great Divide* to your safe haven, Christ. And that good decision allows you to continue on to Chapter Nineteen.

NOTES

CHAPTER NINETEEN

NO QUITTERS

Once you start your journey toward sainthood, you can, as we now know, expect and receive a lot of flak from the evil one. It would be no different than a World War II pilot flying over Germany looking for the right place to drop his bombs, expecting the Germans not to do all they could to stop his plane from reaching its target. Flak is the military weaponry that is designed to inhibit bombers from reaching their targets. These explosive devices were sent into the air in barrages at many different altitudes, to increase the chances of one exploding near an enemy plane to take it out of the sky.

It is no different for us in this war of principalities. The enemy does all he can to stop us as we journey towards heaven. I see myself receiving a lot of flak damage and also see others receiving the same damage, even enough to take some out of the sky. This is a rough war, but most on the battlefield don't even think they are in a war.

The pedophile scandal in the Church at the time of this writing shows how deep the enemy has penetrated. And we have not even started to address the dreadful, mortal sin of active homosexuality within the priesthood. The numbers that are involved in this sin, I believe, will not be small. And the parish priest who is loved by all of his parishioners, but is disobedient to the Magisterium – he, too, is a casualty, for he has violated his priestly vows. These have rejected God's grace, allowed Satan to take control, and they have become quitters.

As in all wars, there are heroes. We have lay heroes and we have religious heroes. I especially love the priests who keep an obedient and honorable relationship with their bishops. They are truly heroes. The bishops who align themselves with the Pope are heroes, also - every one of them. They have fought off Satan and sustained.

There is a big difference between priests who surrender to Satan's call and the ones who stay true to the Lord. Even the good and loyal priests come under severe attacks as in the false accusations some suffer. It is easy for someone who has a vendetta against the Church to single out a priest and lie about him, just to cause him and the Church harm. This has happened many times, but a hero does not waver. He weathers the storm and comes out fighting for the Lord. He is not a quitter. He is a survivor and a hero. Thank God for priestly heroes.

There are lay people who go through the same problems as the priests. Some pass the test and some also become quitters. I know, because I have been there. I have been advised not to relate this story here because it could cause doubts about me. I am willing to suffer all for the sake of the truth. This example is one that needs telling so we can be more careful when judging priests, for some must be accused wrongfully.

This is a story about one young lady whom I thought was as close to a saint as anyone I've ever met (keeping in mind that I never met Mother Teresa.) This is my story of flak damage. For the sake of confidentiality, let's call this woman, a former employee of Gospa Missions, Joan, as in 'of Arc.' I think this employee had much in common with Joan of Arc because she started out with a zeal that was beyond anything I had seen before. She seemed to be able to express how she felt with a truth from her heart. I was positive she was being guided supernaturally.

As I watched her handle each and every situation in her life and in her job so well, I was enthralled with how it seemed to come so easily to the young woman. I trusted her with all that I held sacred.

She was the closest thing to a daughter I ever had and I was as proud as I could be when she expressed the desire to pursue a religious vocation. She was saintly and now wanted to give her life to God. Enter the flight/flak scenario orchestrated by Satan. He is the one responsible for destroying vocations. By the way, he is very good at it. People do not give Lucifer enough credit for the damage he inflicts. Many believe he is just a myth and that is just the way he wants it.

Eventually, a young man entered Joan's life and she asked me what I thought of marriage. My explanation was from the words of the apostle Paul when he exclaimed, *"I wish none of you would marry."* Paul conveys to us that marriage is the most difficult path to salvation, although every version of the Bible expresses it differently and there are many versions. Paul is not saying marriage is bad, just very difficult. Many married people will attest to that fact and we can observe this, in this day and age, through the fact that fifty percent or higher of all marriages fail. When this occurs, faith generally crumbles and you have more quitters.

> 1 Cor 7:27-38 *If you are joined to a wife, do not seek to be released; if you are freed of a wife, do not look for a wife. However, if you do get married, that is not a sin, and it is not sinful for a virgin to enter upon marriage. But such people will have the hardships consequent on human nature, and I would like you to be without that.*
>
> *What I mean, brothers, is that the time has become limited, and from now on, those who have spouses should live as though they had none; and those who mourn as though they were not mourning; those who enjoy life as though they did not enjoy it; those who have been buying property as though they had no possessions; and those who are involved with the world as though they were people not engrossed in it. Because this world as we know it is passing away. I should like you to have your minds free from all worry. The unmarried man gives his mind to the Lord's affairs and to how he can please the Lord; but the man who is married gives his mind to the affairs of this world and to how he can please his wife, and he is divided in mind. So, too, the unmarried woman, and the virgin, gives her mind to the Lord's affairs and to being holy in body and spirit; but the married woman gives her mind to the affairs of this world and to how she can please her husband.*
>
> *I am saying this only to help you, not to put a bridle on you, but so that everything is as it should be, and you are able to give your undivided attention to the Lord. If*

someone with strong passions thinks that he is behaving badly towards his fiancée and that things should take their due course, he should follow his desires. There is no sin in it; they should marry. But if he stands firm in his resolution, without any compulsion but with full control of his own will, and decides to let her remain as his fiancée, then he is acting well. In other words, he who marries his fiancée is doing well and he who does not, better still.

My conversation with Joan about marriage led to the deterioration of the relationship between her and me from that day on. She could not believe Scripture would ever caution against marriage and demanded that I show her where it was in the Bible. I showed her the above Scriptures. No kind words came from her direction until we went our inevitable, separate ways. I tried to address the situation a few times, but to no avail.

It is my spirituality and the spirituality of those who work with me, to spend a holy hour in front of the Blessed Sacrament daily. We had a habit of doing this holy hour prior to morning Mass. Joan was one of the most dedicated attendees, but after this incident, she stopped coming. Two times I asked, in a group forum, for better attendance at the holy hour. This seemed to make her even more distant.

The last time I tried to address her absenteeism I said, "All I ever wanted was for you to spend an hour with me . . . ." There was much more I had planned to say. I wanted to tell her how important our group holy hours were for the life of our mission and for her salvation, but I could not go on. I was so heartbroken by her cold stare that I started to cry and I motioned with my hand for her to leave. She not only left my sight, but a few days later she left our little Mission entirely. She never even said goodbye to me. This is not the stuff of which saints are made.

A few days later, Betty, our Mission's dedicated accountant, said she was leaving also. I couldn't believe it. It was like the apostolate was falling apart. I asked Betty for a reason, but a definitive answer was not forthcoming. My persistence in seeking an answer finally paid off. Betty said that Joan related to her that I had made sexual advances toward her. I was aghast! How could someone ever make a false statement like that? But was it a false statement to her? In Joan's precarious mental state, a demon could have slipped in and caused her mind to interpret a conversation in a way it was not meant to be. To make a statement such as the one she made without conferring with a spiritual director is foolhardy. Joan had taken my unfinished sentence about spending an hour with her as something evil and quite different from the holy hour about which I was speaking. Once Satan enters, we are not in control of what we think or say. Judas experienced the same attack by the father of lies.

> 1 Tim 4:1 *Now the Spirit expressly says that in later times some will depart from the faith by giving heed to deceitful spirits and doctrines of demons, through the pretensions of liars whose consciences are seared.*

Poor Joan was fasting so much, praying so much and doing all that seemed so right, but a simple matter of not turning her cheek to a perceived offense can constitute a crucial loss of direction on the path toward salvation. The Our Father Prayer has us asking God to forgive us just as we forgive others. God cannot let her into heaven unless she forgives or accepts forgiveness. Judas would not accept forgiveness and so, we believe, went to hell. So be on your guard all the time, knowing that Satan wants you in hell.

Thank God that Betty, in the end, believed me and stayed at the Mission. Betty's discernment is to her credit and will go far on the Day of Judgment.

> 1 Tim 4:3-14 *If you put these instructions before the brethren, you will be a good minister of Christ Jesus, nourished on the words of the faith and of the good doctrine, which you have followed. Have nothing to do with godless and silly myths. Train yourself in godliness; for while bodily training is of some value, godliness is of value in every way, as it holds promise for the present life and also for the life to come. The saying is sure and worthy of full acceptance. For to this end we toil and*

strive, because we have our hope set on the living God, who is the Savior of all men, especially of those who believe. Command and teach these things. Let no one despise your youth, but set the believers an example in speech and conduct, in love, in faith, in purity. Till I come, attend to the public reading of Scripture, to preaching, to teaching. Do not neglect the gift you have, which was given you by prophetic utterance when the council of elders laid their hands upon you.

There is a way to make your journey a little more flak-proof and hopefully keep you from being a quitter.

> 1 Tim 6:11-21 *But as for you, man of God, aim at righteousness, godliness, faith, love, steadfastness, gentleness. Fight the good fight of the faith; take hold of the eternal life to which you were called when you made the good confession in the presence of many witnesses. In the presence of God who gives life to all things, and of Christ Jesus who in his testimony before Pontius Pilate made the good confession, I charge you to keep the commandment unstained and free from reproach until the appearing of our Lord Jesus Christ; and this will be made manifest at the proper time by the blessed and only Sovereign, the King of kings and Lord of lords, who alone has immortality and dwells in unapproachable light, whom no man has ever seen or can see. To him be honor and eternal dominion. Amen.*
>
> *As for the rich in this world, charge them not to be haughty, nor to set their hopes on uncertain riches but on God who richly furnishes us with everything to enjoy. They are to do good, to be rich in good deeds, liberal and generous, thus laying up for themselves a good foundation for the future, so that they may take hold of the life which is life indeed. O Timothy, guard what has been entrusted to you. Avoid the godless chatter and contradictions of what is falsely called knowledge, for by professing it some have missed the mark as regards the faith. Grace be with you.*

If you allow grace to be a constant companion and take full advantage of all of the sacraments, things will go well - maybe not now, but later, certainly. Many people sin and then refuse to go to confession, and the landslide begins. You can go downhill so fast by just quitting on something that seems to be small. Who makes it seem small? You guessed it, the great destroyer. When you are shooting for the top, for sainthood, take all sin seriously. It is better to get every failure fixed through a Catholic priest as fast as you can. And do not allow some wayward priest to talk you into general absolution. Not only is he tinkering with his salvation, but he may also be tinkering with yours. Live your faith by the book. If you cease to live what the true Church teaches, you become a quitter. There are no quitters in heaven.

A prime example of one who refused to quit is Saint Faustina Kowalska. She is a saint for our time and is the one who gave us the devotion to Divine Mercy.

Faustina had a very difficult time in the convent. The other sisters gave her much trouble. You should read her diary titled *Divine Mercy in My Soul.* One story in the book relates how Sister Faustina opened a door, only to find two nuns involved in an act of mortal sin, as she put it. So we can see things have not changed all that much. I believe the point of her whole book is never to quit. Fight every day for your immortal soul.

I have some good advice for anyone who is contemplating a vocation and is discouraged by recent scandal. I also supply the same advice for those already in the process, but not ordained or professed. If you are stalling on a call to a vocation or you are trying it out and are being oppressed for being orthodox in your faith, hang in there. The problems are not with God not wanting you as a religious. It is Satan who does not want that. *Do not quit!* We need you badly. If there is an attempt to compromise your morality within the seminary or convent, hold your own and pray. If you find the process so liberal that it tests your faith, *do not quit!* Tolerate all that the blind guides throw your way. Pretend to implement their deceitful ways right up to the day you are ordained or processed and then come out of your orthodox closet, to be the best priest or nun this world has ever had. *Just don't quit!*

You are on the home stretch and the race is drawing to an end. If you can hold out a little longer and want to plug into your life what you've been learning; if you are willing to make a firm commitment to wear your flak jacket, defend yourself against Satan's attacks, and run this race to the end, continue to the last chapter.

NOTES

CHAPTER TWENTY

AND THE LIST GOES ON . . .

Please allow me to summarize a bit and add some finishing touches to a subject that I have barely covered. The parameters of salvation are many and you are only one mortal sin away from failure. Be vigilant in your pursuit of sainthood, don't get involved with the constant division, other than fighting against it, and know that with God all things are possible.

The Lord left behind some rather specific assignments that He wanted us to accomplish in our lives. Please go over what I have offered in the way of a list and make a list of your own. Make sure you are working on these constantly. Dive into Scripture and find all of the other parameters for salvation that, through my own ignorance, I have left out. I suggest that you get a computer-based Bible. With it, you can search on any topic and come up instantly with everything the Bible has to offer on any particular subject. The following passages were found on just such a search.

Between the lawyer, the rich man and the scribe, Jesus answered many of our questions in regard to salvation:

> Luke 10:25-27 *There was a scholar of the law who stood up to test him and said, "Teacher, what must I do to inherit eternal life?" Jesus said to him, "What is written in the law? How do you read it?" He said in reply, "You shall love the Lord, your God, with all your heart, with all your being, with all your strength, and with all your mind, and your neighbor as yourself."*

> Mt 19:16-22 *Now someone approached him and said, "Teacher, what good must I do to gain eternal life?" He answered him, "Why do you ask me about the good? There is only One who is good. If you wish to enter into life, keep the commandments." He asked him, "Which ones?" And Jesus replied, " You shall not kill; you shall not commit adultery; you shall not steal; you shall not*

bear false witness; honor your father and your mother'; and 'you shall love your neighbor as yourself.'" The young man said to him, "All of these I have observed. What do I still lack?" Jesus said to him, "If you wish to be perfect, go, sell what you have and give to (the) poor, and you will have treasure in heaven. Then come, follow me." When the young man heard this statement, he went away sad, for he had many possessions.

Mt 22:35-40 *A scholar of the law tested him by asking, "Teacher, which commandment in the law is the greatest?" He said to him, "You shall love the Lord, your God, with all your heart, with all your soul, and with all your mind. This is the greatest and the first commandment. The second is like it: You shall love your neighbor as yourself. The whole law and the prophets depend on these two commandments."*

And here is good advice, also!

James 1:1-27 *James, a servant of God and of the Lord Jesus Christ, to the twelve tribes in the Dispersion: Greeting. Count it all joy, my brethren, when you meet various trials, for you know that the testing of your faith produces steadfastness. And let steadfastness have its full effect, that you may be perfect and complete, lacking in nothing.*

If any of you lacks wisdom, let him ask God, who gives to all men generously and without reproaching, and it will be given him. But let him ask in faith, with no doubting, for he who doubts is like a wave of the sea that is driven and tossed by the wind. For that person must not suppose that a double-minded man, unstable in all his ways, will receive anything from the Lord. Let the lowly brother boast in his exaltation, and the rich in his humiliation, because like the flower of the grass he will pass away. For the sun rises with its scorching heat and withers the grass; its flower falls, and its beauty perishes. So will the rich man fade away in the midst of his pursuits? Blessed is the man who endures trial, for when he has stood the test he will receive the crown of life which God has promised to those who love him. Let no one say when he is tempted, "I am tempted by God"; for God cannot be tempted with evil and he himself tempts no one; but each person is tempted when he is lured and enticed by his own desire. Then desire when it has conceived gives birth to sin; and sin when it is full-grown brings forth death.

Do not be deceived, my beloved brethren. Every good endowment and every perfect gift is from above, coming down from the Father of lights with whom there is no variation or shadow due to change. Of his own will he brought us forth by the word of truth that we should be a kind of first fruits of His creatures.

Know this, my beloved brethren. Let every man be quick to hear, slow to speak, slow to anger, for the anger of man does not work the righteousness of God. Therefore put away all filthiness and rank growth of wickedness and receive with meekness the implanted word, which is able to save your souls. But be doers of the word, and not hearers only, deceiving yourselves. For if any one is a hearer of the word and not a doer, he is like a man who observes his natural face in a mirror; for he observes himself and goes away and at once forgets what he was like. But he who looks into the perfect law, the law of liberty, and perseveres, being no hearer that forgets but a doer that acts, he shall be blessed in his doing.

If any one thinks he is religious, and does not bridle his tongue but deceives his heart, this man's religion is vain. Religion that is pure and undefiled before God and the Father is this: to visit orphans and widows in their affliction, and to keep oneself unstained from the world.

2 Tim 4:1-8 *I charge you in the presence of God and of Christ Jesus who is to judge the living and the dead, and by His appearing and His kingdom: preach the word, be urgent in season and out of season, convince, rebuke,*

and exhort, be unfailing in patience and in teaching. For the time is coming when people will not endure sound teaching, but having itching ears. They will accumulate for themselves teachers to suit their own likings, and will turn away from listening to the truth and wander into myths.

As for you, always be steady, endure suffering, do the work of an evangelist, fulfill your ministry. For I am already on the point of being sacrificed; the time of my departure has come. I have fought the good fight, I have finished the race, I have kept the faith. Henceforth there is laid up for me the crown of righteousness, which the Lord, the righteous judge, will award to me on that Day, and not only to me but also to all who have loved his appearing.

Start making that list now, the list that fights against the *Great Divide*: 1) Go to Mass every day. 2) Pray fifteen decades of the Rosary each day. 3) Fast on bread and water Wednesdays and Fridays. 4) Go to confession once a month. 5) Have conversion of the heart daily. 6) Take care of the orphans and visit the widows and prisoners in their affliction. 7) Feed the poor. 8) Keep oneself unstained from the world, and the list goes on.

I thank you for enduring my book and I believe if you make a commitment to implement what the Lord has placed here, you will exit this life with grace and when that *final Great Divide* comes, you will be with the sheep. I feel a little like I let you down by not helping you enough. There is so much more I wanted to share. But I do hopefully have twelve more books to come. In the meantime, keep in mind that there are no cowards in heaven.

There is only one perfect example of a human being exiting full of grace and she is our shining star. I beseech you to embrace the Blessed Virgin Mary and ask for her constant intercession. With your commitment and her leading you to her Son, Jesus Christ, how can you fail?

Be a survivor of division and crisis. Sainthood is within your grasp.

EPILOGUE

I am always impressed by how God inspires us at just the right moment. When I was finished writing this book, I had an afterthought. When this occurs, a page or two can be added at the end of the book to accommodate that thought, and it is called an epilogue. I placed this thought on paper and after reading it through several times I did not care for it and so I discarded it.

Since it is not necessary to have an epilogue, I just left it out and went on with final proofreading. Something would not let me forget the word 'epilogue', and I did have several pages left at the end of the book. But I resigned myself to the fact I did not have an appropriate afterthought and so, no epilogue.

Lo, and behold the creativeness of our Lord. This last day of final preparation before I sent the manuscript off to be printed, I went to Mass, as I do every day. In the homily, my pastor, Father Bober, said, "Today is the feast of Saint Monica and tomorrow is the feast of her son, Saint Augustine."

Father then related how Saint Monica cried for many years, begging the Lord to save her son. Augustine was a wild and sinful man who refused to get involved with the faith of his mother. She feared for his soul. But Augustine had a game plan. He knew that baptism took away all sin. He cunningly figured that he would go on sinning until he had his fun and then he would be baptized later in life and sail safely into heaven.

What a game plan. Augustine had every thing figured out except for the Scripture that explains that Christ comes like a thief in the night. What if Christ had come before he was baptized? Augustine would have spent all of the days of eternity in hell for hedging his bets. This is what made Monica cry to the Lord. Father explained that she may have given up personally on her son, but never gave up on the Lord. Her prayers were answered, not quickly, but answered in God's time.

Augustine happened upon Saint Ambrose as he was evangelizing in Milan and the hook was set. Augustine had a conversion at age thirty-three and handed his life over to the Lord. He is now called Saint Augustine.

The feast day of Saint Augustine is on the very day this book goes in the mail to the printer. My thought, and the reason I believe God knew all along that this epilogue would be placed here on this very day is this: The Lord wants everyone to experience conversion and would like that to occur today. Too many people, like Augustine, put off for tomorrow what could be accomplished sooner and put themselves at great risk. Please do not play Augustinian roulette with your soul. This epilogue is half for those who procrastinate and half for those who pray for the conversion of a loved one.

For you procrastinators, dissenters and liberals who are putting off surrender to God until a later date, please read a book called *Hell* by Fr. F. X. Schouppe, SJ, Tan Publishing. I am sure if this book did not bring about your conversion, that book will.

For you who pray for the conversion of someone or are praying for the Church to return to something beautiful and full of reverence, and seem to see no results, take the example of Saint Monica to heart. It will take a lot of perseverance in prayer and fasting to weather this storm caused by this *Great Divide.*

An Invitation

As a disciple of Jesus, your responsibility is great, so I invite you to accept the challenge of doing much more for God. Your first priority should be the honest support of your parish and diocese. With so few attending Mass in so many parishes, the collections are down in many places and there are fewer people to volunteer their time.

After fulfilling your commitment to the Church, I invite you to become part of Gospa Missions (Our Lady's Missions) and be an Apostle of the Last Days. You can do this in several ways. If you have the ability to lay your current life aside, if you are healthy and financially solvent, think about coming to Gospa Missions to work with us. We need a few good professionals to work at the Mission headquarters. Local volunteers are always welcome to help out a few hours or a few days a week at our religious store or in the office. Contact us to see if your talents will fit into our needs.

Shopping for all of your religious goods at our *Amazing Grace* store in Evans City, PA, on the internet at www.gospa.org or www.catholicbookstore.org, or through our Gospa Missions mail order department, will have you involved in God's work. How? Because we are a nonprofit organization and all proceeds support the Mission and our humanitarian activities. God asks for a fair percentage of our time, talent and treasure. I am only suggesting ways to do just that.

It is people like you who set up all of the places where I speak. You could invite me to your conference, set up one presentation or a whole tour in your area. Contact me for a speaker portfolio. So all you have to do is pick a subject, call me to set the date, and find a place to do it. I can give up to five different talks which can be your parish mission or Life in the Spirit seminar. I could give a presentation at your grade school, high school or CCD program. I love speaking to kids. The talks I have delivered to prison inmates have been very special to me, as well. I do not charge a stipend and the airfare is not even always required, so it could cost you nothing.

You could support this Mission through the Gospa Missions newsletter. It is one of the best periodicals in the business. The short and simple teachings, devotions, prayers, information on the saints, book and video reviews and hard-hitting editorials will help you to stay rooted in your faith. Consider subscribing.

Financial assistance for our orphanage in Ogoja, Nigeria, Africa, or sponsorship of a child would be great.

I ask people who want to support my evangelizing or see that the book gets into the hands of people who cannot afford it, to send a $30 donation. I ask $30 from all of you who read the book (even if it was just loaned to you or if you already paid for it,) if it helped you in your spiritual journey. Be willing to help us help others.

Donations have come. From $20 to a high of $7000 at one time, came in envelopes, as people voiced their support for Catholic evangelists and expressed their desire to help spread the Good News. They added their prayers and they made Gospa Missions grow to be a powerful force against Satan. With their help, we distributed 25,000 free copies of *Apostles of the Last Days*. We have sent books, tapes, and videos to prisons, the military and to the less fortunate all over the world. You can continue this tradition by sending a donation yourself. Send what you can and we will maximize your gift. This means that your donation will not go to furnish some executive with a big salary. The highest paid person at Gospa Missions receives only nine thousand dollars a year. I, myself, did not receive a paycheck for more than eight years. I will be prudent with your donation.

If you would like to write me, my address is:

Thomas Rutkoski
333 Wilderness Trail
Evans City, PA 16033

Whatever you decide to do, may God bless you.

In the love of Christ,

Thomas Rutkoski
Founder, Gospa Missions

Other Works By Thomas Rutkoski

Books

Apostles of the Last Days
Miracles, and How To Work Them
The Contextual Rosary of Scripture

Video Tapes

Conversion Story
The Responsibility of Being Catholic

Audio tapes

Conversion Story
The Responsibility of Being Catholic
Miracles in My Life
Tom Talks to Kids (7-14)
Tom Talks to Teens (15-20)
God's Winning Team
In Giving, You Receive

Popular Products from Gospa Missions

Crucifix-medal of St. Benedict
Our Lady of Grace (The Tihaljina statue)
Image of Jesus Prints
The Pope with the Blessed Mother Prints

Above products, all titles mentioned in this book, and over 3000 other items are available through Gospa Missions by mail or on the web at **www.gospa.org** or **www.catholicbookstore.org**

The Contextual Rosary of Scripture

We all should know after reading *Great Divide* how important it is to pray the Rosary in these days. If many great saints prayed the Rosary, then we should ask ourselves, "Why not me?"

Praying the Rosary is more than just picking up your beads and saying a bunch of Hail Marys. *The Contextual Rosary of Scripture* is an aid, in booklet form, to maximize the power of the Rosary, by helping you meditate on the life, death and resurrection of Jesus Christ.

In this little book you are presented with the Scriptures in context to make them flow with each Hail Mary you pray. This book was originally created to be included in each box of *The Chocolate Rosary* mentioned in these pages. We hope that you will want all of your friends to have one, so they are available to be purchased separately for $4.95.

This pocket size book is easily carried on your person, to be ready as a serious prayer form, in those times of great need.

St. Joseph Orphanage/School

A project of Gospa Missions

In 1995, Thomas Rutkoski, the founder of Gospa Missions, and his wife Mary, visited Ogoja, Nigeria at the request of Father Peter Abue. They became aware of hundreds of children in the area who were living in desolation. Then Tom promised that Gospa Missions would do something to help them if they prayed enough. When they returned home, they began soliciting funds to build an orphanage in Ogoja to supply food, clothing, shelter, schooling, and ultimately, hope.

Today, more than 400 children pray for our intentions as St. Joseph Orphange/School is completed.

Gospa Missions has developed a program which allows you to sponsor one of our orphans. For $240 a year, you can help provide a child with food, clothing, shelter, and an education. Only 65 cents a day! One hundred percent of the funds go to help the children at the St. Joseph Orphanage/School in Ogoja.

As a sponsor, you will be able to choose the age range and gender of your child. Gospa Missions will provide you with a Sponsor Kit that includes:

- ✔ A color photo of your child
- ✔ Biographical information about your child
- ✔ Instructions on how to write to your child
- ✔ Informational about region and the orphanage

You can pay one lump sum of $240 a year or send $20 a month by check, money order or we can automatically charge your credit card each month. Donations are tax deductible.

As Fr. Peter said, "know that without Gospa Missions there is no help for these children."

For more information on
St. Joseph Orphanage contact:
Gospa Missions
230 East Main Street
Evans City, PA 16033
724.538.3171 or www.gospa.org

SOURCES AND SELECTED BIBLIOGRAPHY

Comfort My People by Steve Bell, © Signpost Music, Winnipeg, MB, R3E 2T1, Canada ,1989.

Butler's Lives of the Saints on CD-ROM, Harmony Media, Inc, Salem, OR 97305

My Imitation of Christ, Thomas a Kempis, Confraternity of the Precious Blood, 5300 Fort Hamilton Parkway, Brooklyn, NY, 11219, 800-404-3943.

God's Way recorded by David Parkes, Irish Records, Pembroke, MA 02359

Bible passages taken from *The Holy Scriptures* Bible Study Software Program by Christian Technologies, Inc, Independence, MO 64055

Catechism of the Catholic Church, 1994, Apostolate for Family Consecration, Bloomingdale, OH 43910

Code of Canon Law: A Text and Commentary, 1985, Paulist Press, Mahweh, NJ, 07430